HOW THE SPECTER OF COMMUNISM IS RULING OUR WORLD

FIRST EDITION

———————

PUBLISHED BY
THE EPOCH TIMES
229 W 28TH ST, 7TH FLOOR
NEW YORK, NY 10001

———————

PRINTED BY
EPOCH PRESS, INC.
7 HIGHPOINT DRIVE
WAYNE, NJ 07470

———————

ISBN 978-1-947150-09-6

How The

SPECTER OF COMMUNISM IS RULING OUR WORLD

From The
Editorial Board of
"NINE COMMENTARIES ON
THE COMMUNIST PARTY"

VOLUME II

An Epoch Times Special Publication

Table of Contents

The specter of communism did not disappear with the disintegration of the Communist Party in Eastern Europe

Preface

THOUGH THE COMMUNIST REGIMES of Eastern Europe have disintegrated, the specter of communism has not disappeared. On the contrary, this evil specter is already ruling our world, and humanity must not harbor a mistaken sense of optimism.

Communism is neither a trend of thought, nor a doctrine, nor a failed attempt at a new way of ordering human affairs. Instead, it should be understood as a devil — an evil specter forged by hate, degeneracy, and other elemental forces in the universe.

In another dimension, not visible to us, it took the form of a serpent, then that of a red dragon, and it keeps company with Satan, who hates God. It exploits low-level beings and demons to wreak havoc on humankind. The goal of the specter is to ruin humanity. While the divine offers salvation, communism tells people not to believe in the divine, attacks human morality so as to make people abandon tradition, and causes people to disregard the divine's instruction and, ultimately, to be destroyed.

The communist evil specter, with its countless mutations,

is full of guile. Sometimes it uses slaughter and violence to destroy those who refuse to follow it. Other times, it takes recourse in the language of "science" and "progress," offering a wonderful blueprint of the future in order to deceive people. Sometimes it presents itself as a profound field of learning and makes people believe that it is the future direction of mankind. Other times, it uses the slogans of "democracy," "equality," and "social justice" to infiltrate the fields of education, media, art, and law, bringing people under its banner without their awareness. At yet other times, it calls itself "socialism," "progressivism," "liberalism," "neo-Marxism," and other leftist terms.

Sometimes it holds up seemingly righteous banners such as pacifism, environmentalism, globalism, and political correctness. Other times, it supports vanguard art, sexual liberation, legalization of drugs, homosexuality, and other indulgences in human desires, giving the mistaken impression that it's part of a popular trend.

Extremism and violence aren't its only expressions — sometimes it pretends to care for the welfare of society. Yet its root purpose is to destroy, by whatever means, everything that is traditional, whether it be faith, religion, morality, culture, the institution of the family, art, pedagogy, law — whatever it takes to have man fall into a moral abyss and be damned.

Communism and its various mutations are now found around the world. China and Cuba publicly proclaim themselves to be led by communist regimes. Even the United States — the leader of the free world — has fallen prey to attacks by the evil specter. Europe embraces socialism, and Africa and Latin America are enveloped in communist influence. This is the startling reality humankind now faces: The evil specter's conspiracy to destroy humankind has almost succeeded.

Humans instinctively desire to benefit themselves and flee from danger. Instinct urges them to escape from suffering, to make a name for themselves, to establish prosperous enterprises, or merely to enjoy life. It is human to have these thoughts. However, if humans distance themselves from the divine, the evil specter can latch onto and intensify these thoughts to control people.

The hubris of the specter's revolt against divinity also makes those it controls experience a sense of hubris. These individuals then try to play God through the exercise of power, capital, and knowledge, with the aim of ruling the fates of millions and influencing the course of history through social movements.

Humans are created by the divine and have both good and evil in their nature. If people abandon evil and choose compassion, they can return to the divine. What awaits on the opposite side is evil personified — the devil. The choice resides solely with the individual.

Many fundamentally kindhearted people have unknowingly become the communist specter's agents or the targets of its manipulation — what Vladimir Lenin called "useful idiots." Though society as a whole has ended up on the verge of destruction because of the specter's inducements and temptations, very few people have willingly pledged their souls to the devil and chosen to deliberately corrupt mankind. For most, the kindness innate in human nature remains, giving them an opportunity to rid themselves of the specter's influence.

The purpose of this book is to set out this complex and tangled issue in plain language as truthfully as possible. Then people will be able to see the communist specter's tricks. More importantly, this book seeks to present the moral, cultural, and artistic traditions that the divine laid down for mankind. Individuals may then choose between the divine and the evil specter for themselves.

When a person's kind thoughts emerge, the divine will help free him from the devil's control. But the process of seeing the devil for what it is requires that one think deeply and discern clearly. This book seeks to reexamine the tides of history over the last several centuries and, from a high level and with a broad perspective, assess the multifarious masks and forms the devil has adopted in order to occupy and manipulate our world.

The goal of this effort is not to simply recount history, but to understand how we can stop the devil from ever ruling the world again. This relies on each individual's enlightenment, proactive abandonment of evil, and return to the traditions and way of life that the divine laid down for man.

The divine will triumph over the devil. Which side we stand on will determine our eternal destiny.

Chapter Nine

The Communist Economic Trap

COMMUNISM'S INFLUENCE IS PRESENT in every sector of our present economic system. With the trend of ever-expanding government being the norm, virtually every country on earth is moving away from classic free-market principles and gravitating toward communist or socialist economics.

Looking at the countries that abandoned communism or the socialist economic model after the fall of the Soviet bloc, one would think that the communist specter had failed in its goals. But the reality isn't so simple. The specter's methods do not follow a rigid pattern. For the sake of a greater objective, it may abandon certain forms while adopting others to suit the historical or social situation. Nowhere is this truer than in the economic sphere.

More than 150 years ago, Karl Marx advocated the abolition of private property and ascendance of state ownership in his book *Das Kapital*. Totalitarian communist states tried to achieve this objective directly, using terror, violence, and mass murder. But as overt communist doctrine lost its appeal, leftists in democratic countries devised nonviolent forms. The multitudinous strains of socialism and communism they created and introduced throughout the years defy easy classification.

In addition to curtailing basic rights to private property and enterprise, communist economic policy fosters corruption and contributes to the erosion of traditional culture. To preserve their prosperity, way of life, and moral foundations, nations around the world must awaken to communist subversion in the economic realm, and take measures against it.

1. State Ownership and Planned Economies: Systems of Slavery

Heaven created man, endowed him with wisdom and strength, and decreed that in his life he would reap rewards for his labor — and thus be able to obtain enough to secure his life. The Declaration of Independence states, "We hold these truths to be self-evident, that all men are created equal, that they are endowed by their Creator with certain unalienable Rights, that among these are Life, Liberty and the pursuit of Happiness." [1] Naturally, these rights include the power to possess and allocate property and assets.

In contrast, Marx and Engels stated in *The Communist Manifesto*, "The theory of the Communists may be summed up in the single sentence: Abolition of private property." [2] This is a reference to state ownership, which, under a planned economy, is mandatory. In communist planned economies, the means of production are directly controlled by the state. The essence of this system violates heaven's principles, runs contrary to human nature, and, ultimately, is a form of slavery.

A. STATE OWNERSHIP: A TOTALITARIAN YOKE

Anti-communist pioneer Fred Schwarz told the following joke

in his book *You Can Trust the Communists … to Be Communists*, about an interviewer who visits first a Soviet automobile plant and then an American one:

"Who owns this factory?"

"We do," they replied.

"Who owns the land on which it is built?"

"We do."

"Who owns the products of the factory when they are made?"

"We do."

Outside in a corner of a large park were three battered jalopies. The visitor asked, "Who owns those cars out there?"

They replied, "We own them, but one of them is used by the factory manager, one is used by the political commissar, and the other is used by the secret police."

The same investigator came to a factory in America, and said to the workers, "Who owns this factory?"

"Henry Ford," they replied.

"Who owns the land on which it is built?"

"Henry Ford."

"Who owns the products of the factory when they are made?"

"Henry Ford."

Outside the factory was a vast park filled with every make and variety of modern American automobile. He said, "Who owns all those cars out there?"

They replied, "Oh, we do." [3]

This story vividly displays the consequences and differences between systems of private and state ownership. Under the system of state ownership, resources and the gains from labor are nationalized. Gone are the mechanisms that motivate individual enthusiasm, ambition, and innovation, along with the sense of responsibility conveyed by personal property rights. In name, state ownership means that the wealth of a country is shared by all citizens, but in practice, it means that the privileged class monopolizes resources and looks after itself first.

The ultimate factor in economic growth is people. State ownership chokes people's vitality and motivation to be productive. It undermines morale, promotes inefficiency, and creates oversupply or gross shortages. From Soviet collective farms to the people's communes in China to failed collectivization in Cambodia and North Korea, the system of state ownership brings starvation wherever it goes. For example, the man-made famine in China killed tens of millions of people between 1959 and 1961.

Both evil and kindness exist in mankind. Private property ownership allows man to develop integrity and encourages labor and thrift. Collective property ownership, however, encourages the evil in human nature, promoting jealousy and laziness.

Austrian economist and philosopher Friedrich Hayek wrote that the growth of civilization relies on social traditions that put private property at the center. Such traditions spawned the modern commercial system and its attendant economic growth. This is an organic, self-generating order that does not require a government to function. Yet communist and socialist movements seek to shape the world according to their wishes — what Hayek called their "fatal conceit." [4]

If private ownership and freedom are inseparable, then the same principle applies to state ownership, wed as it is to dictatorship and suppression. The system of state ownership nationalizes resources, degrades economic productivity, and turns people into the country's servants and slaves. All people must obey the commands of the central party, and any ideas and voices inconsistent with the regime can be shut down. People are then powerless against state intervention.

Thus, the elimination of private ownership and the establishment of state ownership inevitably leads to totalitarian outcomes. Collectivism is a yoke affixed on the necks of humans by a totalitarian state. Freedom is stolen — including the freedom to be upright — and everyone is forced to follow the moral commands of the communist regime.

If power is privatized and wealth collectivized, disaster awaits mankind.

B. ECONOMIC PLANNING: DESTINED TO FAIL

Under a planned economy, an entire society's production, allocation of resources, and distribution of products are based on a plan established by the state. This is completely different from supply and demand economics in a free market.

The planned economy has natural and obvious defects. First, it requires the collection of a huge amount of data in order to make reasonable arrangements for production. For any country, especially a modern state with a large population, the amount of required information is unimaginably large and impossible to process. For instance, the former Soviet Union's commodity pricing bureau had to set prices for twenty-four million different kinds of goods. [5] The complexity and variability of society and people cannot be solved through a unified planned economy. Even with the use of modern big data and artificial intelligence, human thoughts cannot possibly be inputted as variables, and so the system will always be incomplete.

Economist Ludwig von Mises discussed the relationship between socialism and the market in his article "Economic Calculation in the Socialist Commonwealth." [6] He notes that without a real market, a socialist society isn't able to make reasonable economic calculations. Thus, the distribution of resources cannot be rationalized, and the planned economy fails.

Additionally, economic planning requires coercive state control of resources. This ultimately requires absolute power, quotas, and commands. When the requirements of the real world fail to conform to state planning, state power tramples on natural economic trends, thus causing the mass misallocation of capital and all its attendant problems. The planned economy uses the limited power and "wisdom" of government in a doomed attempt to play God.

Moreover, an economics of power is first of all beholden to politics, rather than to the actual needs of the people. Economic planning and authoritarian politics are inseparable. Because national plans are inevitably flawed, when problems arise, the plans will be challenged both inside and outside government. Those in power then feel that their authority is being challenged and will fight back with political pressure and purges. Mao Zedong, for instance, ignored the laws of economics and forced through the Great Leap Forward, resulting in a three-year famine that caused tens of millions of deaths. This led to serious challenges to his leadership position in the Communist Party, which is a key reason he later launched the Cultural Revolution.

The disastrous effects of the planned economy and collective ownership have been fully exhibited in the current conditions of Chinese state-owned enterprises (SOEs). In recent years, a large number of Chinese SOEs have stopped or slowed production, have suffered losses every year, or have become insolvent. They rely on government subsidies and rolling bank credit to maintain operations. They've essentially become parasites on the national economy, and many are widely known as "zombie enterprises." [7] Among the 150,000 state-owned enterprises in China, with the exception of state monopolies in the lucrative sectors of petroleum and telecommunications, other SOEs report minimal profits and suffer serious losses. By the end of 2015, their total assets accounted for 176 percent of GDP, debt accounted for 127 percent, and earnings accounted for only 3.4

percent. [8] Some economists believe that these zombie enterprises have essentially hijacked China's economy, which for many years has remained dependent on cheap manufacturing made possible by extreme exploitation of low-wage workers and a complete disregard for the environment.

Meanwhile, economic planning deprives people of their freedom and forces the state to look after them. All aspects of people's lives come under the control of the state, which locks people in an invisible prison, seeks to abolish free will, and alters the parameters of human life established by the divine. The essence of the project is about turning people into slaves and machines. This is yet another manifestation of the communist revolt against the divine and natural law.

2. Western Countries: Practicing Communism by Another Name

For individuals, Marxism's "abolition of private property" entails the "abolition of bourgeois individuality, bourgeois independence, and bourgeois freedom." For society, it means that "the proletariat will use its political supremacy to wrest, by degree, all capital from the bourgeoisie, to centralise all instruments of production in the hands of the State, i.e., of the proletariat organised as the ruling class." [9]

Many economic policies or structures may not appear socialist on the surface, yet they play the role of restricting, weakening, or depriving people of the right to private property. Others weaken the mechanics of free enterprise, expand government power, and lead society further down the road toward socialism. The methods used include high taxation, generous social welfare, and aggressive state interventionism.

A. HIGH TAXES AND WELFARE

High taxation is a covert way to gradually phase out the system of private ownership. The end result of high taxation is the same as the state ownership and "egalitarianism" imposed by communist regimes, with the only difference being whether nationalization is effected before or after production.

In the West, production is controlled privately, but the revenue is converted into state assets via taxes and redistribution schemes. This wealth-taking is achieved legally through democracy and legislation rather than through killing and violence.

An important feature of the communist or socialist economics seen in Western countries is robust social welfare, which is used to gradually erode moral wisdom and freedom. While some government aid is reasonable — such as social security for victims of disasters or accidents — it is easy for welfare to become a convenient instrument of deception. Its positive aspects become the excuse for increasing taxes and government control. In this regard, generous welfare has already achieved the same destructive consequences to people, society, and moral values as do overtly communist economics, without the need for violent revolution.

Social welfare in developed Western countries consumes a large portion of revenue, which comes from taxes transferred from private wealth. All socialized benefits must ultimately be paid for by the people, via taxes or national debt. There is no other method to maintain this level of government largesse. In the United States, more than half of the tax revenue is spent on Social Security and medical care. More than 80 percent of this money comes from personal income taxes and Social Security taxes; 11 percent is from corporate tax. [10] This kind of massive government spending only began in the past century.

In 1895, the US Supreme Court declared income taxes unconstitutional. The decision stood until the 1913 ratification of the 16th Amendment. Data from fifteen countries in the year 1900 show that only seven imposed an income tax, with Italy leading at a rate of 10 percent. Australia, Japan, and New Zealand had income tax rates of about 5 percent.

By 2016, according to data on thirty-five market economies published by the Organization for Economic Cooperation and Development (OECD), twenty-seven countries had an income tax rate higher than 30 percent. The countries with the two highest income taxes, at 54 and 49.4 percent, are both in Europe. [11] On top of this, eating or shopping in Europe usually adds more than 20 percent in sales tax. Corporate and other taxes further add to the overall tax burden.

High taxation burdens not only the wealthy, but also those at the bottom of the tax scale. While the rich often have various legal means of shielding themselves from taxes, the poor's welfare benefits disappear as their income increases beyond a certain threshold. After taxes, this income is often less than what they received on welfare. People are effectively penalized for working harder and thus incentivized to stay on welfare.

Expansive Welfare

In modern society, vast welfare systems have been expanded to cover unemployment, medical care, pensions, occupational injury, housing, education, child care, and more, far beyond traditional concepts of aid for those in immediate need.

A report from The Heritage Foundation shows that in 2013, more than one hundred million people in the United States, or about a third of the population, received welfare benefits (excluding Social Security and Medicare) worth an average of $9,000 per recipient. [12] According to Census Bureau data from that year, 14.8 percent of the population were classified as living below the poverty line — basically the same rate as in 1967, a few years after President Lyndon B. Johnson declared "unconditional war on poverty in America." This suggests that greatly expanding welfare benefits — as was done under Johnson's administration — hasn't achieved the goal of reducing the percentage of people living below the poverty line.

As of 2014, in the fifty years since Johnson launched his War on Poverty, American taxpayers spent $2.2 trillion on welfare. Yet, as statistics from the US Census Bureau show, the poverty rate has remained steady for the past forty years. [13]

Moreover, poverty is calculated by income and doesn't factor in the various benefits afforded to welfare recipients, such as food stamps, housing subsidies, and education benefits. Over a century ago, French thinker Alexis de Tocqueville said that by only using poverty thresholds to allocate aid, it is impossible to know whether eligible individuals are actually suffering from circumstances beyond their control or if their misfortune is of their own making. [14]

The deliberate categorization of large numbers of people into the "impoverished" demographic provides ample excuse for the expansion of welfare. Living standards in poverty today are far superior to those in the 1960s. According to a government survey conducted in 1999, 96 percent of parents in impoverished households said that their children had never gone hungry due to inability to buy food. Almost 50 percent of impoverished households lived in detached houses, and 40 percent lived in townhouses. Just 9 percent lived in mobile homes. Eighty percent had air conditioning and two-fifths owned widescreen LCD TVs. Three-quarters of impoverished households owned cars. [15]

Even still, the benefits provided by the US government are below average compared with those of other members of the OECD. Most people living in Nordic countries and other Western European nations enjoy far greater welfare than Americans. In Denmark, for example, even the wealthiest citizens enjoy a cradle-to-grave social safety net that includes free medical care, university education, and other generous benefits. Swedes are entitled to 480 days of paid parental leave when a child is born or adopted. Greeks, prior to their country's economic collapse, enjoyed an annual fourteen-month-worth salary and retirement at the age of fifty-seven. The country spent 17.5 percent of its GDP on pension payments.

The expansion of welfare from its traditional role of emergency aid to long-term benefits for entire populations is, in fact, part of the goal of imposing a communist economy.

Social Benefits, Corruption, and Class Conflicts

From an economic point of view, the essence of welfare is to take money from some people and transfer its value to others. However, it is the government that is responsible for distributing the wealth, usually without requiring anything in return—thus de-emphasizing the wisdom that one must work in order to gain. The loss of this moral principle is particularly evident in Northern Europe.

Swedish scholar Nima Sanandaji demonstrated this point using data from the World Value Survey. In the early 1980s, 82 percent of Swedes agreed with the statement that "it is wrong to receive government benefits that you do not deserve." In the 2010–2014 survey, only 55 percent of Swedes agreed with this statement. [16]

Under a generous welfare system, those who work hard receive fewer returns, and those who are less industrious are rewarded with benefits. Over time, this subtly distorts moral traditions, as those who grew up with high government welfare lose the industriousness, independence, responsibility, and diligence of their forefathers. They take the system for granted and consider welfare to be a human right. They have formed a habit of relying on the government and even holding it hostage for continuous aid. Thus, social values are changed almost irreversibly.

Expansive government welfare also squeezes out the role of traditional charities, depriving the donors of the opportunity to do good works and the beneficiaries of the chance to feel gratitude. In traditional society, charity was given by one's own choice, either by giving aid directly to the less fortunate or by donating to charitable organizations such as churches. There were clear donors and recipients, and being able to receive assistance was a privilege, not a right. Recipients felt gratitude for the donors' kindness and would be motivated to use the charity to supplement their own efforts to improve their lot. Those who received charity and turned their lives around would be likely to return the favor when others confronted the same challenges they once faced.

Tocqueville noted that charity combined the virtues of generosity and gratitude, which interact mutually to improve society and exert a positive moral influence. Meanwhile, the relationship between givers and receivers functioned to ease conflicts and antagonism between rich and poor, as charitable behavior on the part of individuals connected members of different economic classes. [17]

The bloated system of modern welfare interrupts the relationship between donors and recipients by bureaucratizing the process of charity. The "donors" of today are taxpayers who are forced to give up their wealth, rather than sharing it voluntarily. Meanwhile, recipients of welfare have no connection to their benefactors and feel no gratitude for their sacrifice.

Tocqueville believed that social welfare exacerbated conflicts between the rich and the poor. Having part of their wealth forcibly confiscated, the wealthy would come to resent welfare recipients. Tocqueville said that the poor, too, would feel discontent if they took their economic relief for granted: "One class still views the world with fear and loathing while the other regards its misfortune with despair and envy." [18]

Bloated welfare also becomes a way for the communist specter to exacerbate jealousy and political conflict. This has been observed in the Greek economic crisis: Among the upper class, tax evasion became a "national sport," according to Greek officials cited by *The Economist*. [19] With reduced tax revenue, the Greek government attempted to cut back on social welfare, only to meet with staunch resistance. So as to not upset its constituents, the government relied on taking out loans to offset diminishing tax revenue, while maintaining the same level of welfare found in other European countries. Greece eventually raised taxes on middle- to high-income earners, farmers, and businesses.

In 2009, an empirical study by Martin Halla, Mario Lackner, and Friedrich G. Schneider showed that social welfare disincentivizes hard work in the long term. The three economists concluded that the dynamics of the welfare state are inimical to the health of a nation's economic base. [20]

The Culture of Poverty

Welfare should be an emergency measure to assist those in genuine need, effective in circumstances such as those involving occupational accidents, epidemics, natural disasters, and so on. It shouldn't become the default form of subsistence, as it is incapable of resolving the dilemma of poverty.

Expanding the criteria that determines who is entitled to welfare creates an atmosphere of negative reinforcement that encourages the misuse of these benefits. For example, the term "disability" is being continually redefined to extend eligibility to more individuals. The result is economic malaise, which causes a regression in social morality.

In 2012, *The New York Times* ran an opinion article titled "Profiting From a Child's Illiteracy," which discusses the impact of welfare policy on low-income families living in the Appalachian Mountain region in the eastern United States. The article describes how impoverished families stopped sending their children to literacy classes in order to qualify for aid. "Moms and dads fear that if kids learn to read, they are less likely to qualify for a monthly check for having an intellectual disability," the article states. "Many people in hillside mobile homes here are poor and desperate, and a $698 monthly check per child from the Supplemental Security Income program goes a long way — and those checks continue until the child turns 18." [21]

The program began about forty years ago with the goal of helping families whose severely physically or mentally challenged children made it difficult for parents to work—about one percent of poor children. By 2012, more than 55 percent of qualifying children were categorized as mentally challenged, but did not have a defined diagnosis. Across the United States, there are now a total of around 1.2 million "mentally challenged" children for whom taxpayers provide $9 billion annually. [22]

Here, welfare and the flaws of human nature feed each other in a downward spiral. While those who advocate and devise welfare policy may do so with good intentions, the effects of these policies are often detrimental, both to individuals and society as a whole.

Welfare abuse doesn't just tie down public finances; it also affects the futures of children who grow up inside its system. Research conducted in 2009 found that two-thirds of people who received welfare as children continued to receive it into adulthood. [23]

According to American economist William A. Niskanen, the welfare system has spawned a culture of poverty, which in turn has fed a vicious cycle of dependence on government aid, children born out of wedlock, violent crime, unemployment, and abortion.

Niskanen analyzes state data for 1992 and estimates the potential effects of increasing Aid to Families with Dependent Children benefits by 1 percent of the average personal income. He determined that the number of recipients would increase by about 3 percent; the number in poverty would increase by about 0.8 percent; births to single mothers would increase by about 2.1 percent; and unemployment would increase by about 0.5 percent. Abortions and violent crime would both increase by just more than 1 percent each. [24] Niskanen's findings suggest that a robust welfare system fosters dependence on the system and discourages personal responsibility.

The disintegration of families is a chief ingredient in the culture of poverty. In a study of historical and contemporary poverty among blacks, economist Walter E. Williams found that in 1925 New York City, 85 percent of black families were two-parent. By 2015, black single-parent households had reached nearly 75 percent. The welfare system incentivizes this phenomenon, as it provides considerably more benefits to single mothers than to those who marry. By purposely remaining single, a parent can access more government subsidies, including welfare payments, housing subsidies, food stamps, and medical care. Welfare has been instrumental in pushing single parenthood, which has proven to cause more poverty. Alternatively, Williams found that the poverty rate among black married couples had remained in the single digits since 1994. [25]

The Left's Use of Welfare Policy to Gain Votes

While welfare has been ever-expanding over the last few decades, the gap between rich and poor has also continuously increased. The average wage, adjusted for inflation, has increased at a snail's pace, while wealth flows to the most wealthy, resulting in a larger class of working poor. The Left weaponizes these societal issues to push for a bigger government, higher taxation, and more welfare to combat poverty, exacerbating the problems even further.

Leftwing politicians use a variety of election slogans to convince voters of their noble intent, portraying themselves as possessing the moral high ground, despite that they are draining taxpayer money to fund their programs. Their method is to seize the wealth of the upper and middle classes and distribute it among the poor. This system of forced charity conceals the relationship between the donors (taxpayers) and the recipients. Politicians present themselves as the benevolent givers and receive the recipients' gratitude in the form of votes, while telling the recipients that they should resent the "rich" — the actual donors.

B. AGGRESSIVE ECONOMIC INTERVENTIONISM IN WESTERN COUNTRIES

In Western countries, the state, which traditionally only passed and enforced laws, has now become a leading participant in the economic arena. Like a referee joining a soccer match, the state has become responsible for controlling and regulating capital in what used to be a mostly self-regulating economy.

At present, governments in the free world are already practicing interventionism in their national economic systems. One driver of this trend came out of the Great Depression in the 1930s. Following the crisis, Western society was deeply influenced by the economic theory developed by British economist John Maynard Keynes. Keynesian economics advocates active state intervention and regulation of the economy through finance. In his seminal book, *The General Theory of Employment, Interest and Money,* Keynes opposes free market self-regulation and instead favors increased government spending and interventions such as bailouts to stabilize the market.

In a healthy society, the government's role is limited. Only in exceptional situations should the state interfere in the economy, such as during natural disasters or other crises. But today, Keynesian theory has taken root around the world. Governments of virtually all countries are racing to take greater control over their respective economies.

When governments play an active role in the economy, each action creates a massive ripple effect in the markets. New policies and laws can make or break entire industries, forcing many businesses and investors to become overly beholden to government decisions.

Active financial control combined with high-welfare policies has caused many governments to incur huge debt. According to data from the OECD, more than one-third of its member states have government debts higher than 100 percent of GDP. One country's debt has exceeded 237 percent of its economic output. [26] This presents a major vulnerability for the social and economic futures of many countries.

Nobel Prize-winning economist Ronald Coase wrote multiple research papers on the impact of government intervention.

In his work, Coase found that interventionist policy almost always produces negative results. The most probable explanation, he said, is that "the government now operates on such a massive scale that it [has] reached the stage of what economists call negative marginal returns. Anything additional it does, it messes up." [27]

The Consequences and Reality of Interventionism

There are at least two major consequences of extensive government intervention. First, the power of the state expands in terms of its role and scale. Government officials develop increasing hubris about their ability to interfere with the economy and have the state play the role of savior. After handling a crisis, the government is wont to retain its expanded powers and functions.

Second, interventionism creates more reliance on the government. When the populace encounters challenges, or when the free market cannot provide the desired benefits, the people will lobby in favor of more government intervention to satisfy their demands.

As the power of the state increases, private enterprise weakens and the free market has less space in which to function. People who have benefited from and grown dependent on politicians will increasingly demand that the government take responsibility for allocating wealth, and enact laws to enforce this.

In the West, there is a strong political current pushing society toward the Left. This encompasses followers of the original left wing, including socialists and communists, as well as those not traditionally associated with the Left but who have been co-opted by it. This emboldens leftist politicians to take greater measures to intervene in the economy and interfere with the functioning of private enterprises. This erosion of normal economic activity appears to be caused by various social movements, but in fact, it is the specter of communism that pulls the strings.

Western governments wield their authority under the banner of equality and other political excuses to increase intervention, while enacting laws to give themselves more permanent power. There is no doubt that this behavior deprives market economies of their principal arbiters — the free will of the people.

The state is essentially expanding its authority over the free market to turn it into a command economy. The long-term implications are that all aspects of the economy and popular livelihood will come under state control. Economic means will be used to consolidate political power, enslaving society and its citizens.

C. HOW SOCIALIST ECONOMICS LEADS TO COMMUNIST TOTALITARIANISM

High taxes, high welfare, and widespread state intervention are manifestations of socialism within Western economic systems. As things stand, the only difference between the planned economies of communist countries and heavy state interventionism in the West is the law and some basic aspects of the system are protecting human rights from total government control.

Hayek, the economist and philosopher, cautioned against state-controlled planning and wealth redistribution, saying that it would inevitably tamper with the market and lead to the rise of totalitarianism, regardless of whether the system was democratic or not. Hayek believed that although the socialism practiced in Europe and North America was different from state ownership and planned economies, it would nevertheless arrive at the same outcome — people would still lose their freedom and livelihood, just in a slower and more indirect fashion. [28]

As has been discussed earlier in this book, Marx, Engels, and Lenin all saw communism as the final goal, with socialism a mandatory step on the journey. A train's destination will not be affected by its stopping at a station along the way — in fact, it might pick up more passengers. Likewise, the specter of communism is the driving force behind a country's move toward socialism. Once humanity forsakes tradition, whether in the economic sphere or in other areas, and accepts communist ideology, the pace of this development is irrelevant.

The destination at the end of this path is not heaven on earth, but the destruction of humanity. The specter is not concerned with whether "heaven" is realized or not — this promise is merely bait to lure people to their doom.

3. The Dystopian Socialism of the Chinese Communist Party

In 1978, after state ownership and the planned economy had reduced China to a poverty-stricken disaster, the Chinese Communist Party (CCP) was compelled to introduce economic reforms to keep its hold on power. Embarking on a process of "reform and opening up," the CCP introduced elements of a free market. This led many to believe that the Party had become capitalist, but this was far from the truth.

A. THE CHINESE ECONOMY: NO RELAXATION OF COMMUNIST CONTROL

Out of expedience, the CCP liberalized some aspects of the Chinese economy, such as allowing private business. But the communist cadres have not loosened their grip. Although private enterprises exist, the CCP has never promised the people any fundamental right to private property. All resources and land remain ultimately at the Party's disposal.

At the same time, the CCP imposes strict controls on economic matters, including large-scale national planning. The market is only a means used by the state to stimulate production; it is not truly independent, and neither are there institutions in place to support a free market.

The Chinese communist model is a monstrous combination of socialism, statism, and market economics. There is no rule of law or clear system of property rights. The exchange rate is not allowed to adjust itself naturally. The flow of wealth in and out of the country is controlled, and international firms operating in the country are tightly restricted. The CCP uses government subsidies and export tax rebates to boost exports with the aim of defeating competitors with a price war. This has disrupted the normal order of world trade. It is precisely for these reasons that the World Trade Organization has long refused to acknowledge China as a market economy.

Many in Western governments harbored the naive hope that economic development would bring political liberalization and democracy to China. Instead, with greater financial means, the CCP subjected its people to more brutal and sophisticated forms of repression. In July 1999, the regime launched the persecution of one hundred million people in China who practiced the spiritual discipline Falun Gong. In order to carry out the nationwide campaign, the CCP greatly expanded and empowered its security forces, pouring funds into advanced surveillance systems and promoting those responsible for "successful" persecution to high-ranking positions. This war against the universal principles of truthfulness, compassion, and tolerance continues to this day. Inevitably, the instruments used to persecute Falun Gong were repurposed to repress other faiths and the general population. Since 2009, the CCP has spent far in excess of 500 billion yuan (US$75 billion) annually to cover the costs of "maintaining stability," that is, policing the Chinese population.

B. THE TRUTH BEHIND CHINA'S ECONOMIC RISE

Because of China's rapid GDP growth over the past forty years, many have come to believe in the superiority of socialist economics. It has made many Westerners, including elites in political and academic circles, marvel at the efficiency of the totalitarian system.

In fact, the economic model the CCP has built cannot be

replicated. On the one hand, despite its economic rise, the socialist system has great internal instability. On the other hand, the Party's model enshrouds an abundance of corruption created by its unscrupulous political system. China's economic growth has been based in large part on the following factors.

First, the relaxation of the state-owned economy and central planning, and the revitalization of the private sector gave the Chinese economy a powerful productive drive. The Chinese people, who had their industrious potential stifled for decades, showed their desire to rise out of poverty and their drive to do business. Moreover, China's vast population of more than one billion provided a pool of almost inexhaustible cheap labor.

A second factor was the massive influx of Western capital and technology into China during the reform era. Under the command economy, China's vast expanses of underutilized land, labor, and markets were like gold for which prices were not yet determined. The combination of capital investment and undeveloped resources ignited the blaze of China's economic growth. Had it not been for the Party's totalitarian rule, this fire could have started decades earlier, and in a much more controllable and sustainable fashion.

The scale of Western investment in China is immense. According to published figures, American annual direct investment in China reached almost $117 billion in 2018, up from $11 billion in 2000. [29] The total value of foreign capital entering China from 1979 to 2015 amounted to about $1.64 trillion, according to China's Ministry of Commerce. [30]

Western countries gave the People's Republic of China preferential trade status along with broad market access. In May 2000, the US government granted Beijing "permanent normal trade relations." On December 11, 2001, China formally entered the World Trade Organization and joined the international market. Consequently, a huge amount of Western wealth was transferred to China, making it the "world's factory."

However, it cannot be forgotten that the PRC's economic power fed on unethical practices: the extreme exploitation of workers, the use of sweatshops and of forced labor in prison camps across the country, the demolition of housing and forced relocation of the occupants, and the like. For the sake of short-term growth, the CCP welcomed environmental destruction and ignored public health hazards in order to squeeze every last drop of profit from its land, people, and resources. The Communist Party took advantage of Western capital, technology, markets, favorable trading status, and cheap domestic production costs to make vast sums in foreign reserves. The trade deficit between the United States and China rose from about $83 billion in 2000 to more than $345 billion in 2019.

Eventually, the CCP overturned the conventions of international trade and took full advantage of the opportunities available to it, regardless of whether they were legitimate. It adopted a national strategy of plagiarizing intellectual property in attempts to overtake other countries in industry and technology. This constitutes the biggest case of theft in history. A 2017 report by the Commission on the Theft of American Intellectual Property stated that China's fake goods, pirated software, and stolen trade secrets caused the United States a loss of between $225 billion and $600 billion every year, a figure that did not include losses due to the theft of intellectual property. The report states that over the three preceding years, the United States lost $1.2 trillion due to intellectual theft, the majority of which was perpetrated by China. [31] A report by the Office of the Director of National Intelligence stated that 90 percent of cyber attacks on US businesses originated from the Chinese regime and inflicted an estimated $400 billion in total economic damage every year. [32]

The PRC's economic model utilizes state authority to induce rapid economic development while employing underhanded tactics to increase its competitiveness. It also has encouraged other countries to adopt heavier state intervention. These countries have made the grave mistake of idolizing the Party's model as a success while ignoring the human and moral tragedies it created.

C. CONSEQUENCES OF THE CHINESE ECONOMIC MODEL

The CCP's economic model has put society in moral freefall, exactly in line with the communist specter's aim of destroying humankind. The Party's economic power goes hand in hand with the erosion of morality as it drags people into a bottomless sea of indulgence, toward eventual annihilation.

Today's China is inundated with fake goods, poisonous food, pornography, drugs, gambling, and gangs. Corruption and debauchery have become achievements to take pride in, while social trust is virtually nonexistent. The widening gap between rich and poor is accompanied by social strife and abuse of justice. In the PRC's economy of power, Party officials use their authority to amass wealth. The severity of the corruption increases with rank. The misappropriation of billions is a normal occurrence. There is simply no government as corrupt or morally degenerate as the Chinese communist regime.

Within this environment of corruption, citizens turn a blind eye to the suffering of their compatriots. In October 2011, the world was shocked by the death of Yueyue, a two-year-old girl in Guangdong Province who was hit by a truck. Instead of getting out to help, the driver rode over Yueyue again as he left the scene. Minutes later, another vehicle ran over her legs. Eighteen people walked by without helping Yueyue, until a scrap collector finally moved the crying toddler to safety. She later died in the hospital. International media wondered if China had lost its soul. It might be understandable that people are reluctant to come to the aid of others when there is danger involved, such as in an armed robbery, yet Yueyue did not pose any conceivable threat to anyone as she lay dying in the street.

The communist movement leads to enormous destruction

of traditional values and culture, and in communist China, moral standards have already dropped far beyond what one can easily imagine. The harvesting of organs from living people, good people who practice spiritual cultivation and strive for self-improvement, has become a state-sanctioned industrial operation. An unknown number of prisoners of conscience have been killed on operating tables as their organs were plundered for profit. Communists have turned medical personnel, who are supposed to help people, into murderers. The CCP's evil has reached across the world; through economic incentives, the Party entices countries that are supposed to be upholding human rights to turn a blind eye to its crimes.

Economic growth without morality is chaotic, unsustainable, and disastrous. Under the inhumane policies of the CCP, social conflicts abound, and the environment is on the verge of collapse. The consequences of moral decay are fatal. China calls itself a strong country, but its strength is an illusion. Its superficial prosperity, built upon the reckless pursuit of wealth, is doomed to collapse.

There is no good future in store for China if it cannot escape the snare of the CCP. The specter of communism has no intention of implementing healthy and sustainable growth, as its true goal is to destroy China, and the world.

4. The Ravages of Socialism in the Developing World

A. EASTERN EUROPE: HAUNTED BY SOCIALISM

Nearly thirty years after the fall of the Soviet Union, communism continues to haunt Eastern Europe, as there has never been a full reckoning of the crimes committed by former communist regimes.

The lingering presence of communism can be seen in various facets of Eastern European politics and economics. Russia and Belarus, for example, retain powerful state-owned enterprises, high welfare, and aggressively interventionist policies.

During the transitional period from communism, Eastern European countries experienced crises of slow economic growth and high unemployment. All this encouraged the relapse of communism and socialism in new forms. Left-wing parties were animated with renewed vigor, feeding off a sense of nostalgia for the socialist past. [33] The ghost of communism has not been banished.

B. HOW SOCIALIST ECONOMICS FAILED DEVELOPING NATIONS

In the developing nations of Asia, Latin America, and Africa, many newly independent countries had declared their allegiance to socialism by the 1960s, with disastrous results. In the early 2000s, Venezuela's economy collapsed as a direct result of its socialist policies. Once the richest in Latin America, the country is now rife with poverty, crime, and starvation. Zimbabwe was once the richest country in Africa; today, it has sunk into complete catastrophe, with inflation spiralling beyond imagination.

Venezuela: How Socialism Bankrupted a Prosperous Country

Venezuela is blessed with considerable oil reserves. In the 1970s, it was the fastest-growing economy in Latin America, enjoying the lowest level of income inequality and the highest per capita GDP in the region. [34] Venezuela's relatively free economy attracted skilled immigrants from Italy, Portugal, and Spain. Together with the protection of property rights, these factors enabled the nation's economy to grow rapidly from the 1940s to the 1970s. [35]

In 1999, when the new president took office, he embarked on an ill-fated program of nationalization that eventually threw the Venezuelan economy into chaos. The president publicly declared: "We must transcend capitalism. But we cannot resort to state capitalism, which would be the same perversion of the

Soviet Union. We must reclaim socialism as a thesis, a project, and a path, a new type of socialism, a humanist one, which puts humans and not machines or the state ahead of everything." [36]

To build socialism, the Venezuelan government requisitioned or nationalized many private companies across industries including oil, agriculture, finance, heavy industry, steel, telecommunications, energy, transportation, and tourist enterprises. This process was ramped up following the president's 2007 reelection. His government expropriated 1,147 private companies between 2007 and 2012, with catastrophic effects.

Companies in once-productive industries were shut down and replaced by inefficient state-owned enterprises, scaring off investors. As production sank, Venezuela turned to relying heavily on imports. Coupled with a series of government interventions involving foreign reserves and price controls, disaster inevitably struck when the price of oil dropped. Some attributed this tragedy to the oil crisis, but according to data provided by the World Bank, seven countries that relied even more heavily on oil exports than Venezuela continued to experience economic growth from 2013 to 2017. [37]

The root cause of Venezuela's dramatic failure was the socialist economic system. Venezuela's economic policy essentially marched to the tune of the ten revolutionary demands Marx proposed in *The Communist Manifesto*, starting with abolition of private ownership and high taxes and moving to a centralized economy and means of production. [38] Venezuela met its economic fate at the hands of the communist specter.

Zimbabwe: From Africa's Breadbasket to Land of Famine

After Zimbabwe's declaration of independence in 1980, it endeavored to build a socialist state according to Marxist-Leninist principles. Its first prime minister was a Marxist believer and his guerrillas, guided by Mao Zedong Thought, received unconditional assistance from the PRC. Unlike other African countries that implemented socialism, Zimbabwe did not immediately impose policies of nationalization.

Zimbabwe's economic woes began in 2000 following the start of land reform. Land belonging to white farmers was seized and redistributed among landless blacks, as well as politically connected individuals. Many were inexperienced in farming, and the result was a sharp decline in agricultural productivity. In an attempt to evade the crisis, the Reserve Bank of Zimbabwe printed more money, leading to endless hyperinflation. Figures from the central bank indicate that in June 2008, the country's annual inflation reached 231 million percent. By mid-November 2008, inflation peaked at nearly 80 billion percent, after which the authorities gave up publishing monthly statistics. [39]

In 2008, a great famine struck Zimbabwe. Of the country's sixteen million people, five million were threatened with starvation. Today, malnutrition is chronic and widespread.

Communism plagues the world in ways that can be observed or foreseen across all countries. Developed Western countries are beginning to experience crises. Meanwhile, the tragedy of socialism is already a reality in the developing world. This is the principle: The communist specter uses economics to promise comfort and satisfaction, then lures people into moral degradation and the abyss of poverty.

5. Marx's Theory of Exploitation: An Inversion of Good and Evil

Through a set of elaborate theories, Marxism deceives people into replacing traditional morals with its ersatz standards that invert right and wrong. In the Marxian view, whether an individual is good or bad is based not on his morality and actions, but rather on his place in the (inverse) hierarchy of capital.

One who belongs to what Marxists call the "capitalist" class is guilty of exploiting the proletariat, and since the proletariat is supposedly the oppressed and exploited class, its members naturally occupy the moral high ground. No matter how they treat business owners, property owners, and the affluent, they can hold their heads high. Marxism turned the possession of property into a crime and advocated violent expropriation.

Marx said that only labor creates value. If a company owner invests $10 million in a company in a year, and the revenue that year is $11 million, in the Marxian view, this $1 million in profit is "surplus value" created by the employees but unfairly expropriated by the "capitalist" company owner. Thus, Marx claimed that exploitation was the secret to how capitalists made money and, therefore, the "original sin" of the bourgeoisie. Marx concluded that to eliminate this sin, the entire capitalist society must be destroyed — that is, the bourgeoisie would be eliminated and their assets confiscated, while the vanguard of the party would collectivize property and institute communism.

Marx's theory of exploitation divides people into two opposing classes: the bourgeoisie with capital, and the proletariat without. In fact, since industrialized societies came to the fore, class mobility has increased rapidly. The class mobility in Marx's era (the early 1800s to the 1850s) was similar to that in the 1970s in both the United Kingdom and the United States. [40] The interchange between classes is a dynamic process; a supposed member of the proletariat is no longer among the proletariat if he buys public equity in a company, for example. If one's class assignment can be changed so easily, attempts at dividing people into groups like this have no other purpose than to incite class hatred.

In China, the Soviet Union, and the communist states of Eastern Europe, the communist parties stole land, lynched landlords, and robbed business owners of their factories. They murdered "class enemies" and confiscated generational wealth, waging campaigns of state terrorism against the people. All this evildoing was a result of communism's hate-filled theories. Meanwhile, traditional moral standards, as well as belief in the divine, saints, and classical sages, were branded as belonging to "the exploiting classes" and were to be attacked and eradicated.

Marx's theories have been widely criticized in economic and philosophical circles. The following are merely a few examples that illustrate the absurdity of Marx's theory of exploitation.

Marx argues that labor creates value, and that value is determined by the labor time necessary for production. This is a ridiculous theory. The value of a commodity is not one of its intrinsic properties. Most of the time, humans add a subjective element to each commodity — most saliently, supply and demand.

Many economists have explored the process of valuation, and unlike Marx's narrow doctrine, most economic thinkers agree that numerous factors are involved in the creation of value — including land, capital, labor, science and technology, management, the risk of investment, and so on. Economic activities are a complex system, involving different links in the chain of production. Different factors of production have certain managerial requirements, and different people play different roles, which are indispensable to the whole chain and contribute to the creation of "residual value."

For example, a business owner plans to spend $1 million hiring two engineers to design and produce a certain new toy. A marketer also is hired to promote the new toy. Two years later, the new toy gains popularity and earns a profit of $50 million. Is it the labor of the engineers and marketer that created the residual value of $50 million? Of course not. The reason the new toy earned millions is that people wanted it. The business owner's insight into the market, ability to organize and manage others, and courage to take a risk all contributed to the value of the toy.

Suppose the creativity in the toy came from one of the engineers — then, does the residual value of the $50 million come from the fact that the business owner exploited the engineer's creativity without giving anything in return? Of course not. If the engineer thinks his creativity was not being adequately rewarded, he could find another company that offers higher pay.

In a free market, a balance will ultimately be struck in matching skills and ambition with capital. Business owners who demand unreasonable profits will lose to the competition or be unable to attract talent. In addition, since waiting for a return on invested capital delays spending or other enjoyment of that capital, the profits are also due to the efforts of the investor. Therefore, it's normal that an additional sum will be gained in return. The principle is no different than lending at interest.

There also are many "accidental" factors involved in deciding the value of a commodity. Such accidental factors can only be reasonably explained by a frame of reference founded on traditional beliefs and culture.

In certain situations, the creation and destruction of value can be entirely unrelated to the question of labor. A diamond worth $10 million today may have been worthless five thousand years ago because no one wanted it. A barren patch of land inherited from a grandfather could suddenly be one hundred times more valuable due to the prosperity of a nearby city or the discovery of rare-earth metals underground. Here, the increase in value involves no labor. Such vast, unexpected wealth is simply a matter of good fortune. Both Western and Eastern cultural traditions recognize that fortune is a form of divine blessing.

In order to demonstrate the "rationality" and "necessity" of state ownership, Marx concocted the exploitation theory based on surplus value, which turned the economic activities that people engage in as a normal part of life into negative and unethical behavior. His theory poured hatred and scorn on the existing economic order as part of his attempt to undermine and overthrow it.

In fact, the employers and the workers, the landlords and the peasants, form a community of shared interests. Their relationship should be one of cooperation and interdependence; each group supports the other to survive. Marx deliberately exaggerated the differences between classes, seeing them as absolutes — like the antagonism between mortal enemies.

There are good and bad people among employers, just as there are among workers. In economic exchange, what should really be exposed and sanctioned is anyone who violates ethical standards. The basis of judgment should be moral character, not wealth.

People can change their economic and social status through their own efforts. Workers can become investors through the accumulation of wealth. Investors can become workers due to failures in their investments. The role of labor and investors in modern society often changes. Most people also play both roles — putting the profits they made into future productive capacity, thus creating employment, increasing social wealth, and benefitting the general public. Even the founder of the US labor union movement said, "The worst crime against working people is a company which fails to operate at a profit." [41]

The absurd "surplus value theory" affixes the label of "exploitation" to the normal activities of landowners and capitalists. It has incited incalculable hatred and struggle, muddled thinking, and has destroyed the lives of millions.

6. Hatred and Jealousy: The Origin of Absolute Egalitarianism

Communism advocates absolute egalitarianism. Superficially, this may sound like a high-minded aim, leading many to blindly believe it is righteous. In reality, it evokes hatred and jealousy, as people believing in absolute egalitarianism can't tolerate the success of others, or others being wealthier and having better lives, easier work, and more luxurious living conditions. Everyone must be equal, and believers say, "I should have what you have, and I can get what you get." In such a worldview, everyone is equal and the whole world is the same.

Absolute egalitarianism manifests in at least two main ways. First, when people are not yet equal, they are encouraged to be dissatisfied with their economic status. People come to covet what others have and even seek it through improper or violent means. In extreme cases, they destroy others' property and even kill to get rich.

The worst manifestation of these tendencies is violent revolution. In order to provoke dissatisfaction, Marx divides society into two opposite classes: those who own the means of production, and those who don't. In the countryside, this was the landlord and the peasant; in the city, it was the business owner and the worker. The aim was to incite class hatred and use the supposedly disenfranchised members of society to carry out violent revolution. The peasants are poor and landlords are rich — seize their wealth! Everyone should be rich! Thus, the CCP called on peasants to engage in "land reform" — that is, attack landlords and divide up their land. If the landlords refused to comply, they were killed. The Party did this by first inciting hooligans to start trouble, then encouraging the peasantry to join them in rising up and attacking the landlord class. The heads of millions of landowners fell.

Second, once groups have basically achieved a state of "equality" — in which any benefits are divided up among everyone — anyone who stands out is penalized. Everyone is treated the same whether one works more, works less, or doesn't work at all. This fails to acknowledge a universal principle: While people may appear to be the same on the surface, in truth, each individual's personality, intellect, physical strength, morality, occupation, role, education, living conditions, endurance and perseverance, inventiveness, and so on are all different, and what one contributes to society is also different. Thus, why should the same outcome be applied to all? In this sense, inequality is actually true equality, while the equality pursued by communism is true inequality and true injustice.

The ancients in China said that heaven will reward one according to the effort one puts in. Absolute egalitarianism is impossible in the real world.

Under the cover of egalitarianism, the lazy benefit, while the capable and the hardworking are penalized and even resented or hated. Everyone slows their pace to match the speed of the slowest. This causes everyone to become lazy, waiting for someone else to contribute so that one can take advantage and jump on for the ride, gaining something for nothing or stealing from another. The result is widespread moral decline.

The hatred and jealousy that drive absolute egalitarianism are the poisonous roots of communism's economic perspective. Human nature has both good and evil inherent in it. Western faiths refer to the seven deadly sins, while Eastern culture teaches that man has both Buddha nature and demon nature. Buddha nature manifests itself as kindness, the ability to endure hardship, and consideration for others. Demon nature manifests as selfishness, laziness, jealousy, malice, hatred, rage, lust, and tyranny, as well as having a disregard for life, inciting discord, spreading rumors, getting something for nothing, and so on.

The economic perspective adopted by communism deliberately stimulates demon nature, amplifying people's jealousy, greed, laziness, and other evil factors, causing people to lose their humanity and forsake the traditional values held for thousands of years. It amplifies the worst in human nature and turns people into communist revolutionaries.

In *The Theory of Moral Sentiments*, eighteenth-century economist and philosopher Adam Smith said that morality is the foundation of mankind's prosperity. Observing common rules of morality "is required for the very existence of human society, which would crumble into nothing if mankind were not generally impressed with a reverence for those important rules of conduct." [42]

Lawrence Kudlow, director of the US National Economic Council, believes that morality must exist alongside economic prosperity. He wrote in 1997 that if the United States could abide by the "foremost principle" — to adhere to the moral values the nation was founded on — the development of the United States would be limitless. [43]

A. ECONOMIC EGALITARIANISM:
A STEPPING STONE TO COMMUNISM

Under the influence of absolute egalitarianism, vigorous calls ring out in the West for "social justice," as well as minimum-wage laws, affirmative action, and other demands. What lies behind these is a desire for equality of outcome, of which communist elements can take advantage. From the communist perspective, it doesn't matter whether these vulnerable groups obtain equality or if their social status improves. They are merely pawns for inciting resentment.

If communists get what they demand, then they simply make new demands for equality — there is no end to it. If they don't achieve their demands, they strengthen people's notions about the justice of equality and turn this into a major platform upon which to gain more influence. Because communism incites resentment in multiple fields and via so many different means, if it's allowed to spread unchecked, the inevitable result is social turmoil. Communists will always be able to find vulnerable groups and demand financial or social equality for them, repeating the process until the path toward communism is paved.

Moreover, the implementation of these policies often results in the opposite of what is promised. Those who are supposed to be protected by these policies instead lose out. Take minimum-wage laws, for example: On the surface, its goal is to protect the rights of workers, but the effect is that many businesses simply stop hiring because it is uneconomical for them to do so. As a result, workers lose their jobs. Eliminating lower-wage jobs also means the loss of skill-building, as young people and those new to an occupation then have few opportunities to be trained and work their way up to higher-paying jobs. The one-size-fits-all approach also violates economic theory and results in excessive government intervention.

People also use the excuse of "equal pay for equal work" to demand social revolution based on fighting racism and sexism. They cite statistics that, for example, the average wage of black males is less than the average wage of white males, that the average female wage is less than the average male wage, and that these discrepancies are the result of racism and sexism. In reality, such comparisons are not appropriate. When comparing apples to apples, the results are different. Some scholars' research has found that college-educated, married black couples earned slightly more than their white counterparts. [44] After decades of communist tactics to destroy the traditional family and promote welfare, black families of this type are relatively fewer, and this is the main reason why there are overall discrepancies between the races regarding income. Making meaningful and accurate comparisons should be common sense, but communist elements tend to incite discord and struggle, which leads people to look at things irrationally.

Communism does not care about the well-being of vulnerable groups. It is simply interested in slogans that drag people down the road to destruction.

B. COMMUNISM'S USE OF UNIONS TO UNDERMINE FREE SOCIETIES

The loss of US manufacturing jobs in the past few decades is a well-known phenomenon, but many people don't realize that unions, hijacked by leftist causes, are one of the main culprits. Many of today's unions claim to help obtain benefits for the working class, but they often do the opposite. This is evident in the history of unions and the transformation of their mission.

Trade unions were initially founded by members of the working class with few or no skills, for the purpose of negotiating with management. To a certain extent, a trade union is able to broker and resolve conflicts between workers and owners. But communist elements took unions and turned them into tools to promote communist policies and movements. The unions became a powerful weapon for destroying free enterprise and carrying out political struggle.

Friedrich Engels wrote on the topic, "The time also is rapidly approaching when the working class will have understood that the struggle for high wages and short hours, and the whole action of Trades Unions as now carried on, is not an end in itself, but a means, a very necessary and effective means' but only one of several means towards a higher end: the abolition of the wages system altogether." [45]

Lenin believed that the formation and legalization of trade unions was an important means for the working class to wrest control from the "capitalist" class, and that the unions would become the pillar of the Communist Party and a key force in class struggle.

In a speech, Lenin proposed that trade unions become "a school of administration, a school of economic management, a school of communism," and a link between the Communist Party and the masses. The daily work of the trade union was to convince the masses to transition from capitalism to communism. "The trade unions are a 'reservoir' of the state power," he wrote. [46]

In the mid-to-late nineteenth century, communist and left-wing forces used trade unions to incite workers to go on large-scale strikes, make harsh demands on owners, and even take violent measures, such as destroying machinery and factories. In October 1905, more than 1.7 million workers in Russia participated in a nationwide political strike that paralyzed the country's economy. During this time, a particularly aggressive union, the Central Workers' Group, was formed and became the main precursor to the Petrograd Soviet, a "council" of workers and soldiers that played a central role as the vehicle for the Russian Revolution. [47]

Trade unions in Western and developed countries also have been widely infiltrated and used by communist elements. The relationship between employers and employees is a symbiotic one, yet communists try to provoke, expand, and intensify discord between them. Unions are used to escalate conflicts during the bargaining process between management and workers. Additionally, unions rationalize and intensify the confrontational side of the management–worker relationship and use this to legitimize their own existence. From there, they inflame workers' dissatisfaction and blame the "capitalists" for any problems. This has been key to unions' survival.

On the surface, trade unions are fighting for the interests of workers, but in reality, they are undermining industrial competitiveness. There are two reasons for this. First, under the pretext of protecting workers' rights and interests, unions make it difficult for enterprises to lay off employees who don't perform well and who achieve little. This gives rise to a culture of laziness. Not only is this unfair to employees who work diligently, but it also makes them less proactive. The most important factor in the growth of a company is its workers, but with the union's umbrella of protection over employees who fail to perform, enterprises lose their competitiveness. Enterprises that fail to meet these union demands are then the targets of struggle, including strikes and protests, which further disable the business. The powerful United Auto Workers union routinely called for strikes in Detroit. Prior to the 2008 financial crisis, the union demanded $70 an hour in wages and benefits. Consequently, the US automobile manufacturing industry was on the brink of bankruptcy. [48]

Second, under the pretext of protecting employees' welfare (including pensions, health insurance, and the like), unions constantly raise costs for enterprises. This forces companies to curtail growth and to cut their investment in research and development, which hurts competitiveness. It also results in companies having to increase product prices, which harms consumer interests. Studies show that this is why companies without unions, such as Toyota and Honda, were able to produce high-quality cars at a lower cost, and why Detroit-based automobile factories with labor unions became less competitive. [49]

As Edwin Feulner, founder of US think tank The Heritage Foundation, said of unions, "They function like an albatross around a company's neck — making it less flexible, less able to react wisely to the demands of a changing marketplace." [50]

While the loss of job opportunities in the US manufacturing industry has been recognized and discussed for decades, many people don't know that unions are a key driver of the job losses. Unionized manufacturing jobs fell by 75 percent between 1977 and 2008, while nonunion manufacturing employment increased by 6 percent over that time, according to a report by The Heritage Foundation.

The situation in the construction sector is similar. A report by Heritage Foundation research fellow James Sherk states: "Unlike the manufacturing sector, the construction industry has grown considerably since the late 1970s. However, in the aggregate, that growth has occurred exclusively in nonunion jobs, expanding 159 percent since 1977. Unionized construction jobs fell by 17 percent." [51]

In addition, labor unions are the tools employed by communist elements to promote egalitarianism in enterprises. Sherk notes that unions demand that companies pay wages according to the length of service of the employee (the same is done in socialist countries), without regard to the employee's contribution to the company or performance. "Union contracts compress wages: They suppress the wages of more productive workers and raise the wages of the less competent." [52]

The idea at work here is the same as absolute egalitarianism under communism, which is effectively the redistribution of wealth among employees within the enterprise. The interference in the internal decision-making of enterprises and the monopoly of the labor market erodes the free market.

Unions' aggressive advocacy for what they describe as

workers' welfare ends up favoring some workers over others and puts a drag on individual companies and the economy as a whole. A survey conducted in 2005 showed that "most union households disapprove of American unions" and that "the main reason for their disapproval is never openly discussed in union media or addressed at union conventions." [53]

Labor unions infiltrated by communism, and under the guidance of the progressive movement, have often become tools to wage struggle against the free market. Corruption and vested interests are common among union leaders. Their single-minded battle against what they call injustice in the workplace creates a burden on industry and productivity, preventing corporate reform and rational attempts to stream-line manufacturing, services, education, government bureau-cracy, and other fields. Politically, the Left draws support from unions to promote their social movements and drive wedges in society.

7. Communist 'Ideals': Tempting Man Toward His Own Destruction

Although communist theory is full of loopholes and contra-dictions, many are still deceived by it. This is because Marx described a utopian communist paradise that people all over the world could enjoy. This is the central fantasy and delusion. His depiction included "overwhelming material abundance" and much higher moral standards for society. Each person would work "according to his ability" and receive "accord-ing to his need." There would be no private ownership, no gap between the rich and the poor, no ruling class, and no exploitation. There would be freedom and equality for all, and each person would be able to develop his or her partic-ular talents. Life would be wonderful.

This set of deceitful arguments attracted many to fight for it. Many Westerners today have never had the tragic experience of living in a totalitarian state. They continue to harbor an illusory hope for a communist paradise, and therefore fan the flames by advocating communist and socialist ideas.

In fact, all the ideas put forward by Marx are dangerous illusions. Marxism claims that a communist society will enjoy a superabundance of material goods. However, human desires and human wants are endless. Under the constraints of limited human knowledge, limited working hours, and limited resources, shortages and deprivations are inevitable. This is the most basic starting point for all economic studies. Without these constraints, people wouldn't have to explore which kind of production method was most efficient, as the supposed superabundance would provide for all and could be squandered at will.

Marxism also claims that moral standards would be greatly improved in a communist society. However, as good and evil coexist in each person, the improvement of moral standards in a society requires the guidance of upright beliefs and values, as well as personal efforts in self-cultivation. What Marxism preaches is atheism and class struggle, which enlarge the evil side of humans. People are not allowed to have freedom of belief, and religion is only a political tool of the Communist Party. What's more, under communism, religious institutions are used to safeguard tyranny, to mislead the world, to resist and oppose the divine, and to turn people further away from the divine. Without righteous belief in the divine and self-discipline, morality can only decline. Moreover, once in power, all communist leaders prove to be tyrants — arrogant, lewd, and completely unethical. To expect their followers to be so vastly improved in moral standards runs counter to reason.

Marxism also proclaims there will be equality for all. But as discussed earlier, socialism inevitably leads to totalitarianism. Power is the basis of resource distribution, yet the distribution of power under a totalitarian state is most unjust.

Therefore, resource distribution under totalitarianism also will be most unjust. In all countries where socialism rules or has ruled, people see a privileged stratum form, as well as extreme gaps between the rich and the poor and the suppression of people by the state. Resources are exhausted for military purposes, and people's belongings are robbed to make the privileged class more powerful, while the majority are left to labor in poverty.

Marxism deceives with the promise of "from each according to his ability, to each according to his need." [54] Communism deceives people by promising that every member of society can give full play to his or her abilities. In socialist economies, people are unable to act at will according to their own ability, as they do not have basic freedoms.

Marxism says that the division of labor creates alienation. But in fact, division of labor is necessary for any society. Smith argues in *The Wealth of Nations* that a division of labor can greatly increase productivity and promote prosperity. The differences created by the division are not necessarily conflicts, nor do they necessarily lead to alienation and depersonalization. People from all walks of life, regardless of their station, can contribute to society, elevate their morals, and help to bring happiness to humankind.

However, communism uses individuals' pursuit of goodness to mislead them into becoming religious fanatics for communist ideology. It uses the pursuit of goodness as its banner to pull people away from the divine. It pollutes people's minds, strengthens their evil nature, and leads them to commit all manner of crimes. Under this influence, people indulge in material enjoyment, casting aside loftier and nobler beliefs in the higher purpose of life. Communism poisons everything it touches and slaughters people by the millions, as seen in every country where it came to power. If the world's people do not wake up now, they will face horrifying consequences.

8. Morality, Prosperity, and Peace

Striving for happiness is human nature. A prosperous economy can bring happiness, yet the economy does not exist in a vacuum. When the path of economic development deviates from ethics and morality, an economic crisis may follow. A society that is merely wealthy is not only incapable of bringing joy and happiness, but its prosperity will also be short-lived. As the foundation of ethics and morality crumbles, a disastrous outcome awaits.

In 2010, *People's Daily*, a mouthpiece for the Chinese regime, reported that despite economic development, China had been declining for years on the Forbes' Gross National Happiness Index. The world's second-largest economy is plagued with corruption, environmental pollution, and food-safety incidents, making the Chinese people extremely insecure about their lives. In this case, wealth has increased as morality and happiness have declined.

This reflects the fatal flaw in communism: Human beings are composed not only of flesh, but, far more so, of mind and spirit. The divine laid down the path that man's life would take. The Chinese say "every bite and every sip is preordained," which is analogous to the Western spiritual belief in the concept of fate, or that lives are preordained. People who believe in the divine understand that wealth is a grace bestowed upon them by their Creator. They value having a humble and thankful heart, and hence they are content and happy.

Among those aboard the doomed Titanic as the ship sank in 1912 was millionaire John Jacob Astor IV, whose fortune could have built thirty Titanics. Yet when facing death, he chose what he thought was morally correct and protected women and children — he gave his spot in the final lifeboat to two terrified children. [55] Similarly, Isidor Straus, co-owner of Macy's department store, said, "I will not go before the other men." His wife, Ida, also refused to get on a lifeboat, giving her place to

Ellen Bird, their new housemaid. Ida chose to spend her final moments with her husband. [56]

These people of great wealth chose to put traditional values and faith before the opportunity to save their assets and lives. Their choice of morality and justice manifests the radiance of human civilization and human nature: A noble character is more valuable than life, which is yet more valuable than wealth.

Mr. Li Hongzhi, the founder of Falun Gong, wrote in "Wealth With Virtue":

> *It is the duty of the ruler and officials to bring wealth to the populace, yet promotion of money-worship is the worst policy one could adopt. Wealth without virtue (de) will harm all sentient beings, while wealth with virtue is what all people hope for. Therefore, one cannot be affluent without advocating virtue.*
>
> *Virtue is accumulated in past lives. Becoming a king, an official, wealthy, or nobility all come from virtue. No virtue, no gain; the loss of virtue means the loss of everything. Thus, those who seek power and wealth must first accumulate virtue. By suffering hardships and doing good deeds one can accumulate virtue among the masses. To achieve this, one must understand the principle of cause and effect. Knowing this can enable officials and the populace to exercise self-restraint, and prosperity and peace will thereby prevail under heaven.* [57]

If humankind maintains the aforementioned values for wealth and life, the economic challenges rooted in human beings' greed, sloth, and jealousy will be reduced considerably. Once mankind suppresses its selfish desires, the ideology of communism will no longer be able to lure the human heart, and moral standards will remain high.

The communist specter has made intricate arrangements to destroy mankind. Its economic arrangements are only one part of the story. To free ourselves from the control of communist "ideals," we need to expose the conspiracy, identify the fraudulent messaging, and stop putting hope in this bankrupt ideology. We also need to restore traditional values and recover morality and virtue. Thus, humanity will be able to embrace everlasting prosperity and happiness and obtain true peace. Human civilization will then radiate with new vitality.

Chapter Ten

Corrupting the Legal System

1. Law and Faith

LAW IS THE IRON FORCE of fairness and justice that affirms good and punishes evil. What is good and what is evil must be understood by those who write laws. From the perspective of faith, these criteria come from the divine. The teachings of sages and religious scriptures provided the basis for the laws that govern human society.

The Code of Hammurabi, enacted in ancient Babylon, is one of the earliest sets of written laws that have been found. Engraved in the stone tablet above the code itself is a powerful scene: Shamash, god of the sun and justice, bestowing the laws upon King Hammurabi. This is the depiction of a god granting a human sovereign the authority to govern his people using the rule of law.

For Hebrews, the Ten Commandments in the Old Testament were considered to be both divine and secular law simultaneously — a tradition that became the foundation of Western legal culture. From fourth-century Roman emperors, to the East Roman Justinian I and his successors, to the first of Britain's Anglo-Saxon kings, Alfred the Great, the legal system took the Ten Commandments and Christian doctrine as its inspiration. [1]

Followers of religion believe that in order to be considered legitimate, the law must accommodate divine standards of good and evil, as well as religious teachings. The thinking behind nonviolent civil disobedience in the United States can be traced back to early Christian doctrine. When Roman emperor Gaius Caligula commanded that statues of Caesar be erected within the Temple walls in Jerusalem and that Christians must worship Roman gods, Christians opted to face crucifixion or be burned at the stake rather than obey. To have followed the command would have meant violating the first two Commandments — in other words, the emperor demanded that secular law take precedence over divine commandment, which is sacred and inviolable.

In general, the Ten Commandments can be divided into two categories. The first four describe the relationship between man and God — that is, what constitutes the appropriate reverence for God. The other six govern relationships between people and, at their core, reflect the teaching to love others as you love yourself. Reverence for God is an imperative that enables humanity to maintain, unchanged, the principles of fairness and justice.

The same was true in ancient China, where historically the law was promulgated by imperial decree. The emperor, or "Son of Heaven," was required to follow providence and the principles of heaven and earth. This is the "Tao," or Way, imparted by Lao Zi and the Yellow Emperor. The Han Dynasty Confucian scholar Dong Zhongshu said: "The greatness of Tao originates from heaven. Heaven never changes, and neither does the Tao." [2] In ancient Chinese usage, "heaven" is not an abstraction of natural forces, but refers to the divine. Faith in the Tao of heaven forms the moral bedrock of Chinese culture. The imperial legislative systems derived from this belief influenced China for thousands of years.

American legal scholar Harold J. Berman believed that the law coexists with the overall principles of social morality and faith. Even under the separation of church and state, the two are mutually dependent. In any society, the concepts of justice and legality must have their roots in what is considered holy and sacred. [3] The modern legal system retains many facets of religious ceremony that strengthen its power.

2. *Law Under Communist Tyrannies*

Communist parties are anti-theist cults. They aim to sever a society's links to its ancestral culture and traditional values, and they will never follow the teachings of righteous gods in their legislative principles. It was never realistic to expect that communist parties would make any sincere attempts to maintain fairness or justice.

A. EXTRALEGAL POLICIES OF STATE TERROR

Traditionally, Christians talk about loving others as we love ourselves, and Confucian teachings say that the benevolent man loves others. Here, love is not limited to the narrow concept of love between a man and a woman, or the love that exists among family members or friends. Love also encompasses benevolence, mercy, justice, selflessness, and other virtues. With this cultural foundation, not only is the law sacred, but it also embodies the spirit of love in human society.

No legal system can hope to account for any and all possible forms of conflict and provide judgments for each. Thus, laws must factor in the subjectivity of all parties. A judge must follow the spirit of the law to give a verdict that abides by the principle of benevolence.

In the Temple of Jerusalem, Jesus admonished the Pharisees for their hypocrisy, for despite strictly adhering to the words of Moses, they had ignored virtues required by the code, such as justice, mercy, and truthfulness. Jesus himself healed on the Sabbath and sat with gentiles, for what he cared about was the spirit of kindness embodied within the doctrines, not only the literal meaning.

By contrast, communism is rooted in hatred. It not only hates God, but also hates the culture, lifestyle, and traditions that the divine established for humanity. Marx did not mince words in expressing his desire to doom himself to ruin and bring the world down with him. He wrote to his future wife, "Jenny, if we can but weld our souls together, then with contempt shall I fling my glove in the world's face, then shall I stride through the wreckage a creator!" [4]

Sergey Gennadievich Nechayev, a communist terrorist in czarist Russia, wrote in his pamphlet *The Revolutionary Catechism* that the revolutionary "has broken all the bonds which tie him to the social order and the civilized world with all its laws, moralities, and customs, and with all its generally accepted conventions." The revolutionary, according to Nechayev, should see himself as the archenemy of this world and its conventions, and "if he continues to live with them it is only in order to destroy them more speedily." [5]

Nechayev's use of the clerical term "catechism" for his lawless vision hints at the cult-like disdain that communism harbors for humanity and the divine. "He is not a revolutionary if he has any sympathy for this world," Nechayev wrote.

Lenin expressed a similar view: "Dictatorship is rule based directly upon force and unrestricted by any laws. The revolutionary dictatorship of the proletariat is rule won and maintained by the use of violence by the proletariat against the bourgeoisie, rule that is unrestricted by any laws." [6]

Wielding political power to kill, torture, and mete out collective punishment in the absence of legal restraints is nothing other than state terrorism, and it is the first step taken by communist regimes when they come to power.

In the months following the Bolshevik overthrow of the Russian government in 1917, hundreds of thousands of people were killed in the course of the political struggle. The Bolsheviks established the All-Russian Extraordinary Commission for Combating Counter-revolution and Sabotage, abbreviated Cheka, and endowed it with powers of summary execution. From 1918 to 1922, the Chekists killed no less than two million people without trial. [7]

Alexander Nikolaevich Yakovlev, former propaganda minister of the Central Committee and member of the Politburo and Secretariat of the Communist Party of the Soviet Union, wrote that in the 20th century alone, sixty million people in Russia had died as a result of war, hunger, and repression. Using public archives, Yakovlev estimated that the number of people killed in Soviet persecution campaigns was twenty million to thirty million. In 1987, the Politburo of the Soviet Union set up a committee, of which Yakovlev was a member, to review miscarriages of justice under Soviet rule. After reviewing thousands of files, Yakovlev wrote: "There's a feeling that I've long been unable to shake. It seems that the perpetrators of these atrocities are a group of people who are mentally deranged, but I fear that such an explanation runs the risk of oversimplifying the problem." [8]

To put it more plainly, Yakovlev saw that the atrocities committed in the communist era were not the result of mere impulses, but rather careful planning. These crimes were committed not for the greater good of the world, but from a deep hatred of life itself. The drivers of communism commit atrocities not out of ignorance, but out of malice.

B. EVER-CHANGING STANDARDS
OF RIGHT AND WRONG

While communism ignores the rule of law to perpetrate acts of state terror, it puts on a show in front of Western countries by claiming it's committed to upholding the law. It does this so that it can engage, infiltrate, and subvert free societies through the avenues of trade and economic partnerships, cultural exchange, and geopolitical cooperation. For instance, at the onset of China's reform and opening up in 1979, the Chinese Communist Party (CCP) passed a "criminal procedure law," ostensibly to strengthen the judiciary. But this law has never been seriously enforced.

According to Marx, the law is a product of "class contradiction" and a tool that embodies the will of the ruling class. The laws of a communist party come neither from God, nor from a genuine love of the people, nor from a desire to maintain a fair and just society. The interests of the ruling group, that is, the communist party of a given country, are all that matter. As the goals and interests of the party change, so change its laws.

Naturally, once the CCP seized power, it adopted class struggle as its guideline and proceeded to rob the entire citizenry. It promulgated laws against the crime of "counter-revolutionary activity," which applied to everyone who opposed the Party's policies of theft. The CCP punished counter-revolutionaries with incarceration or death.

After completing the process of mass robbery to implement public ownership, the CCP needed a way to keep what it had stolen. It shifted its priorities toward economic development and implemented laws that protected private property. In essence, this means little more than protecting the Party's vested interests. For example, the widespread compulsory demolition of Chinese people's homes to make way for development projects illustrates the regime's continued infringement on the right to private property.

In March 1999, the CCP announced the need to "rule the

country according to law." [9] A few months later, it began the nationwide persecution of Falun Gong and established a Gestapo-like extrajudicial body, the 610 Office, to carry out the brutal campaign. To fulfill its mission, the 610 Office was given the authority to bypass all laws and judicial procedures, allowing it to manipulate the public security apparatus and judicial system to suppress Falun Gong.

The Party periodically conjures up new enemies so as to renew its tyrannical rule over the Chinese people. The targets of persecution are ever-changing and include the campaigns against landlords and capitalists, the 1989 massacre of students in Tiananmen Square, and the suppression of Falun Gong practitioners and human rights lawyers.

Accordingly, the law must be changed frequently. In seventy years of rule, the Party has promulgated four constitutions, the last of which has undergone four revisions since its introduction in 1982. Gaining experience from multiple political campaigns, the CCP has used the law to adjust and disguise its motives and actions. Sometimes it does not even bother to apply this camouflage.

C. IGNORING THE CONSTITUTION

The Constitution of the People's Republic of China is replete with verbose language in an effort to show that the CCP is committed to the rule of law and civilized international norms. In practice, however, the constitution is never strictly followed, and basic rights such as freedom of speech, belief, and association are not actually protected.

According to Marxist theory, law reflects the will of the ruling class, rather than objective justice. For a communist party, then, passing and amending laws to suppress its enemies and impose its will on society follow as a matter of course. Under this kind of system, anyone who dares to challenge the "will of the ruling class" — that is, anyone who opposes the interests of the communist party — is subject to legal persecution as a class enemy, whether they are unemployed workers, demobilized soldiers, farmers whose land was expropriated, human rights lawyers, or simply those struggling to make ends meet.

To lawyers practicing in communist countries, the laws on the books always make way for the interests of the regime. If a lawyer tries to cite the law and argue in favor of justice, the judge and prosecution will shut him down by talking about the supposed spirit of the law. They even blatantly say that the court is run by the communist party and must follow its orders. Whatever the thoughts of these individual court workers, what they say indeed reflects the spirit of law that exists under communist regimes.

In the Chinese court system, during hearings involving persecuted Falun Gong practitioners, the judges may say things like the following: "Why are you bringing up the law? I care only about politics." "The Party doesn't allow defense. The leaders' words are the law." "The Communist Party leads the court, so we need to follow the Party line." "No legal procedure is necessary for Falun Gong issues." "Don't talk to me about conscience." [10]

English philosopher Francis Bacon once wrote: "One foul sentence doth more hurt than many foul examples. For these do but corrupt the stream, the other corrupteth the fountain." [11]

The laws of the Communist Party, ever-malleable and only selectively practiced, hold no sanctity from which to derive legitimate authority. Over the past century, the spirit of the law that governs the Party's legal system has brought about countless injustices and has overseen the deaths of one hundred million innocent people — a debt of blood for which no representative of the communist cause can ever atone.

"A murderer must pay with his life, just as a debtor with money," a Chinese proverb says. Were the Communist Party to truly enforce the law, it would become liable for its bloody history.

3. How Communism Warps the Law in the West

As with politics, economics, education, and other facets of society, Western rule of law has not escaped infiltration and subversion by the communist specter. In communist countries, the law is manipulated as an instrument for maintaining the regime's rule, reinforcing communist party ideology, and suppressing the people. In free countries, the specter's aim is to use the law to distort the standards of good and evil, to subvert traditional faith and the law's moral foundations, and to seize the powers of legislation and enforcement, thus putting demonic norms into practice.

The communist specter's influence over the rule of law can be found all across the West. As the United States is the leader of the free world, this section focuses on the erosion of US legal institutions.

A. SUBVERTING THE MORAL FOUNDATIONS OF THE LAW

As communist parties and their various followers around the world promoted atheism and the theory of evolution, the connection between the law and divine principles was steadily rejected. The spirit of the law began to shift from its divine role of maintaining fairness and justice to expressing the will of political interests and radical ideology. The law has been largely reduced to an instrument of revenge, arbitration, bargaining, and the allocation of benefits. This opened the door for those poisoned by communism to pass laws to undermine society and move humanity closer to destruction.

Liberalism and progressivism reject traditional faith and moral judgment, seeing morality as a secular agreement that changes according to the development of society. Marriage, for example, is regarded as a simple contract between two people who are willing to state their commitment to each other, rather than a vow made before the divine. Recognition of same-sex marriage is based on the ostensible premise of freedom and progress — a premise that is malleable and will inevitably result in the corruption of the law. The separation of traditional morality from justice was reflected in an abortion case that reached the Supreme Court in 1992. Three justices stated: "Some of us as individuals find abortion offensive to our most basic principles of morality, but that cannot control our decision. Our obligation is to define the liberty of all, not to mandate our own moral code." [12]

Put another way, the law prioritizes freedom over morality, and the values of liberty and morality are separate. But liberty, as established by the American Founding Fathers, is a "self-evident" principle, that is, it is bestowed by God — or as the Declaration of Independence puts it, "their Creator." Rejecting the universal standards set by the Creator in order to increase the range of so-called freedoms is a method the devil uses to distort the law and lead humanity to its downfall.

B. SEIZING THE POWERS OF LEGISLATION AND PROMULGATION

Before a new law takes effect, it goes through multiple stages, including its drafting, endorsement by politicians, passage by the legislature, and implementation by law enforcement officials. There also may be court rulings over its legality. During this process, individuals or groups in academia, media, legal circles, and even the entertainment industry exert influence over the preparation and enactment of the law. The communist specter has found representatives across society to help it take control of the legislative process. Various lobbyists have done their best to fill government agencies with leftists. In the judicial branch, they became judges, prosecutors, and other officials responsible for the carriage of justice.

Presidents will do everything in their power to appoint like-minded justices to the Supreme Court, or use executive powers to circumvent the legal system. Historically, liberal US presidents have tended to grant more pardons. In a recent administration, the president commuted the sentences of 1,385 convicts and granted a total of 212 pardons, the greatest number since the administration of President Harry Truman. [13] In one of his final acts before leaving the White House, the president commuted the sentences of 209 individuals and granted pardons to 64 others. Most of those who received pardons were nonviolent drug offenders, but one exception was a man who had been charged and found guilty of leaking 700,000 classified military documents. With presidential clemency, this man's sentence was reduced, and he served less than 7 years of his 35-year sentence. [14]

While the president has the constitutionally ordained power to grant pardons, overuse of this power works against the function and purpose of the law, which is to punish wrongdoing and support upstanding citizens. In 1954, then-Sen. Lyndon B. Johnson of Texas, who later served as the 36th president of the United States, introduced the Johnson Amendment, a provision in the tax code that prohibits nonprofit organizations, including churches, from engaging in certain activities. Violators can have their tax exemptions revoked. Wary of this, some Christian churches have instructed their ministers to avoid certain topics when speaking at the pulpit, including controversial social issues such as abortion, homosexuality, euthanasia, stem cell research, and so on.

The communist specter has also manipulated all political groups in an attempt to change law enforcement through prosecutorial elections. One district attorney, sent to his position by progressive patrons and political groups, fired thirty-one prosecutors during his first week on the job. Calling for an end to "mass incarceration," he also ordered the remainder of his staff to stop prosecuting people for marijuana possession. Similar situations exist in other states. The president of the union for deputy district attorneys in Los Angeles County said that it was as if prosecutors were being called on to "pick and choose" which laws to enforce. In her opinion, it's a "slippery slope" when elected officials are asked to ignore the laws they swore to uphold. [15]

Judges also have jurisdiction to cancel orders from administrative departments. For instance, US immigration law gives the president the right to deny entry to foreigners in emergency situations. However, some judges influenced by liberalism considered a recent travel ban issued by the president to be religious discrimination. Their rulings delayed the ban for over four months until the executive action was upheld by the Supreme Court.

Since lawyers greatly influence court rulings, the political leanings of a legal association can have a direct impact on whether the spirit of the law can be followed. The founder of one lawyers' association with a nationwide presence was a self-avowed socialist who believed in public ownership and said that his ultimate goal was to establish communism. [16] The association boasts a membership in the tens of thousands across the country and an annual budget in the hundreds of millions. It files lawsuits to support causes such as abortion rights, same-sex marriage, and the right of homosexuals to adopt children.

Followers of liberalism and progressivism occupy key political positions across the United States and dominate academia, the media, and social movements. This has allowed the communist specter to wield unprecedented power over the legislative and judicial processes.

C. TWISTED COURT INTERPRETATIONS

Traditional religions emphasize the importance of personal accountability. In the Bible, the book of Ezekiel uses father and son as a parable to depict good and bad. Though they are father and son, they bear the consequences of their respective conduct and are not personally responsible for each other's actions. As the Bible says, "For whatsoever a man soweth, that shall he also reap." Likewise, the Chinese believe that goodness begets goodness and that evil will be punished by heaven.

Liberty means responsibility. A person has the right and freedom to choose his ideas, speech, and actions. He also needs to be responsible for his own choices. Once a person has committed a crime, he should be punished accordingly. This is the principle of justice. Liberal judges, however, encourage people to shirk their responsibilities and shift accountability to prevailing social conditions, such as their economic or racial background, physical and mental health, education, and other demographic parameters, allowing criminals to escape legal punishment.

Prohibiting Public Expressions of Faith

God is everywhere in American life. The nation's motto is "In God We Trust," which is even written on the dollar bill. The US Declaration of Independence states that human rights are what the Creator has given us. All US government officials, including the president and judges, say "So help me God" when they are sworn in. The most common ending to presidential speeches is "God bless America." The Pledge of Allegiance, recited in public schools, describes the United States as "one nation under God."

Some of these traditions have lasted for more than two hundred years, almost as far back as the founding of the United States. But in the past sixty years, they have been constantly challenged by communist followers.

One national lawyers' association aims to remove the Ten Commandments from public display across the United States. The most famous case occurred in Montgomery, Alabama. In 2001, the association called for the removal of a slate bearing the Ten Commandments that was located in the rotunda of the state court. The group found a judge who had been appointed by a Democratic president to hear the case. In a seventy-six-page verdict, the judge ruled in favor of the lawyers' association.

The specifics of the ruling may sound ridiculous. For example, the judge claimed that the "solemn ambiance of the rotunda," the frescoes behind the slate, and the atmosphere created by a picture window featuring a waterfall constituted sufficient reason to have the Ten Commandments removed. The judge also said that the slate's "sloping top" resembled an open Bible and gave viewers cause to "feel as though the State of Alabama is advancing, endorsing, favoring or preferring, Christianity." [17]

As early as 1980, the Supreme Court had banned the Ten Commandments from being displayed in public schools. This decision was the catalyst for an overall movement across the country to have the Ten Commandments removed from public view. In Utah, the national lawyers' association even offered a reward to anyone willing to report those plaques and slates that had not yet been taken down. [18]

One US Circuit Court ruled on June 26, 2002, that public schools were prohibited from holding "sworn oaths" because they included the words "under God." This decision was over-turned by the Supreme Court on June 14, 2004. [19]

This is an ongoing legal battle. The American national anthem, motto, Pledge of Allegiance, school prayers, and the like are under siege by atheists and leftist activists. References to "God," or the Creator, as seen in the Declaration of Independence, reflect the divine principles underpinning the US Constitution, and do not violate the rights of Americans. The public display of the Ten Commandments and other religious plaques underscores the deep faith of the American people. In a nation based on strong spiritual traditions, the rise of political movements attempting to prohibit the public expression of belief in the divine indicates the extent to which communism has penetrated the legal system.

Altering the Spirit of the Constitution Through Interpretation and Case Law

In the drafting of the US Constitution, the Founding Fathers established the separation of powers, with the judicial branch originally having the least power. Congress (the legislative branch) is responsible for passing laws; the president (the executive branch) is responsible for executing and enforcing the laws created by Congress; and the Supreme Court (the judicial branch) has neither the power to pass laws nor to govern.

In 2002, while the Supreme Court was hearing a case concerning the Pledge of Allegiance, polls indicated that 90 percent of Americans supported retaining the phrase "under God." In the House of Representatives, there were 416 votes in favor of retention, versus just three against. [20] In the Senate, the result was 99 to zero. [21] The congressional votes reflected the genuine opinion of the American public.

As elected representatives of the people, members of Congress and the president serve terms that range from two to six years before coming up for reelection. As long as the public and mainstream society are guided by divine standards of morality, the extent to which the president and members of Congress can fall toward the left is limited. On the other hand, Supreme Court justices don't need to heed public opinion, since they hold their positions for life. Furthermore, there are only nine justices. It is comparatively easier to influence the decisions made by these nine individuals than it is to alter public opinion.

In the United States, amending the Constitution requires support from two-thirds of Congress, and three-quarters of the states. These strict measures make it difficult to amend the Constitution outright. Therefore, the progressive strategy is not to amend the Constitution directly, but to reinterpret it. They regard the Constitution as a "living" and continually "evolving" document. Using precedent set by the Supreme Court, they encode the views of the Left into law. In this way, they covertly exert their will over the Constitution, which is tantamount to undermining it.

Divine commandment is no longer the highest principle. The Constitution has taken a heavy beating under the gavels of liberal Supreme Court justices, since their rulings are final and must be respected by even the president. The judicial branch is taking an ever-increasing share of authority among the three branches established by the Founding Fathers. In practice, Supreme Court justices have acquired partial legislative and even executive powers.

Liberal Supreme Court justices have brought a number of consequences upon American society that are severe and difficult to remedy. As things stand, the Supreme Court can, through case hearings, order the removal of the Ten Commandments from public schools and spaces, rewrite criminal procedures, raise taxes, recognize rights to abortion and same-sex marriage, allow the publication and display of pornography, and so on.

The growing supremacy of the judiciary combined with the ruling of liberal judges has given the specter of communism an important tool for achieving its designs.

Promoting Obscene Content in the Name of Freedom

The 1960s was an era of deep transformation across American society. Left-wing students drove the anti-war movement, rock 'n' roll, hippie culture, the feminist movement, sexual liberation, and other anti-traditional currents, raising chaos throughout the country.

The chief justice of the Supreme Court in this period was the liberal Earl Warren. During Warren's term as chief justice, the Supreme Court made very influential and far-reaching rulings. This included the prohibition of prayers in public school and the allowance of publications featuring sexually explicit material. [22][23]

In her book *The Supremacists: The Tyranny of Judges and*

How to Stop It, constitutional law expert Phyllis Schlafly provided statistics showing that from 1966 to 1970, the Supreme Court made thirty-four rulings that overruled lower-level court decisions to prohibit obscene content. [24] The Supreme Court's rulings were not signed, and the majority opinion consisted of just one or two lines. Put another way, even the justices themselves didn't bother to rationalize their decisions.

In 1968, Hollywood abandoned its Motion Picture Production Code, lifting its restrictions on obscene content in film. A profusion of various kinds of pornographic works soon followed, and today they have saturated every corner of society.

The First Amendment of the Constitution guarantees freedom of speech. It was intended to guarantee the right to express political opinions, not to manufacture and disseminate pornography.

Legalizing Drug Abuse

As the world got ready to welcome the new year on December 31, 2017, cable news channel CNN broadcast footage with multiple shots of a female reporter smoking marijuana. Visibly under the influence, she appeared disoriented and unaware of her surroundings. The broadcast received widespread criticism. [25]

In 1996, California became the first US state to legalize medical marijuana, and many states soon followed suit. By 2012, Colorado and Washington had legalized marijuana for "recreational use." In these two states, planting, manufacturing, and selling marijuana to adults is completely legal. It has also since been legalized in California. In October 2018, the Canadian government legalized marijuana use.

Aside from causing serious damage to the human body, drugs are psychologically addictive. Once dependent, people can abandon moral inhibitions in order to obtain more of the drug. On the other hand, those who support legalizing drugs believe it would be an effective way to reduce drug trafficking. They say that legalization allows stricter regulation over the drug, and accordingly a reduction in drug-related crime.

Governments anticipate that legalizing drugs would generate billions of dollars in revenue. But it's not hard to see that as greater numbers of people become addicts, lose their desire to work, and suffer poor health, productivity will fall, and the aggregate wealth created by society will shrink. It is self-evident that legalizing drugs cannot increase government revenue in the long term. Furthermore, judging what is right or wrong shouldn't be based on economic profit, but on divine standards. Traditional morality sees the human form as sacred and created in the divine likeness. Western religions believe the body is the temple of the Holy Spirit, while in the East, it was believed that the body can be improved through cultivation to become a Buddha or a Tao. Drug abuse, then, is an act of desecration.

According to a report by the *Los Angeles Times*, one of the important figures lobbying for the legalization of marijuana in the United States is a wealthy progressive. [26] In March 2017, six senators wrote a letter to the US State Department requesting that this individual be investigated for using his foundation to promote progressivism abroad and subvert conservative governments. [27]

The legalization of drugs is an additional step toward encouraging people to lose their inhibitions and cut them off from the divine. As society experiences turmoil and economic downturns, communists seize opportunities to gain political power.

Legalizing Same-Sex Marriage

Schlafly listed twelve methods judges use to undermine morality: rewrite the Constitution, censor acknowledgment of God, redefine marriage, undermine US sovereignty, threaten property rights, promote pornography, foster feminism, handicap law enforcement, invite illegal immigration, interfere with elections, take over parents' rights, and impose taxes. [28]

The book of Genesis describes the destruction of Sodom. One of the crimes the doomed city's residents committed was to engage in homosexuality. This is the origin of the term "sodomy," meaning sexual relations between men. Those with basic knowledge of the Bible know that homosexuality goes against the will of God.

In June 2015, the Supreme Court ruled in a 5–4 decision that same-sex marriage is a right guaranteed by the Constitution. [29] When the ruling was passed, the US president at the time changed the banner on the White House's official Twitter account to the rainbow flag in support of LGBT rights. The Supreme Court's ruling prohibited the thirteen states that still banned same-sex marriage from enforcing their laws. In August 2015, a clerk in Rowan County, Kentucky, refused to issue marriage certificates for same-sex couples due to her beliefs. She was later jailed for five nights for defying a US federal court order to issue the documents. [30] In fact, the court had violated her constitutional right to freedom of belief. Commenting on the clerk's case, former governor of Arkansas and former Republican presidential candidate Mike Huckabee called the Supreme Court's ruling on marriage "judicial tyranny." [31]

As of 2019, twenty-eight countries and territories had officially acknowledged or accepted same-sex marriage, including developed Western countries such as the United States, the United Kingdom, France, Germany, Spain, Norway, Denmark, Finland, Sweden, Portugal, Belgium, Australia, New Zealand, and Canada. The law has the power to reinforce morality or influence its movement in a new direction. To legalize behavior that deviates from traditional moral values is the same as having the government and laws train the people to betray morality and disobey divine commandments.

Under the influence of political correctness, criticism of the chaos that our society finds itself in — whether from the people, civil associations, or religious groups in particular —

can be easily escalated to the level of politics or law, and result in restrictions on free speech or other punishments. Following the legalization of immoral behavior, those who make any comments or criticisms on related issues are often accused of violating laws, such as those concerning gender discrimination. The law has been twisted into a means of strangling people's ability to make moral judgments. It is essentially promoting homosexuality and encouraging people to give themselves to endless desire and degeneracy.

D. RESTRICTING LAW ENFORCEMENT

Under liberal influence, many judges or legislative agencies deliberately curtail the legitimate power of law enforcement, effectively turning a blind eye to crime. The communist specter's aim in doing this is to paralyze the state apparatus in order to stir up social turmoil, which in turn creates excuses either for the expansion of government, or the necessary conditions for a coup or revolution.

Many states have passed far-left laws, a typical example being "sanctuary state" policies. Among other provisions, sanctuary states often prohibit federal immigration officials from arresting illegal immigrants in local prisons, including those with outstanding warrants for arrest. Local police are barred from cooperating and communicating with federal agents to enforce immigration laws.

This poses a serious security risk for the public. In July 2015, illegal immigrant José Inez García Zárate shot and killed a young woman who was walking along a pier in San Francisco. Zárate had a history of crime: He had been charged with seven felonies involving drugs and robbery, and possession of weaponry, and had been deported five times. Under San Francisco's sanctuary laws, officials released Zárate from custody three months before the fatal shooting, rather than transfer him to federal immigration authorities, who had requested custody of him for deportation.

When a criminal stands trial, extremely strict standards are placed on the prosecution. This is ostensibly to protect the legitimate rights of the suspect, but often the result is that criminals are able to take advantage of loopholes in the law. Cunning suspects, or those who enjoy status or privileges, who understand the law and regulations, or who hire capable attorneys, can drag out the legal process, at great cost to the judicial system. It can be very difficult to bring guilty suspects to justice.

Influenced by the spread of "sexual liberation," verdicts in cases involving sex crimes often cite findings in research by Alfred Kinsey or activists who follow him to argue that the damage caused by sex abuse is little or nonexistent. Many cases have been settled by reducing the sentences of sexual predators. [32] Many ordinary criminals also have had their original sentences reduced, ostensibly owing to budget shortages or on account of prisoners' rights. The real motivation, though, is to use political correctness to weaken the power of the law, disturb social order, and pave the way for further expansion of government.

For the law to be fair, it must administer strict punishments to those who commit unpardonable crimes. Since antiquity, murder has been punishable by death. But today, some countries and territories have abolished capital punishment on such grounds as "humanity," "tolerance," or a supposed respect for life.

Under the influence of twisted liberalism and progressivism, some people give undue weight to prisoners' rights — no matter the severity of their crimes — while remaining strangely silent regarding the victims. If a murderer is fed and housed by taxpayer money, his loss of freedom is hardly a fair trade for the death of the victim and the trauma it causes to loved ones.

Many researchers in the United States have found that capital punishment is effective in deterring crime. David Muhlhausen, a senior policy analyst in The Heritage Foundation, testified in front of the Senate Judiciary Committee in 2007 that capital punishment has a deterrent effect and can save lives. In the 1990s, three professors, including Paul Rubin at Emory University, examined twenty years of crime statistics from three thousand cities and towns across the United States and concluded that "each execution results, on average, in 18 fewer murders — with a margin of error of plus or minus 10." [33]

Even scholars who are against capital punishment must concede that it has a deterrent effect. By pushing the concepts of freedom and legality to extremes, the Left has distorted the law and robbed it of its sanctity.

E. USING FOREIGN LAWS TO WEAKEN US SOVEREIGNTY

When liberal judges can't find wording in the US Constitution to support their personal opinions, they use laws passed in other countries to sustain their arguments.

For instance, in the Supreme Court case of *Lawrence v. Texas* (2003), the liberal justices wanted to repeal a Texas statute banning consenting homosexual adults from engaging in sexual acts, but they could not find anything from the Constitution to support this case. They then quoted an "authoritative" agency outside of the United States as saying that homosexuality was "an integral part of human freedom in many other countries," and successfully repealed the law. This case resulted in repeals of similar statutes in thirteen other states. [34]

Communist thought has spread around the world in different forms. The socialist trend throughout Asia and Europe is plain to see, and it has great influence in Africa and Latin America as well. Countries such as Zimbabwe and Venezuela are socialist countries in all but name. Even Canada is not free of its influence.

Commerce and globalization have brought the United States in closer connection with other countries. In order to introduce elements of socialism domestically, liberal judges leverage the excuse of conforming to international convention and then use case law to alter the spirit of the Constitution. If even the United States, as the leader of the free world, can't maintain basic, traditional standards, the entire globe will be lost to communism.

4. Restoring the Spirit of the Law

Today, the law has been turned against the divine teachings that originally inspired it. Legality has become a tool the communist specter uses to trample upon the moral foundation of human society, bringing it to the brink of destruction. Anti-traditional and immoral legislation has weakened the ability of the law to maintain social order, leaving the expansion of state power as the only "solution" to the malaise.

Under a legal system controlled by the communist specter, people would be left with only two options: Either refuse to follow the authorities and their degenerate laws, or betray their morality in order to comply. The former would mean the destruction of law in practice, for as jurist Harold Berman put it, "The law must be believed in; otherwise, it exists in name only." [35] The latter option entails a slippery slope of moral decline, creating a downward spiral in which the law and the state of society compete in a race to reach rock bottom. In either case, society at large would have no way out of this demonic vortex.

The 1958 book *The Naked Communist* lists forty-five goals pursued by communism in order to infiltrate and undermine the United States. Seven of them concern the legal system. [36]

The sixteenth goal consists of using the courts' technical decisions to weaken important US institutions by claiming that their conduct infringes upon civil rights.

The twenty-fourth goal is to abolish all laws restricting indecent content by portraying them as censorship that violates free speech and expression.

The twenty-ninth is to challenge the Constitution as flawed, obsolete, or incompatible with international practice.

The thirty-third is to abolish all laws that interfere with the communist apparatus.

The thirty-eighth goal is to make it legal for non-police agencies to carry out arrests. All behavioral problems are to be delegated to mental health workers.

The thirty-ninth is to wrest control over the field of psychiatry and impose mental health laws to control individuals who oppose communist aims.

The forty-fifth goal is to abolish the Connally Reservation, also known as the Connally Amendment. This regulation gives the United States the right to favor domestic jurisdiction over rulings by international courts. The purpose of this goal is to prevent the United States from protecting its domestic sovereignty and to instead have international bodies such as the International Court of Justice overrule the US judiciary.

Looking at the goals listed above and comparing them with what has already been implemented, it is apparent that communism is well-placed to continue undermining US law and justice.

Be it state-sponsored policies of hatred in countries controlled by communist regimes, or regulation in Western countries where communist ideology has hollowed out the legislative and judicial institutions, in both cases the target is the spirit of the law — that is, reverence for the divine and traditional morality.

If we are unable to maintain the moral standards dictated by divine commandment as our criteria for recognizing ultimate good and evil, society will continue to pass laws that conform to communist ideology, favoring the wicked and suppressing the righteous. Society will lose its divine principles of justice and liberty and succumb to the communist specter's tyranny.

Chapter Eleven

Desecrating the Arts

1. Art: A Gift From the Divine

OVER THE MANY YEARS of human civilization, man has contemplated what constitutes true beauty. People of faith know that all the wonders of the world come from the divine. Profound art is an attempt to emulate and display the beauty of heaven in the human world. Inspiration comes from the divine, and artists can become outstanding figures in their fields if they receive divine blessings and wisdom.

With strong faith in and devotion to the divine, great artists during the Renaissance plumbed their ingenuity to create works in praise of God. Artists in the mid-Renaissance period, including Leonardo da Vinci, Michelangelo, and Raphael, grasped techniques that far exceeded those of their predecessors and their peers, as if by miracle. Their masterpieces

— including paintings, statues, and architecture — became timeless classics of the art world.

For centuries, these works of art set a noble example for humanity. By appreciating this art, not only can the artists of later generations study pure artistic technique, but members of the public can truly feel and see the presence of the divine. When these works, the techniques that created them, and the spirit that infused the artists are all preserved, human society is able to maintain a connection with the divine. Then, even as humanity goes through its periods of decadence and decline, there will be hope for a return to tradition and a path to salvation.

The same principles prevail in the sphere of music. As the saying (reportedly, from a German opera house) goes: "Bach gave us God's word. Mozart gave us God's laughter. Beethoven gave us God's fire. God gave us music that we might pray without words." For his entire life, Johann Sebastian Bach considered devotion to God and the praise and worship of God to be the highest principles in the creation of his music. On all of his important musical scores, the letters SDG can be seen — an abbreviation of "Soli Deo gloria," meaning "glory to God alone."

The highest level an artist can reach is through the materialization of heavenly objects in the human realm through divine revelation. The great paintings and statues, and the most sublime scores in the early, baroque, and classical canon, were all created by religious believers and represent the pinnacle of artistic work attained by man.

The three most important elements in artistic creation are representation, creation, and communication. All artistic creations contain a theme, that is, the message the artist seeks to communicate, regardless of the form the work takes — whether it be a poem, painting, statue, photograph, novel, play, dance, or film. The artist delivers the theme to the hearts of the reader, listener, or viewer. This process is the communication

— the transmission of the artist's mind to the recipient.

To achieve the goal of communication, artists must possess a superb ability to imitate and represent, with the object of imitation being the world of gods or of man, or even the underworld. Artistic creation is a process of refining the deeper or more essential elements of an object of representation. It requires artists to strengthen their own ability to communicate and to touch people's hearts. If the artist possesses righteous faith in the divine and in morality, the divine will endow him with the inspiration to create. Such works will be divine, pure, and benevolent — beneficial to both the artist and society.

On the other hand, when the artist abandons moral standards, negative elements hijack the creative process, with evil forces exerting influence and using the artist to depict hideous creations and grotesqueries from the underworld. Works of this kind harm their author and the wider society.

The value of the orthodox, traditional arts thus becomes clear. Divine culture and art in the East and the West were connections woven between the divine and human civilization, and were meant to bring them into contact. The ideas and messages transmitted through this art are beauty, benevolence, light, and hope. On the other hand, corrupt works of "art" are created by those under the control of evil elements. They drive a wedge between man and the divine, and drag humans closer to evil.

2. Art's Immense Influence on Humanity

Great works of art transmit heritage, disseminate knowledge and wisdom, and fortify character. They hold exalted positions in the great civilizations of the West and the East.

The ancient Greek mathematician and philosopher Pythagoras believed that the secret of music was in its imitation of the harmony of the heavenly bodies, which itself reflects the harmony of the universe.

The Chinese held similar views. The *Treatises on Music and Harmony* discuss music's correspondence with the five elements (metal, wood, water, fire, and earth), and how musical instruments are constructed to represent and emulate the patterns of heaven and earth. Only in this way can "music of the grandest style" be achieved, that which exhibits "the same harmony that prevails between heaven and earth." [1] This kind of music is able to not only attract divine birds like the crane and phoenix, but also serve as an invitation to deities to grace the occasion with their presence.

Confucius once said: "[The Zhou Dynasty] surveyed the two dynasties that went before; its ways are refined and elegant. I follow Zhou." [2] He admired how the legendary Chinese rulers governed with ritual and music: "The Sage-Emperor Shun invented a five-stringed musical instrument, which he called qin, sang to its tune about the gentle summer breeze from the south, and lo and behold, his empire ran smoothly [under the influence of his music]." [3] These examples illustrate the edifying effects of pure, upright music.

The "Music of Prince of Qin Breaking Up the Enemy's Front," composed by the great Tang Dynasty emperor Li Shimin, won the deep respect of ethnic groups living on the periphery of the Tang realm. The *New Book of Tang* recorded that on the journey to seek Buddhist scriptures from the West, monk Xuanzang was told by a king in a remote Indian state, "Your emperor must be a saint, for he composed the 'Music of Prince of Qin Breaking Up the Enemy's Front.'" [4]

During the reign of Louis XIV, the French royal court displayed great elegance through dance and art. Dance contains not only the techniques of movement, but also social etiquette and norms. Louis XIV inspired Europe through the art and culture of his court and was emulated by other courts and the population at large in Europe.

Not only was Frederick the Great of Prussia an outstanding king, but he was also an accomplished musician, composer, and flautist. He ordered the construction of the Berlin opera house, personally supervised the opera, and opened it to a wider set of social classes. To this day, opera remains an important part of German culture. These few examples make clear the long-lasting influence that orthodox art can exert on society.

Upright art conforms to natural law, imitates divine wisdom, and brings with it special energy and effects. It benefits people by feeding both the senses and the soul. The greatest artists work not only on the physical, technical level, but also, more importantly, on the spiritual level, in their communion with the theme of the work. Such artists sometimes express a sense of experiencing a higher force beyond this physical world. The effect is similar to that of singing an ode to God — a solemn and divine experience that transcends human language. Behind true art lies the accumulated wisdom of a people, their creativity, and their inspiration. There are often profound meanings that go far beyond what is seen on the surface. Some works transmit a special kind of spiritual energy. All of this has an effect on viewers at a deep, spiritual level. The effect is singular and irreplaceable by any other means.

A superb artist can influence the morality of society by instilling values into people's hearts through poignant stories and images. Even people without deep learning or education can gain insight, inspiration, and moral lessons from traditional art. In traditional Western societies, consider how many learned right from wrong, good from evil, through the medium of folk tales such as "Hansel and Gretel" and "Snow White."

In China, many generations learned from the four great novels (*Water Margin*, *Journey to the West*, *Romance of the Three Kingdoms*, and *Dream of the Red Chamber*) and from the traditional arts of storytelling and drama. Such works allow people to feel divine greatness and make them yearn to assimilate to heavenly principles.

Degenerate values also exert an invisible influence through art. Screenwriting lecturer Robert McKee wrote in his book *Story: Substance, Structure, Style and the Principles of Screenwriting*: "Every effective story sends a charged idea out to us, in effect compelling the idea into us, so that we must believe. In fact, the persuasive power of a story is so great that we may believe its meaning even if we find it morally repellent." [5]

Art can have tremendous impacts — both positive and negative — on human morality, thought, and behavior.

"The Mozart effect," for instance, has attracted worldwide attention, with the scientific community conducting a number of studies on the positive influence of Wolfgang Amadeus Mozart's music on people and animals. In 2016, a more in-depth study of the Mozart effect found that the composer's music has positive effects on human cognitive function and behavior. Surprisingly, playing Mozart's music in reverse has the opposite effect. Austrian composer Arnold Schoenberg's modern atonal music has an effect similar to that of playing Mozart backwards, which demonstrates its negative qualities. [6]

Compared with atonal music, rock 'n' roll can have an even greater negative effect. One researcher compiled data from two similar cities and found that the city in which a large number of rock songs were broadcast via radio and television saw 50 percent more cases of pregnancy out of wedlock, dropouts, youth deaths, crimes, and so on. [7] Some rock music even glorifies suicide. One commentator, referring to a song by a famous rock star who faced several lawsuits from parents of young listeners, wrote, "Its dark rhythms and depressing lyrics certainly can be taken as an encouragement for suicide, and it is an irrefutable fact that young people have snuffed out their lives while listening to it repeatedly." [8] It is not uncommon for teens who commit suicide to do as described in rock lyrics, and numerous rock musicians have themselves descended into depression and drug abuse, or taken their own lives.

Another well-known example of art put to negative use is the Nazi propaganda film *Triumph of the Will*. Despite director Leni Riefenstahl's argument that she had merely created a documentary, the propaganda film exhibits superb artistic mastery. The grand scenes and displays of strength made audiences resonate with the energy and power behind it. Her many innovative shooting techniques and technical prowess influenced film for decades to come. Yet the work also became a crucial piece of propaganda for Hitler and Nazi Germany and is known as one of the most successful works of propaganda in history. An obituary for Riefenstahl published in the British newspaper *The Independent* in 2003 stated, "*Triumph of the Will* seduced many wise men and women, persuaded them to admire rather than to despise, and undoubtedly won the Nazis friends and allies all over the world." [9]

Understanding the great power of art can help us better understand the importance of traditional art and why evil elements want to undermine and sabotage it.

3. Communism's Sabotage and Abuse of Art

Since art has such a tremendous effect on society, it's not surprising that communism uses art to achieve its aim of socially engineering humans and leading them toward destruction.

A. ART IN COMMUNIST COUNTRIES

Communist parties know the power of art and they turn all art forms into tools for advancing their brainwashing. Many people have ridiculed the Chinese Communist Party (CCP) for having singers and actors become military generals. They wonder how civilians who have never been trained in arms or warfare could be qualified to be generals. The CCP believes that these people are just as important as trained military personnel in promoting and upholding the communist cult — or perhaps even more crucial. In this sense, its military ranks conform perfectly with Party principles. As Mao Zedong said, "We must also have a cultural army, which is absolutely indispensable for uniting our own ranks and defeating the enemy." [10]

Artistic performances in communist countries are designed to have people forget the miseries they suffer under communist rule and to cultivate their loyalty to the communist party through art. This propaganda effect — called "thought work" — cannot be achieved by mere martial power.

One can compare the CCP's grand opening ceremony at the Beijing Olympics, which was put on at enormous cost to the taxpayer, to North Korea's large-scale song and dance festival Arirang and the former Soviet Union's ballet troupes. All served the needs of the party.

In September 2011, the CCP's Ministry of Culture held a so-called Chinese culture festival, China: The Art of a Nation, at the John F. Kennedy Center for the Performing Arts in Washington, DC. It included the CCP's signature propaganda piece, the ballet *Red Detachment of Women*, which promotes class hatred and violent revolution.

If upright art that was close to the divine and promoted traditional values were allowed to exist simultaneously with party-controlled art used for brainwashing the public, then the latter would lose its monopoly and have no effect. This is why all communist countries maintain strict censorship over the arts and the publishing industry.

B. COMMUNIST ELEMENTS BEHIND THE AVANT-GARDE MOVEMENT

For centuries, classical art has been passed down from generation to generation. This tradition continued until the twentieth century, when it came to an abrupt end. The transmission and inheritance of art were disrupted by a radical avant-garde movement and began to quickly degenerate. As artist Robert Florczak said: "The profound, the inspiring, and the beautiful were replaced by the new, the different, and the ugly. ... Standards declined until there were no standards. All that was left was personal expression." [11] Humanity thus lost its universal sense of the aesthetic.

The source of this battery of new artistic movements is closely connected to ideological trends influenced by communism. Many of these artists were either avowed communists or para-communists of one kind or another, or they were subject to the sway of these ideologies.

Georg Lukács, the Hungarian cultural commissioner of the Communist International and founder of Western Marxism, created the Frankfurt School. One of its tasks was to establish a "new cultural form" by abandoning traditional culture. This new cultural form set about excluding art that sought to represent the divine. As Herbert Marcuse, a German socialist and a representative of the Frankfurt School, wrote: "Art both protests these [existing social] relations, and at the same time transcends them. Thereby art subverts the dominant consciousness, the ordinary experience." [12] That is, Marxists enlist art in the revolt against the divine and the subversion of morality. Views of this sort dominate the direction of modern art.

Gustave Courbet, the founder of the French realist school, was a participant in the Paris Commune. He was elected as a committee member of the Commune and the chairman of the radical Federation of Artists. Courbet devoted himself to transforming the old system and establishing new artistic directions. He ordered the Federation to demolish the intricate neoclassical Vendôme Column (which was later rebuilt). Courbet denied that human beings were created by God, and he was determined to use art to express the worldview of the proletariat, as well as materialism. He is known for saying, "I have never seen either angels or goddesses, so I am not interested in painting them." [13]

Courbet believed that reforming the arts was really waging a revolution. In the name of painting what he called "reality," he replaced beauty with ugliness. His nude paintings, for instance, focused in particular on depicting the female genitalia — a supposed revolutionary act — as a way of rebelling, transgressing against tradition, and somehow further inciting communist activism. The thinking and life of Courbet illustrate the close link between the communist ideology of revolution and modern art.

Under the influence of modernist thought, the revolutionary fervor of artists from the late nineteenth century brought about a series of movements in the art world. Unlike traditional schools of artistic expression, these were avant-garde movements that explicitly sought to rupture tradition. The term "avant-garde" was first used by socialist scholars to describe artistic movements that matched their own political aspirations.

In the late nineteenth century, these influences brought about impressionism. Ever since, modern artists have abandoned the demands of traditional oil painting, including precision, proportion, structure, perspective, and transitions between light and shade. Neoimpressionism (pointillism) and postimpressionism then emerged, centering their works on the exploration of the personal feelings of the artist. Representative figures in this school include Georges-Pierre Seurat and Vincent van Gogh, both of whom were inclined toward socialism. Van Gogh abused alcohol and suffered mental illness later in life, and his paintings appeared to reflect the world that people experience while under the influence of drugs.

Works of art contain the messages their creators wanted to convey. Artists during the peak of the Renaissance conveyed compassion and beauty to their audiences. Compare this to contemporary artists, who exude negative and dark messages. Modern artists abandon their own thoughts and allow themselves to come under the control of low-level and ghostly entities. They themselves are often incoherent and confused, and their works are similar — dark, negative, hazy, gray, depressed, decadent, and disordered.

After impressionism came expressionism and fauvism, followed by Pablo Picasso's cubism. In 1944, Picasso joined the French Communist Party. In his letter *Why I Became a Communist*, he wrote: "My joining the Communist Party is a logical step in my life, my work and gives them their meaning. ... In my own ways I have always said what I considered most true, most just and best and, therefore, most beautiful. But during the oppression and the insurrection, I felt that that was not enough, that I had to fight not only with painting but with my whole being." [14]

Picasso encouraged a break with the classical methods of painting. For him, everything was a piece of dough to be picked up and shaped as he pleased. The eerier his works became, the happier he appeared to be. The process of creating monstrous images is the process of destroying an image, to the point where no one can understand it. Even Georges Braque, the modern artist who co-founded cubism with Picasso, on viewing Picasso's *Les Demoiselles d'Avignon,* was "horrified by its ugliness and intensity." Picasso had been "drinking turpentine and spitting fire," acting more like a carnival performer than an artist, he said. [15]

Marcel Duchamp, an early member of the dada art movement, also sought to subvert and rebel against tradition with his display and use of readymade objects. He repurposed found or factory-made items and turned them into so-called art installations. Duchamp, who was called the father of conceptual art, advocated the idea that anything could be called art. The dadaist movement is itself a communistic project, as evidenced by the manifesto of the Berlin dadaists, who called for an "international revolutionary union of all creative and intellectual men and women on the basis of radical Communism," as well as "the immediate expropriation of property (socialization) and the communal feeding of all" and "the erection of cities of light, and gardens which will belong to society as a whole and prepare man for a state of freedom." [16]

Dadaism's criticism of tradition evolved into surrealism in France, as represented by the communist André Breton, who advocated revolution. He was against the supposed suppression brought by reason, culture, and society — a view typical of the modern artists in Europe at the time.

The artistic movements that extended these principles include abstractism, minimalism, pop art, and postmodernism. Abstractism is about the emotional expression of rebellion, disorder, emptiness, and escapism. The ugly trampling of moral values is evident in these "-isms" in the arts today. At their most outrageous, these artists create works that openly desecrate religious figures like Jesus Christ.

Not all modern artists support leftwing politics, but there is a clear ideological commonality with communist thought — that is, the rejection of the divine, and the aim to replace the divine as the starting point for understanding human life. These "-isms" came to exert increasing influence in the public sphere and ultimately have led to the complete marginalization of classical art.

C. THE INVERSION OF TRADITIONAL AESTHETICS: THE UGLY AS ART

The numerous schools of modern art that have appeared and developed share several things in common: They invert conventional aesthetics; they take ugliness as beauty; and they aim to shock, even to the point of being as ghastly as the artist's imagination allows.

Marcel Duchamp signed his name on a urinal and named it *Fountain*, to be put on display for the public in New York. Though the object was never put on display, Duchamp's action was considered a clever joke among his peers in the art world, and later artists and academics have thought it the height of creativity. This is the environment in the art world, whereby classical easel painting has been marginalized and installation art has risen to prominence. In 1958, Yves Klein held his exhibition *The Void* at the Iris Clert Gallery in Paris. The displayed works turned out to be empty, white walls.

A major figure of the postwar German avant-garde, Joseph Beuys, covered his head with honey and gold leaf and murmured nonstop for three hours to a dead hare in his arms in the 1965 work *How to Explain Pictures to a Dead Hare*. In Beuys's view, anyone could be an artist. One anecdote goes that a frustrated questioner once shouted at him, "You talk about everything under the sun, except art!" Beuys reportedly responded, "Everything under the sun is art!" [17]

In 1961, Piero Manzoni, a key figure of the avant-garde, claimed he had put his own feces in ninety cans, called them artwork, and put them up for sale under the name *Merda d'artista* ("Artist's Shit"). In 2015, one of the cans was sold in London for a record price of 182,500 pounds, or about US$240,000, hundreds of times the price of the same weight in gold. He also signed his name on the bodies of nude women as part of a series he called *Sculture viventi* ("Living Sculpture").

In China, there was a nude "artist" who coated his body with honey and fish oil to attract flies. Desecration of the body seems intended to communicate the idea that life is cheap, ugly, and disgusting. In the BBC documentary *Beijing Swings*, about "extreme artists" in China, so-called performance art included the performative consumption of a human fetus. Amidst public condemnation that such art was "hideous," art critic Waldemar Januszczak, the presenter of the documentary, inadvertently revealed its true nature in saying, "It is worth trying to understand why China is producing the most outrageous and darkest art, of anywhere in the world." [18] In fact, this is a result of the pursuit of the demonic. Some of these modern, so-called works of art are so filthy and shameless that they exceed the mental endurance of normal people. Such behavior of the avant-garde is the Cultural Revolution of the art world.

Those who support modernism have taken to the trend like ducks to water, but painters truly proficient in the technical skill of painting have a tough time. Painters and sculptors who adhere strictly to tradition, who master their craft through painstaking practice, have been squeezed out of the art world. John William Godward, the English Victorian neoclassicist painter associated with the Pre-Raphaelite Brotherhood, felt that he was discriminated against given that his style of realistic classical painting fell out of favor with the rise of Picasso's modernist works. In 1922, he committed suicide and was said to have written in his suicide note, "The world is not big enough for myself and a Picasso." [19]

Similar methods were adopted to ruin music. Authentic music conforms with musical theory and order. Musical tuning and the keys and modes it produces are all derived from harmonious natural patterns. The universe created by the divine is harmonious. Humans are able to appreciate and participate in the harmony of the universe, and thus create beauty, since humans are also created by the divine.

Modern atonal music rejects ideas like tonality, chords, and melody, and lacks order in its structure. Such music is a revolt against divinely imparted classical music. Atonal music violates the harmony in the universe, which is why many audiences find it unpleasant. Modernist musicians argue, based on their warped theories of aesthetics, that audience members must train their ears to get used to such music so that they can enjoy it.

Schoenberg, one of the founders of modern music, introduced his "twelve-tone system," a fundamentally atonal structure that marked the creation of anti-classical musical technique. Schoenberg's music was considered the negation of all German musical culture until then — the betrayal of taste, feeling, tradition, and all aesthetic principles. His music was called "cocaine" by Germans at the time: "To perform Schoenberg means the same as to open a cocaine bar for the people. Cocaine is poison. Schoenberg's music is cocaine." [20] In later generations, a music critic assessed him thus: "It is a measure of the immensity of the man's achievement that, fifty years after his death, he can still empty any hall on earth." [21]

What led to the widespread acceptance of Schoenberg was the musical theories of Theodor W. Adorno, an important figure in the Frankfurt School. In Adorno's 1949 work *Philosophy of Modern Music*, he portrayed Schoenberg as the "quintessential exponent of modernism in music" and explained Schoenberg's twelve-tone compositional method as the culmination of the attempt to grant music "an autonomous status and structural self-sufficiency in response to the omnipresent domination of capitalistic ideology." Adorno's philosophical support for Schoenberg set the stage for the widespread acceptance of Schoenberg's system by later generations of composers and music critics. [22] Since then, numerous musicians have emulated Schoenberg, and his avant-garde style has had a major impact on the postwar music world.

After destroying tradition with modern music, avant-garde art used rock 'n' roll to supplant the role of classical music in people's lives. Sidney Finkelstein, the leading music theorist of the Communist Party USA, openly declared that the boundaries between classical and popular music should be eliminated. At around the same time, strongly rhythmic rock music was gaining an increasing foothold in the United States, as classical and traditional music was squeezed out and marginalized.

The characteristics of rock 'n' roll include inharmonious sounds, unstructured melodies, strong rhythmic beats, and emotional conflict — quite similar to the communist idea of struggle. According to the *Records of the Grand Historian* by China's foremost ancient historian, Sima Qian, only when sound conforms to morality can it be called music. Typically, the lives and compositions of rock 'n' roll musicians are centered around sex, violence, and drugs.

Rock 'n' roll, along with other modern sounds such as rap and hip-hop, continued to gain popularity in the United States. Rappers flaunt their rebellion against tradition and society with their casual use of drugs, obscene language, and unruly, violent behavior. As the morality of society as a whole declines, such "art forms," previously regarded as the product of subcultures, have made their way into the wider society and are even sought-after by mainstream performance venues.

We have so far focused on the current circumstances in the worlds of art and music. In fact, the entire artistic world has been greatly impacted, and the influence of the modern art movement can be seen in the deviation from traditional ideas, methods, and skills in areas like sculpture, architecture, dance, decoration, design, photography, movies, and more.

Many people who are engaged in modern art are strongly influenced by communist ideology. For example, the founder of modern dance, Isadora Duncan, was openly bisexual and an atheist. She objected to ballet, calling it ugly and unnatural. In 1921, she and 150 children with barely any dance training performed her work "Internationale," set to the communist anthem, in Moscow for Communist Party elites, including Vladimir Lenin. [23]

As for why these deviations exist and become trendy, or even mainstream, it is closely related to communism's corruption of divinely inspired traditional arts. On the surface, of course, this is not apparent, and the situation seems to be a form of self-deception that has been widely accepted — the notion that if there's a theory behind it, then it's art.

If people look closely at the differences between avant-garde and traditional art, they will find that the artists of the Renaissance not only used art to praise God, but also presented beauty in an uplifting manner that engendered feelings of truth and goodness in the human heart. In doing so, their art helped maintain the morality of society.

On the other hand, the various mutated forms of avant-garde try to upend all the achievements of the Renaissance, "to destroy the uplifting — therefore, bourgeois — potential of art, literature, and music, so that man, *bereft of his connection to the divine*, sees his only creative option to be political revolt." Ugliness that is "so carefully nurtured by the Frankfurt School [has] corrupted our highest cultural endeavors," and popular culture in turn, becomes "openly bestial," wrote one academic. [24] Admiring and idolizing such ugliness brings forth the dark side of people; decadent, depraved, violent, evil, and other negative kinds of thoughts gain ascendancy. The pursuit of such ugliness has led to deconstructing and uglifying scenes of the divine, humanity's own divine nature, morality and society, and even direct blasphemy against the divine. Not only has this alienated humans from the divine, it has also alienated them from their innate divine nature, society, and traditional values.

D. THE PERVERSION OF LITERATURE

Literature is a special art form. It uses language to pass on the wisdom that the divine has bestowed upon humankind, as well as record the formative experiences of humankind. The two great epics of ancient Greece, *The Iliad* and *The Odyssey*, both portray the complex series of events surrounding the Trojan War, vividly depicting a historical epic of gods and men. The virtues of courage, generosity, wisdom, justice, and temperance that were praised in the epics became an important source of values for the Greek world and all of Western civilization.

Due to the great influence literature has, evil elements use it to control people, concocting and promoting written works that impart the ideology of communism, slander traditional culture, destroy people's morality, and spread pessimism and an attitude of passivity and meaninglessness toward life. Literature has become one of the key tools communism uses to control the world.

During the history of the Soviet Union and the CCP, in order to brainwash the general public, the respective communist parties instructed their intellectuals to portray, using traditional techniques, the lives of the proletariat and the concept of class consciousness in order to explain the ideology and policies of the communist party. This gave rise to a large number of propagandistic literary works, including the Soviet novels *The Iron Flood* and *How the Steel Was Tempered*, and the CCP works *The Song of Youth*, *The Sun Shines on the Sanggan River*, and others, all of which had an enormous impact. Communist parties call this style of work "socialist realism." Mao generalized its function as "serving the workers, peasants, and soldiers," serving "the proletariat." [25] The ability of this type of literature to instill ideology is obvious and well-understood. However, communism's use of literature to destroy humanity is not limited to this type.

The following summarizes some of the major aims and effects of communist-influenced literature.

Using Literature to Destroy Tradition

A major step in the destruction of humanity has been to slander the traditional civilizations that the divine bestowed on mankind. Whether in China or the West, communist elements use intellectuals with modern thoughts to create and promote works that distort or slander traditional culture.

During China's New Culture Movement, the author Lu Xun became famous for viciously attacking tradition and denouncing Chinese antiquity. In his first novel, *A Madman's Diary*, he had the protagonist declare that all of Chinese history could be summed up in two characters: "man eating." Lu Xun was praised by Mao as "the greatest and most courageous standard-bearer of this new cultural force" and "the chief commander of China's Cultural Revolution." Mao also said, "The road he took was the very road of China's new national culture." [26]

In Europe in 1909, Italian poet Filippo Tommaso Marinetti published the *Futurist Manifesto*, calling for the total rejection of tradition and the celebration of machinery, technology, speed, violence, and competition. Russian poet and communist Vladimir Mayakovsky published the manifesto *A*

Slap in the Face of Public Taste in 1913, in which he expressed his resolve to break away from traditional Russian literature.

Defending Hideous Portrayals as 'Reality'

Today, intellectuals and artists use literature and the arts to portray things or scenes that are ugly, strange, and terrifying, using the excuse that they are merely showing things as they really are.

Traditional art conveys harmony, grace, clarity, restraint, propriety, balance, universality, and ideals, which require selection and choice. In the view of modern artists, such works cannot be considered real. This view, however, comes from a misunderstanding of the origin and function of art. Art originates from everyday life, but it should transcend everyday life so that it may both delight and instruct. Because of this, during the creative process, artists must select, refine, and process what to portray.

Blindly focusing on this understanding of realism artificially restricts the boundaries of life and art. If this type of realism is art, then what everyone sees and hears is all art — in which case, why spend time and money training artists?

Corrupting Moral Values

Pretexts such as "expressing one's true self" and giving free rein to one's "stream of consciousness" have led people to abandon traditional moral standards and indulge in the demonic side of human nature.

French communist and poet André Breton defined surrealism as "psychic automatism in its pure state, by which one proposes to express — verbally, by means of the written word, or in any other manner — the actual functioning of thought. Dictated by thought, in the absence of any control exercised by reason, exempt from any aesthetic or moral concern." [27]

The "stream of consciousness" writing and surrealist "automatic writing" are closely related. Influenced by Sigmund

Freud's psychopathology, some writers in the West started to experiment with stream-of-consciousness writing from the beginning of the twentieth century. Such writings usually have simple storylines and focus on the inner and private thought processes of insignificant characters (anti-heroes) through narratives composed of meandering thoughts.

Human beings simultaneously contain the potential for both kindness and evil. A life should be dedicated to the constant elevation of moral standards and cultivation of virtue through self-restraint. In modern society, many people experience ill thoughts and desires. Putting them on display for public consumption is equivalent to polluting society.

Unleashing Man's Dark Side as 'Criticism' and 'Protest'

Writers and artists in the Western free world, under the influence of anti-traditionalist sentiment, consider all laws, regulations, and moral codes to be restrictive and suppressive. They see problems with modern society and the weaknesses of human nature, but instead of dealing with them rationally, they promote extreme individualism via criticism and protest, indulging in their personal desires.

They use degenerate means to express so-called resistance, while strengthening the dark side of their nature, indulging in hatred, laziness, desire, lust, aggression, and pursuit of fame. A lack of moral self-restraint won't solve any social issues; it can only worsen them.

During the counterculture movement of the 1960s, the American poet Allen Ginsberg became the representative of the Beat Generation and is still venerated today by those who wish to rebel against society. His poem "Howl" depicts extreme lifestyles and mental states, including alcoholism, sexual promiscuity, drugs, sodomy, self-mutilation, prostitution, streaking, violent assault, theft, vagabonding, and madness.

As the counterculture movement became institutionalized, "Howl" came to be regarded as a literary classic and was included in numerous literature collections. Ginsberg admitted that he was a communist when he "was a kid" and held no regrets. [28] He idolized Fidel Castro and other communist dictators and widely promoted homosexuality and pedophilia. Ginsberg is a clear representative of the common ground between communism and extreme individualism.

Spreading Pornography

Since the beginning of the twentieth century, explicitly sexual content began to appear in literary works, some of which were filled with such content yet were still praised as classics. Many commentators and scholars abandoned their social responsibilities and praised such pornographic works as real, artistic masterpieces. Much of traditional morality is based on proper relations between the sexes and self-restraint. Breaking such restrictions — with whatever noble-sounding justification — undermines and destroys morality.

Dehumanizing People

In the past several decades, as the culture became more and more confused, a great deal of genre fiction surfaced, including thrillers and works of horror, the supernatural, and fantasy. Through such works, low-level elements can control people's minds and bodies, resulting in the dehumanization of human beings.

A three-foot block of ice does not result from only one day of coldness, as a saying goes. It takes a long period of time, and the involvement of many fields, for literature to degrade so far that it becomes a tool for evil. Romanticism widened literature's coverage of people's private and inner lives, and some ugly and bizarre phenomena — including extreme and insane human mental states — were presented for public consumption. Several British Romantic poets were collectively dubbed "the Satanic School" because of the immoral content of their poems.

Realism uses the excuse of presenting reality to express the degenerate side of human nature. Thus, certain works empha-size warped thoughts and immoral conduct. One critic called realism "romanticism going on all fours." [29]

The philosophy of naturalism, as promoted by Jean-Jacques Rousseau, attributed the decline in human morality to the social environment and family genetics, thus removing the individual's moral responsibility. Aestheticism calls for "art for art's sake," claiming that art is meant to simply provide sensory stimuli and carries no moral imperative.

In fact, all art has subtle, profound, and long-lasting effects on the moral compass. To deny the moral responsibility of art is to open the door for immorality to creep in. Although differ-ent schools of literature generated some high-quality works, they also produced awful works. The negative elements are obviously the result of declining moral standards, and they effectively paved the road for communist ideology to destroy mankind via literature.

When a person writes, his or her moral standard and mental state are reflected in his or her work. With the overall decline of human morality, the negative mindset of writers takes a domi-nant stance. This has created numerous works that, instead of seeking to bring out the goodness in people, pull people down toward hell.

4. Reviving True Art

The power of art is enormous. Good art can rectify the human heart, elevate morality, harmonize yin and yang, and even enable humans to connect with heaven, earth, and divine beings.

In the past century, the specter of communism took advan-tage of man's demon nature and malice, prompting the creation of an enormous variety of so-called "art." People were led to revolt against and blaspheme the divine, oppose tradition, and overturn morality. This had the ultimate effect of turning large parts of society demonic, to a degree that would have been deeply shocking to anyone living in a previous era.

Compared to the beauty of traditional arts, modern works are extremely ugly. Human aesthetic standards have been destroyed. The avant-garde has become mainstream and commands vast sums of money, while traditional, upright arts have been denigrated.

Arts have been manipulated into a vehicle for people to indulge in their desires and vent their demon nature. The boundary between beauty and ugliness, grace and vulgarity, goodness and evil, has been blurred or even erased. Grotesquerie, chaos, and darkness have taken the place of universal values. Human society is filled with demonic messages, and human beings are being steered along a path of decadence and destruction.

Only by elevating morality and returning to faith and tradition will humankind be able to see another renaissance in the arts. Only then will we all see the beauty, nobility, and splendor of what art can be and is meant to be.

Chapter Twelve

Sabotaging Education

EDUCATION PLAYS AN IMPORTANT ROLE in fostering individual well-being and self-fulfillment, maintaining social stability, and securing the future of a nation. No great civilization in the history of humanity has taken education lightly.

The object of education is to maintain humanity's moral standards and preserve its divinely bestowed culture. It is the means by which knowledge and craftsmanship are imparted and people socialized. Traditionally, the well-educated respect heaven, believe in the divine, and seek to follow the virtue of benevolence. They possess extensive knowledge of traditional culture as well as mastery over one or more trades. Dedicated to their vocations, they believe in treating others with kindness. They serve as the pillars of society, the national elites, and the guardians of civilization. Their extraordinary character and behavior earn divine favor and blessings.

Thus, ruining traditional education is an indispensable

step in the communist specter's plan to sever the connection between man and the divine, thereby destroying humanity. To this end, communism has adopted various strategies to attack and undermine education in both the East and the West.

In Eastern countries that are home to deep-seated cultural traditions, deception alone is insufficient to brainwash the populace. Communist parties have systematically slaughtered the well-educated elites to stop these bearers of culture from imparting the nation's traditional heritage to the next generation. Simultaneously, they bombarded the rest of the population with incessant propaganda.

In the West, the history and roots of cultures are not as deep, comparatively, giving communism fertile ground for covertly contaminating society by subverting and sabotaging education.

The complete breakdown of American education is one of the most distressing things to have happened to the country in the past few decades. It signals the success of communism's mission to infiltrate and corrupt Western society.

This chapter focuses mainly on the United States as an example of how education in free societies has been sabotaged by communism. From this example, readers may infer how education is being undermined in other countries along similar lines.

The communist infiltration of American education manifests in at least five areas:

Promoting Communist Ideology Among the Young.
Communist ideology gradually took over Western academia by infiltrating important traditional fields of study, as well as fabricating new sciences beholden to its ideological influence. Literature, history, philosophy, social science, anthropology, the study of law, media, and other concentrations have become inundated with various derivatives of Marxist theory.

"Political correctness" became the guideline for censoring free thought on campuses.

Reducing the Young Generation's Exposure to Traditional Culture. Orthodox thought, genuine history, and classical literature have been slandered and marginalized in many different ways. Common justifications for this include arguments that the classics are no longer relevant to modern students, or that school curricula need to make room for more "diversity" of thought.

Lowering Academic Standards Starting in Primary School. Because instruction has been progressively dumbed down, students of the new generation are becoming less literate and mathematically capable. They possess less knowledge, and their ability to think critically is stunted. It is hard for these students to handle key questions concerning life and society in a logical and forthright manner, and even harder for them to see through communism's deceptions.

Indoctrinating Young Students With Deviated Notions. As these children grow older, the concepts instilled in them become so strong that it is nearly impossible to identify and correct them.

Feeding Students' Selfishness, Greed, and Indulgence. This includes conditioning them to oppose authority and tradition, inflating their egos and sense of entitlement, reducing their ability to understand and tolerate different opinions, and neglecting their psychological growth.

Communism has achieved its objectives in nearly all of these five areas.

1. Communist Elements in Primary and Secondary Education

Although communism is most obvious at the university level, it has deeply influenced primary and secondary school education. Its influence has undermined children's intellectual development and maturity, making them more susceptible to leftist influences in college. It has caused generations of students to have less knowledge and a diminished ability to reason and engage in critical thinking. The progressive education movement led by John Dewey initiated the trend more than a century ago. Subsequent education reforms have generally followed in the same direction.

In addition to instilling atheism, the theory of evolution, and communist ideology in students, primary and secondary education in the United States employ psychological manipulation that destroys students' traditional beliefs and morals. It instills moral relativism and modern concepts that convey a corrupt attitude toward life. This occurs across all sectors of education. The sophisticated measures used make it almost impossible for students and the public to guard against the trend.

KGB defector Yuri Bezmenov, introduced in Chapter Five, described in 1985 how communist ideological infiltration in America was nearing completion: "Even if you start right now, here this minute, you start educating [a] new generation of Americans, it will still take you fifteen to twenty years to turn the tide of ideological perception of reality back to normalcy and patriotism." [1]

A third of a century has passed since Bezmenov gave his interview. During this period, even as we witnessed the downfall of the Soviet Union and other socialist regimes in Eastern Europe, communism's infiltration and subversion in the West didn't stop. Communist elements in the West set their sights on education as a primary target. They took over all tiers of the institution, promoting their own twisted theories on education, pedagogy, and parenting.

A. DUMBING DOWN STUDENTS

The United States is a constitutional republic. Presidents, lawmakers, town mayors, and school-district committee members are all elected by the voting public. Whether such a political framework can be pursued in a manner that is truly beneficial to all depends not only on the moral level of the people, but also on the level of their knowledge and discernment. If voters are not well-versed in history, political and economic systems, and social issues, they will have difficulty electing officials whose platforms are based on the long-term and fundamental interests of the country and society. This puts the country in a dangerous situation.

In 1983, a group of experts commissioned by the US Department of Education wrote the report *A Nation at Risk* after eighteen months of research. The report stated:

> *For our country to function, citizens must be able to reach some common understandings on complex issues, often on short notice and on the basis of conflicting or incomplete evidence. Education helps form these common understandings, a point Thomas Jefferson made long ago in his justly famous dictum: "I know no safe depository of the ultimate powers of the society but the people themselves; and if we think them not enlightened enough to exercise their control with a wholesome discretion, the remedy is not to take it from them but to inform their discretion."*

Individuals with little knowledge and poor critical thinking abilities are unable to recognize lies and deception. Education plays an enormous role. Thus, when communist elements penetrate all levels of the education system, students become foolish and ignorant and thus vulnerable to manipulation.

The report makes these additional points:

The educational foundations of our society are presently being eroded by a rising tide of mediocrity that threatens our very future as a Nation and a people. ... If an unfriendly foreign power had attempted to impose on America the mediocre educational performance that exists today, we might well have viewed it as an act of war. As it stands, we have allowed this to happen to ourselves. We have even squandered the gains in student achievement made in the wake of the Sputnik challenge. Moreover, we have dismantled essential support systems which helped make those gains possible. We have, in effect, been committing an act of unthinking, unilateral educational disarmament. [2]

The report quoted analyst Paul Copperman as saying, "For the first time in the history of our country, the educational skills of one generation will not surpass, will not equal, will not even approach, those of their parents."

The report cites some shocking findings: In addition to US students' grades often being at the bottom compared to those of students in other nations, 23 million American adults are functionally illiterate — that is, only possessing the most basic everyday reading, writing, and comprehension skills. The rate of functional illiteracy is 13 percent among 17-year-olds and may reach as high as 40 percent among minority youth.

From 1963 to 1980, scores on the Scholastic Aptitude Test (SAT) declined dramatically, with the average verbal score dropping by more than 50 points, and the average math score dropping by nearly 40 points. "Many 17-year-olds do not possess the 'higher order' intellectual skills we should expect of them. Nearly 40 percent cannot draw inferences from written material; only one-fifth can write a persuasive essay; and only one-third can solve a mathematics problem requiring several steps." [3]

In the 2008 book *The Dumbest Generation: How the Digital Age Stupefies Young Americans and Jeopardizes Our Future*, Emory University professor Mark Bauerlein compiled data on the knowledge gaps of American students in the subjects of history, civics, math, science, technology, fine arts, and more. He gave the example of the history exam in the 2001 National Assessment of Educational Progress, on which 57 percent of students scored "below basic" and only 1 percent achieved an "advanced" score. Surprisingly, on a multiple-choice question on which country had been a US ally in World War II, 52 percent chose Germany, Japan, or Italy instead of the Soviet Union. Results in other areas were equally disappointing. [4]

The decline in the quality of education in the United States is obvious. Since the 1990s, the term "dumbing down" has appeared in many books on education and has become a concept American educators cannot avoid. John Taylor Gatto, a senior teacher and educational researcher in New York City, wrote, "Pick up a fifth-grade math or rhetoric textbook from 1850 and you'll see that the texts were pitched then on what would today be considered college level." [5]

To avoid making the American education system look bad, in 1994 the College Board redefined the scores of the SAT, the university entrance examination. When the modern form of the SAT began to be adopted in 1941, the average score of the language exam was 500 points (top marks are 800 points). By the 1990s, the average score had dropped to 424 points; the College Board then redefined 424 as 500 points. [6]

The decline in the quality of education is not just reflected in the decline in students' literacy. Due to a lack of basic knowledge, the critical thinking faculties of American students have fallen sharply. American scholar Thomas Sowell observed: "It is not merely that Johnny can't read, or even that Johnny can't think. *Johnny doesn't know what thinking is*, because thinking is so often confused with feeling in many public schools." [7]

The reason for the decline of grades is not that students today are not as intelligent as before, but because communism is quietly carrying out a war against the next generation, using the education system as its weapon. Charlotte Thomson Iserbyt, a former senior policy adviser to the US Department of Education, wrote in 1999, "The reason Americans do not understand this war is because *it has been fought in secret* — in the schools of our nation, targeting *our children* who are captive in classrooms. The wagers of the war are using very sophisticated and effective tools." [8]

B. THE DESTRUCTIVE NATURE OF PROGRESSIVE EDUCATION

The backlash against tradition in American primary and secondary schools began with the progressive education movement of the early twentieth century. The following generations of progressive educators concocted a series of sham theories and discourses that served to alter curricula, water down teaching materials, and lower academic standards. This wrought enormous damage to traditional education.

From Rousseau to Dewey

Dewey, the father of American progressive education, was greatly influenced by the ideas of the eighteenth-century Swiss-born philosopher Jean-Jacques Rousseau.

Rousseau believed that people are good by nature and that social ills are responsible for moral decline. He said all men were free and equal at birth and that given a natural environment, everyone would enjoy their innate rights. Inequality, privilege, exploitation, and the loss of man's innate kindness were all products of society. For children, Rousseau advocated a model of "negative education" that would leave them to their own discovery. This education was to be absent of religious, moral, or cultural teaching.

In fact, humanity is endowed with both benevolence and

wickedness. Without nurturing benevolence, the wicked aspects of human nature will dominate to the point where people consider no method too base and no sin too evil. With his elegant rhetoric, Rousseau attracted many misguided followers. The deleterious influence his pedagogical theory has had on Western education is hard to overestimate.

About a century later, Dewey picked up where Rousseau had left off and furthered the destructive work. According to Dewey, who was influenced by Darwin's theory of evolution, children should be weaned from the traditional tutelage of parents, religion, and culture and given free rein to adapt to their environments. Dewey was a pragmatist and moral relativist. He believed that there was no unchanging morality and that people were free to act and behave as they saw fit. The concept of moral relativism is a critical first step in leading humanity away from the moral rules set by the divine.

Dewey was one of thirty-four people who signed their names to the original *Humanist Manifesto*, penned in 1933. Unlike the humanists of the Renaissance, twentieth-century humanism is, at its core, rooted in atheism. Based on modern concepts such as materialism and the theory of evolution, it regards the universe as self-existing rather than created and holds that human beings are the product of a continuous biochemical process.

In this calculus, the object of education is to mold and guide students according to the educator's wishes — something not fundamentally different from Karl Marx's "new man." Dewey himself was a democratic socialist.

American philosopher Sidney Hook said, "Dewey had supplied Marxism with the epistemology and social philosophy that Marx had half seen for himself and had half sketched out in his early works but had never adequately spelled out." [9]

In 1921, as civil war raged across Russia, the Soviets took the time to produce a sixty-two-page pamphlet featuring excerpts from Dewey's *Democracy and Education*. In 1929, the rector of the Second State University of Moscow, Albert P. Pinkev-ich, wrote, "Dewey comes infinitely closer to Marx and the Russian Communists." [10] Biographer Alan Ryan wrote that Dewey "supplied the intellectual weapons for a decently social democratic, non-totalitarian Marxism." [11]

Progressive educators make no pretense about their goal to transform students' attitudes toward life. To achieve this aim, they have overturned all aspects of learning, including class structure, teaching materials and methods, and the relationship between teachers and students. Personal experience is considered superior to knowledge learned from books. Lectures have taken a backseat to projects and activities.

The conservative American website Human Events listed Dewey's *Democracy and Education* as number five on its list of the ten most harmful books of the nineteenth and twenti-eth centuries. It pointedly observed that Dewey "disparaged schooling that focused on traditional character development and endowing children with hard knowledge, and encouraged the teaching of thinking 'skills' instead." [12]

Astute critics have taken to task the progressive bent in education from the very beginning. Mortimer Smith's 1949 book *And Madly Teach: A Layman Looks at Public School Education* provides a concise and comprehensive rebuttal to the principal tenets of progressive education. [13] Progressive educators have dismissed such critics as "reactionaries" and used various means to suppress or ignore them.

Dewey spent 25 years as a tenured professor at Columbia University. During the period in which he taught the philosophy of education at the Teachers College, at least one-fifth of all primary and secondary school teachers received instruction or advanced degrees at Columbia. [14] In contrast to figures like Marx, Engels, Lenin, Stalin, or Mao, Dewey appears to have had no aspiration to become a revolutionary guru or take over the world, but the system of education he created became one of communism's most potent tools.

Indulging Students

According to Rousseau's theory of education, humans are born good and free, but are made bad by society. Therefore, the best method of education is to give children free rein and yield to the child's own whimsical development. Under the influence of Rousseauean thought, progressive educationists since Dewey have often echoed these ideas: One should not force the values of parents or teachers upon students; children should be allowed to make their own judgments and decisions while growing up.

English poet Samuel Taylor Coleridge once elegantly gave the following retort to this sort of view: "[British radical John] Thelwall thought it very unfair to influence a child's mind by inculcating any opinions before it should have come to years of discretion, and be able to choose for itself. I showed him my garden, and told him it was my botanical garden. 'How so?' said he, 'it is covered with weeds.' — 'Oh,' I replied, 'that is only because it has not yet come to its age of discretion and choice. The weeds, you see, have taken the liberty to grow, and I thought it unfair in me to prejudice the soil towards roses and strawberries.'" [15]

The quick-witted poet used the analogy to convey to his friend a principle: Ethics and wisdom are painstakingly cultivated. Not overseeing a garden will cause an overgrowth of weeds. Abandoning children is akin to giving them over to ever-present forces for ill. It amounts to extreme negligence and irresponsibility.

Good and evil are simultaneously present in human nature. Though children are by comparison simpler and purer than adults, they also are susceptible to laziness, jealousy, combativeness, selfishness, and other negative traits. Society is a big dye vat. If children are not properly raised, then by the time they have come to their "age of discretion and choice," they will have long been contaminated by bad thoughts and bad habits. Attempts to educate them at that point will be too late.

This indulgence of students reached its peak in the pedagogical literary work *Summerhill: A Radical Approach to Child Rearing*, published in 1960. The book's author, A. S. Neill, established in 1921 an English boarding school, Summerhill, whose students at the time ranged in age from five to sixteen. The school gave children complete autonomy. Children were allowed to decide whether they wanted to go to one class but not another, or no class at all. Neill's views on education were heavily influenced by Wilhelm Reich, a Frankfurt School philosopher and vigorous proponent of sexual freedom, and the two often corresponded.

Besides academics, the school was extremely lax on ethics, discipline, and male–female relations; it followed all anti-traditional values. According to a former student who attended in the 1960s, male and female students were allowed to have mock weddings and sleep together. Neill allowed staff and students to swim naked together in an outdoor swimming pool, and some staff members were permitted to date students. His thirty-five-year-old stepson, who taught ceramic art, would often bring upper-grade girls back to his room. [16]

In his book, Neill says, "Every older pupil at Summerhill knows from my conversation and my books that I approve of a full sex life for all who wish one, whatever their age." He has even hinted that, if not prohibited by law, he would have openly permitted boys and girls to sleep together. [17] When *Summerhill* was published, it quickly became a bestseller. In the 1960s alone, it sold more than three million copies and became required reading at teachers' colleges.

An ancient Chinese saying says, "A strict teacher produces outstanding students." Studies in the West have found that strict teachers get better results in the classroom. They also have a more positive influence on their students' conduct. [18] Sadly, in the United States and other Western countries, under the influence of progressivism and educational autonomy, laws have been enacted that limit the scope of parents and teachers in managing students. This has caused teachers to become afraid to discipline students. Students' bad habits are not corrected in a timely manner, or at all, thus leading to a precipitous decline in their sense of morality as well as their academic performance.

Student-Centered Education

The most important function of education is to maintain and pass on the traditional culture of human civilization. Perhaps nowhere was this more the case than in ancient China, where educators and scholars were held in the highest regard. "A teacher is to pass on the Dao, teach the learnings, and clear up confusion," as a Chinese saying goes. Dewey's progressive educational thought removes the authority of teachers and downgrades their importance. His stance is anti-intellectual and against common sense — in essence, against education itself.

Advocates of progressive education claim that students must be placed at the center and allowed to explore on their own, to reach their own answers. The real intention of progressive education is to cut students off from their bond with traditional culture. Traditional curricula contain knowledge accumulated over thousands of years of human civilization. A negation of teachers' authority in the process of education is a negation of their role in carrying forward the knowledge of civilization. This is the ulterior motive of communism.

Daisy Christodoulou's 2014 book *Seven Myths About Education* analyzes and refutes seven widely spread misconceptions about modern education, including claims that "facts prevent understanding," "teacher-led instruction is passive," "projects and activities are the best way to learn," and "teaching knowledge is indoctrination." [19] Most of these myths stem from progressive education and have been passed down for several generations, becoming a plague on educational culture. For instance, take the first misconception, that fact-learning prevents true understanding. Modern American education has degraded traditional methods of attention to memorization, reading aloud, and practice, characterizing them as "mechanical memorization," "rote learning," and "drill to kill." Rousseau attacked memorization and verbal lessons in his 1792 novel *Emile, or On Education*, and Dewey's progressive educators furthered such theories.

In 1956, American educational psychologist Benjamin Bloom and collaborators published a framework for categorizing educational goals, widely known as Bloom's Taxonomy. It divided human cognition into six levels, from low to high. In 2001, the levels were revised to be "remember, understand, apply, analyze, evaluate, and create." The latter three are regarded as higher-order thinking because they involve comprehensive analysis. We are not analyzing the strengths and weaknesses of the Bloom classification itself, but merely pointing out that since the framework was proposed, progressive educators have used the pretext of cultivating "higher-order thinking" to weaken the teaching of knowledge in schools.

Anyone with common sense knows that having certain basic knowledge is the foundation of any intellectual task. Without a reserve of knowledge, the so-called higher-order thinking, critical thinking, and creative thinking can only serve to deceive oneself and others. Bloom's classification system provides a seemingly scientific excuse for the inexplicable approach of progressive educators.

One of the planks of the theory of student-centered instruction is that students should choose what they learn, according to their own interests. The theory also states that teachers should educate students only in what the students are interested in.

To have students learn in an enjoyable way is what every teacher wants, but children have shallow knowledge and limited vision, and they're unable to discern what is important to learn and what isn't. Teachers must take responsibility for guiding students so that they can transcend their superficial interests and broaden their vision and understanding. Simply catering to the superficial interests of students will only lead to their permanent infantilization. By espousing student-centered instruction, educators are deceiving students and parents, which is ultimately irresponsible to society.

Studies have found that there is a tendency in American society for adults to remain in a state of adolescence longer than in other populations. The National Academy of Sciences, Engineering, and Medicine in 2002 defined adolescence as a period from twelve to thirty years of age. Research supported by the MacArthur Foundation went even further and said, based on traditional markers of adulthood, a person nowadays may not be considered an adult until age thirty-five. [20] The education system and media bear the responsibility for this extended period of adolescence that many adults have found themselves in.

One of the excuses given by progressive educators for lowering teaching requirements is that with higher enrolments in secondary and post-secondary schools and with students coming from across society, the average level of attainment cannot be as high as it was in the past. This understanding is wrong. In a democratic society, the object of public schooling is to allow those who otherwise wouldn't have the means to receive an education the opportunity to do so — not to lower academic standards, which causes everyone's learning to suffer. Progressivism claims to replace "useless" classical courses such as Greek and Latin with more contemporary courses, but in the end, most schools don't end up introducing high-quality courses useful for modern life, such as in-depth courses in mathematics, economics, and modern history. The curriculum and teaching-method reforms advocated by progressive educators deceive students who are not yet well-informed, as well as parents who defer to schools, teachers, and so-called experts.

Some teaching methods proposed by progressive education

are useful when applied to some subjects and areas of learning. However, when we look at the progressive education movement and its specific background and outcomes, it becomes clear that progressive education sets itself up in opposition to traditional education, thereby mutating education and ultimately ruining students.

C. RUINING STUDENTS' MORAL CHARACTER

On April 20, 1999, two students at Columbine High School in Colorado murdered twelve students and one teacher and injured at least twenty more in a carefully planned massacre. The tragedy shocked the nation. People wondered why the two students would carry out such a cold-blooded attack, murdering their classmates and a teacher they'd known for years.

By comparing social phenomena in different historical periods, educators noticed that up to the 1960s, common problem behaviors among US students were minor, like tardiness, talking in class without permission, or chewing gum. After the 1980s, there were worse problems, like excessive drinking, drug abuse, premarital sex, pregnancy, suicide, gang activity, and even indiscriminate shootings, which have only increased in frequency since Columbine. These downward trends are a concern to millions in the United States and other countries, but few understand the real roots of these developments, and no one is able to prescribe an appropriate treatment for the disorder.

The distortion and downward spiral of the moral standards of American youth are no accident.

Atheism and Evolution

Fred Schwarz, a pioneer of anti-communist activism, observed, "The three basic tenets of Communism are atheism, evolution, and economic determinism." [21] All three key elements of communist ideology have been adopted in American public schools.

The divine created humankind and laid down the moral standards that should regulate human life. Belief in the divine lays the foundation of morality for society and underpins the existence of the human world. Communism forcibly spread atheism and the theory of evolution in schools as a means of destroying morality. This is to be expected in communist states like China and the former Soviet Union, but in the United States, it was carried out covertly.

Under the pretext of separation of church and state, leftists oppose the teaching of creationism in American public schools, while on the other hand promoting the theory of evolution. This education inevitably leads the number of religious believers to decline, as children are indoctrinated with the idea that the theory of evolution is scientific truth and not to be questioned.

Since the 1960s, courts around the United States have shut down Bible study in public schools, again under the pretext of separation of church and state. An appeals court ruled in 1981 that students enjoyed freedom of speech, unless the speech was a prayer, at which point it became unconstitutional. [22]

In 1987, students in Alaskan public schools were told not to use the word "Christmas" since it contained the word "Christ." They were also told they couldn't exchange traditional Christmas cards or presents. In 1987, a federal court in Virginia ruled that homosexual newspapers could be distributed on a high school campus, but religious newspapers were banned. In 1993, an elementary school music teacher in Colorado Springs was prevented from teaching Christmas carols because of alleged violations of the separation of church and state. [23]

Teaching and test materials in the United States have undergone extensive revision due to the anti-theist orientation of the education system, in combination with decades of political correctness. In 1997, Diane Ravitch, an education historian, was a member of the National Assessment Governing Board, which administered federal tests in schools. She noticed that passages in reading tests had been scrubbed by editors to remove white males as heroes or any references to Christianity. The maxim that "God helps those who help themselves" was changed to "People should try to work things out for themselves whenever possible." [24]

On the one hand, the American public education system ejected belief in God from schools under the pretext of upholding the separation of church and state. On the other hand, evolution, with its unresolved gaps, was held to be a self-evident truth to be instilled in children who had no mental preparation or defense. Children tend to believe in the authority of their teachers.

Parents with religious beliefs teach their kids to respect others, but children who are instilled with the theory of evolution are likely to challenge the religious education given by their parents. At the very least, they will no longer take their parents' religious instruction as seriously. The result is that education pulls children away from parents with religious beliefs. This is the most challenging problem that families with religious beliefs face when it comes to their children's education, and it's the evilest aspect of the anti-theistic education system.

Communist Ideology

Chapter Five of this book illustrates the nature of political correctness: It works like the thought police of communism, using a set of distorted political standards to replace authentic moral standards. Since the 1930s, political correctness has played a dominant role in the American education system. When put into practice, it comes in different forms, some of which are extremely deceptive.

E. Merrill Root, author of *Brainwashing in the High Schools: An Examination of Eleven American History Textbooks,* published in 1958, conducted research into eleven sets of history teaching materials used in Illinois between 1950 and

1952 and found that they characterized American history as a power struggle between rich and poor, between the privileged few and the underprivileged. This is the essence of Marxian economic determinism. [25]

In 2013, a school district in Minnesota adopted a project named All for All, which shifts the focus of teaching toward racial and income inequalities. This ideology blames the poor performance of students on systemic racial or income discrimination. The project demanded that all teaching activities be based on advancing racial and income equality and that only teachers and administrators who were deeply aware of the issues associated with these inequalities be employed.

The project was designed for students from Pre-K through Grade 12. Tenth-grade English classes focus on the themes of colonization and immigration, as well as "social constructions" of race, class, and gender. The eleventh-grade framework claimed, "By the end of the year, you will have ... learned how to apply marxist [sic], feminist, post-colonial [and] psychoanalytical ... lenses to literature." [26]

In July 2016, California adopted a new social science framework for public elementary and high schools. The original left-leaning framework was made to look even more like left-wing ideological propaganda. Content that should be emphasized in history and social science courses — like the founding spirit of America, and military, political, and diplomatic history — was watered down or ignored. In contrast, the values of the 1960s counterculture were passionately highlighted and made to seem like the nation's founding principles. The curriculum also articulated a clearly anti-traditional framework of sex and family.

Take the eleventh-grade courses, for example. The new framework claimed its focus was on the rights movements of minority races, tribes, and religions, as well as women and lesbian, gay, bisexual, and transgender (LGBT) Americans. In reality, religion was seldom mentioned, but much was written about sexual minorities. LGBT groups were included first and were given a significant share of the eleventh-grade history courses. The LGBT portions were written in a tone clearly supportive of "sexual liberation." For example, in a discussion on AIDS, it was suggested that people's fear of AIDS weakened the civil rights and sexual liberation movements. [27]

Sexual content occupied many chapters, squeezing out other content far more worthy of attention for young people. For example, in the course on World War I, students hardly learn about the critical role played by the US Army, but are taught that American soldiers found European sexual customs satisfying. [28] This left-leaning framework is full of distortion and bias, guiding students to hate their own country. Though the framework was adopted only in the state of California, its approach had a national impact.

D. PSYCHOLOGICAL MANIPULATION

Another method through which students have been extensively morally corrupted is psychological conditioning, used to inject them with moral relativism.

In 1978, hundreds of parents and teachers attended hearings for the Protection of Pupils' Rights Amendment, a federal law that affords certain rights to parents of minor students with regard to surveys that ask questions of a personal nature. The hearing testimonies totaled more than thirteen hundred pages. In her 1984 book *Child Abuse in the Classroom*, conservative activist Phyllis Schlafly summed up the issues described in the testimonies, including the use of "education as therapy." Unlike traditional education, which aims to impart knowledge, education as therapy focuses on changing students' emotions and attitudes. This kind of education uses teaching to play psychological games on students. It has them fill out surveys on personal issues and asks them to make adult decisions, weighing in on issues like suicide and murder, marriage and divorce, and abortion and adoption. [29]

Such courses weren't set up for the students' psychological health — they were intended to change the values of students through psychological conditioning.

Psychology and Education

Modern education is heavily based on philosophy and psychology. In addition to Dewey's progressive education, other theories that have had a significant impact on the US education system include Sigmund Freud's psychoanalysis, Carl Rogers's humanistic psychology, and the Frankfurt School's critical theory, which combines theories from Marx and Freud. Herbert Marcuse, a theorist of the Frankfurt School, called for the removal of all inhibitions so that young people could let loose their natural instincts and indulge their personal whims. [30] It was this thinking that helped accelerate the birth of the counterculture of the 1960s.

Deeply influenced by the above-mentioned schools of thought on psychology, the first director general of the World Health Organization, Canadian psychiatrist Brock Chisholm, proposed a shocking theory: In order to release the individual from psychological pain, morality and the concept of right and wrong must be neutralized. He said in a 1946 lecture:

> *What basic psychological distortion can be found in every civilization of which we know anything? It must be a force which discourages the ability to see and acknowledge patent facts ... which produces inferiority, guilt, and fear. ... The only psychological force capable of producing these perversions is morality, the concept of right and wrong. ... We have been very slow to rediscover this truth and to recognise the unnecessary and artificially imposed inferiority, guilt and fear, commonly known as sin, under which we have almost all laboured and which produces so much of the social maladjustment and unhappiness in the world. ... If the race*

is to be freed of its crippling burden of good and evil it must be psychiatrists who take the original responsibility. [31]

Chisholm waged war on morality. Seemingly influenced by Chisholm, humanistic psychologist Carl Rogers came up with "values clarification" classes, which served the purpose of eradicating traditional values and the concepts of right and wrong.

Eventually, Dewey's moral relativism, the Frankfurt School's rejection of inhibitions, and Chisholm's psychological theories worked together to attack and undermine traditional values. They destroyed the moral fortifications of public schools in the United States.

Moral Relativism

Americans who attended schools in the late 1970s may remember an imagined scenario many teachers brought up in class, which went like this: As a ship sinks, the captain, several children, a pregnant woman, and a gay man get in a lifeboat. The lifeboat is overloaded and one person must be let go. The teachers would ask the students to discuss and decide who must get off the lifeboat, giving up his or her life. The teacher would not comment on or judge the students' comments.

This story was often used in the values-clarification classes that emerged in the 1970s. Besides being used for values-clarification, the classes were used for decision-making, affective education, the Lions Quest drug-prevention program, and sex education.

William Kilpatrick, author of the 1993 book *Why Johnny Can't Tell Right From Wrong: And What We Can Do About It*, described such classes as having "turned classroom discussions into 'bull sessions' where opinions go back and forth but conclusions are never reached." Kilpatrick wrote:

It has resulted in classrooms where teachers act like talk show hosts, and where the merits of wife swapping, cannibalism, and teaching children to masturbate are recommended topics for debate. ... For students, it has meant wholesale confusion about moral values: learning to question values they have scarcely acquired, unlearning values taught at home, and concluding that questions of right and wrong are always merely subjective. ... It has created a generation of moral illiterates: students who know their own feelings but don't know their culture. [32]

Sowell understood that these sessions utilized the same techniques developed in totalitarian countries to brainwash people:

1. *Emotional stress, shock, or de-sensitization, to break down both intellectual and emotional resistance*

2. *Isolation, whether physical or emotional, from familiar sources of emotional support in resistance*

3. *Cross-examining pre-existing values, often by manipulating peer pressure*

4. *Stripping the individual of normal defenses, such as reserve, dignity, a sense of privacy, or the ability to decline to participate*

5. *Rewarding acceptance of the new attitudes, values, and beliefs—a reward which can be simply release from the pressures inflicted on those who resist, or may take other symbolic or tangible form* [33]

Sowell notes that the sessions encourage students to rebel from the traditional moral values taught by their parents and society. Classes are conducted in a neutral or a "nonjudgmental" way, in which the teacher does not distinguish between right and wrong, but rather searches for what feels good for an individual. "This general approach has been called 'values clarification.' Its focus is on the feelings of the individual, rather than on the requirements of a functioning society or the requirements of intellectual analysis." [34]

Death and Drug-Prevention Education

In September 1990, the US television channel ABC aired a program that concerned many viewers. In it, a school takes students to a morgue as a part of its "death education" and students view and touch corpses. [35]

Common activities of death education classes include asking the students to draw their own tombstones, select their own coffins, arrange their own funerals, and write their own obituaries. Students were to be asked the following questions:

"How will you die?"

"When will you die?"

"Have you ever known anyone who died violently?"

"When was the last time you mourned?
Was it expressed in tears or silent pain?
Did you mourn alone or with someone else?"

"Do you believe in an after-life?" [36]

Obviously, these questions have nothing to do with studying. They are designed to probe the students' outlook on life, their religious beliefs, and their personalities. Some of the questions are aimed to elicit particular reactions and can have a negative impact on teens.

It is said that death education can help students establish the right attitude in the face of death. However, some students who attended these classes have committed suicide. For the same 1990 program, ABC interviewed one student at Columbine High School who said her suicide plans were directly related to the death education she received there. She said the classes made death seem glamorous, "very exciting, [and] very appealing." [37] Although a causal relationship has not been established scientifically, it is certainly reasonable for parents to suspect and fear that by exposing psychologically immature students to confronting information on death and suicide, some students may be more likely to develop depression and hopelessness, which may contribute to reasons for committing suicide.

Drug-prevention education has also become very popular in schools. However, in 1976, Dr. Richard Blum of Stanford University published the results of a four-year study on a drug-prevention education course called Decide. The study found that students who took the course picked up drug use earlier and used drugs more extensively than a control group that did not take the course.

In both 1978 and 1985, professor Stephen Jurs conducted a research project comparing the rate of smoking and substance abuse among students who had taken a self-esteem course called Quest and those who had not. The course was designed to help students make wise and healthy decisions, but the results showed the opposite—participation was followed by an increase in drug experimentation. Those who didn't take the course maintained a steady or lowered rate of smoking and substance abuse. [38]

Neither death education nor drug-prevention education has generated the expected outcome, so what was the real purpose? To pollute children.

Children are very curious but have an immature moral foundation. New and strange content stimulates their curiosity and can lead them down a dark path. In the meantime, such education tends to desensitize students, making them view violence, pornography, terror, and moral decadence as simply normal parts of life. Their tolerance of evil increases in turn. The entire exercise is part of an evil use of art, violence, and pornography to bring about moral decline.

Pornographic Sex Education

Traditionally in both the East and the West, sex has been a taboo topic in public. According to both traditions, the divine established that sexual conduct must take place only within marriage. All other forms of sexual conduct are considered promiscuous and sinful, violating the divine standards of morality. This makes sex and marriage inseparable, and sex can't be a matter of public discussion in a properly function- ing society. In traditional society, the youth received educa- tion in physiology, and there was no need for today's version of sex education.

The modern concept of sex education was first introduced by Hungarian Marxist György Lukács, founder of the Frank- furt School of social theory and philosophy. His purpose was to completely overturn traditional Western values. In 1919, Lukács was appointed minister of culture in the short-lived Hungarian Bolshevik regime. He developed a radical sex-ed- ucation program that taught students about free love, and that marriage was outdated.

In the United States, Alfred Kinsey, financed by the Rocke- feller foundations, published his best-selling Kinsey Reports — two books titled *Sexual Behavior in the Human Male* and *Sexual Behavior in the Human Female* — in the late 1940s and early 1950s. In his since-debunked research, he used pedo- philes to conduct sexual experiments on infants and children. Kinsey's idea that children are "sexual beings" from birth and must be explicitly educated in every manner of sexual activity is the foundation of modern sex education. [39]

The sexual revolution of the 1960s annihilated the remain- ing traditional Western values. Rates of sexually transmitted diseases and teen pregnancy began to rise rapidly. Those who wanted to solve such social problems promoted sex education.

But in the education system that had already deviated from traditional moral teachings, sex education treated intercourse as disconnected from marriage and instead emphasized safety (preventing disease and pregnancy) — thus following the Lukács model of sex education by ignoring all moral aspects of sexual activity.

This form of education then became a tool for destroying youth. Students have also been exposed to the extramarital, promiscuous conduct of homosexuality, thus normalizing such behavior. The result of all this has been that the younger generation indulges in what they think is freedom, while in reality, it is a path that turns away from divinely ordained standards. This sort of sex education from elementary school onward has already destroyed the traditional values of family, individual responsibility, love, chastity, honor, self-control, loyalty, and more.

Dewey's "learning by doing" form of progressive education is a convenient tool for Marxists. The sex-education program Focus on Kids, widely promoted by the Centers for Disease Control and Prevention (CDC), recommends an activity in which teachers organize students to compete in a "condom race." Each student must put a condom on an adult sex toy and then remove it. Whoever finishes fastest wins. [40] In another Focus on Kids exercise, the teacher instructs students to brainstorm ways to be intimate. Be Proud! Be Responsible! is another program endorsed by the CDC and promoted by Planned Parenthood and other organizations. The program requires students to role play — for example, pretending to be two female students discussing having safer sex together. [41] To the majority of people who still have traditional values in their hearts, it is difficult to distinguish these supposedly educational activities from child pornography.

The main proponent of the program, Planned Parenthood, is the biggest provider of sex education in the United States and has a presence in many countries around the world. It also promotes abortion rights. The organization was founded in 1921 as the American Birth Control League. Its founder, Margaret Sanger, was a progressive socialist who traveled to Stalin's Russia, where she solidified her belief in eugenics. "We should breed out the feebleminded families who have done and still are doing much social and racial damage," she said in a draft article. Sanger was also a strong proponent of the sexual liberation movement. She is on record as saying that an extramarital affair she had "really set me free." [42] She even gave her sixteen-year-old granddaughter the advice to engage frequently in sexual intercourse, saying that "three times a day was about right." [43]

Sex education textbook *It's Perfectly Normal* has been translated into twenty-one languages and has sold more than one million copies worldwide. The book uses almost one hundred nude cartoons to depict various normal and abnormal movements, feelings, and physical sensations of masturbation between opposite sexes and homosexuals, as well as birth control methods and abortion. The author claims that children have the right to know all such information. [44] The main theme of the book is that a variety of sexual behaviors are all "perfectly normal" and that none should be subject to moral judgment.

In a widely used high school sex-education textbook, the author teaches children that some religions believe that sex outside of marriage is sinful, then writes, "You will have to decide for yourself how important these messages are for you." [45] To summarize, this worldview holds that all values are relative, and that right and wrong are for children to decide for themselves.

Today, US public schools have two basic types of sex-education classes. One type that's strongly promoted by educational organizations was described earlier: the complete sex-education curriculum, which includes instruction on sexual behavior, birth control, prevention of sexually transmitted diseases, and the like. The other type teaches young people to control their sexual desire, does not discuss birth control, and encourages abstinence from sex until after marriage.

It is undeniable that social morality, especially the general attitude toward sex, has deviated far from traditional, faith-based morality. The media and the internet are flooded with pornographic content, all of which drags children toward the edge of the abyss. In today's educational field controlled by atheism, most public schools that follow "value neutrality" don't want to, or don't dare to, teach children that sex outside of marriage is immoral, nor do they teach children right from wrong based on traditional moral principles.

Sex education remains a controversial topic in society today. There are numerous arguments in different sectors around the issue of safety in sexual activity, focusing on the rates of teenage pregnancy and sexually transmitted diseases. However, the fact that schools are publicly teaching teenagers about sexual behavior will obviously increase sex outside of marriage, which violates traditional sexual morality. Even if there were no teen pregnancies or sexually transmitted diseases, would that mean promiscuity among teenagers would be acceptable? With a decadent attitude toward sexual conduct in ascendance, communism is working to achieve its goal of destroying human morality.

Self-Esteem and Egocentrism

Since the 1960s, a new dogma heavily promoted in schools is responsible for a major downward slide in educational quality: the cult of "self-esteem." On its surface, self-esteem should refer to a feeling of confidence and self-respect that arises from one's own abilities and accomplishments. However, the self-esteem promoted in US schools is something entirely different.

In her book *The Feel-Good Curriculum: The Dumbing Down of America's Kids in the Name of Self-Esteem,* education researcher Maureen Stout writes about a common phenomenon in American schools: Students care about their grades, but don't care about what they learned or how much effort they put in. To satisfy the students' demands for better grades, teachers are forced to reduce the difficulty of exams and assignments. But this only results in even less effort on the part of under-performing students.

Stout asserts that teachers seem accustomed to the phenom-enon and are even of the belief that school should be like the womb — isolated from the outside world so students can gain emotional comfort but not intellectual development or resil-ience. The focus is on students' feelings, rather than their over-all growth. [46]

As many commentators have pointed out, the dogma of self-esteem confuses cause and effect. Self-esteem is the outcome of effort, not a precondition for success. In other words, feeling good does not lead to success, but one feels good after a success.

This misconception of self-esteem is the by-product of the psychotherapeutic style of education ascendant since the 1960s. Psychotherapeutic education ended up indoctrinating a large number of young people with a sense of entitlement and victimhood. Stout delineates the common mindset as "I want to do what I want, how I want and when I want, and nothing and no one is going to stop me." [47]

American education exaggerates the ideas of freedom and self-centeredness in the name of sentimental self-esteem. This style of education produces generations of young people who don't value morality and don't assume responsibility. They care only about their own feelings and not other people's feelings. They pursue enjoyment but try to avoid effort, sacrifice, and suffering. This has wreaked havoc on the morality of Amer-ican society.

E. THE INFILTRATION OF EDUCATION

Control Over US Elementary and Secondary Education

For a long while after the founding of the United States, the federal government was not involved in education; those decisions were the responsibility of state governments. In 1979, the federal government established the Department of Education and its jurisdiction has been enlarged ever since. Currently, its power over education strategies and the allocation of education budgets far surpasses what it previously had. Parents, school districts, and state governments, which used to have a greater say in education, are increasingly compelled to take orders from federal government officials. Parents and school districts have gradually lost their power to decide what gets taught and how it's taught.

Power itself is neutral — those who wield it can do either good or bad. The centralization of power in itself is not necessarily a bad thing, but rather a matter of how the person or institution uses its power and to what end. Centralization in American education has become a major issue due to Marxist infiltration at all levels, especially the central bureaucracy. Under such circumstances, once a wrong decision is made, the impact is extensive and the few clear-headed individuals who remain cannot simply reverse it.

As explained by writer and former teacher Beverly K. Eakman, one of the results from the centralization of power in American education is that the officials in charge can't, over a short time span, see how their educational strategies develop historically and how large of an impact they have over time. Although some strategies may raise doubts, most people do not have the time, energy, resources, or courage to investigate for themselves. Even if their suspicions are aroused in some cases, without other pieces of the puzzle, they can do little more than obey what they're told by their supervisors. Everyone thus becomes part of a gigantic machine. It is difficult for them to see the consequences of their decisions on students and society, and as a result, their moral accountability is attenuated. [48] Communism can take advantage of the weaknesses in this system and break down society's defenses layer by layer.

Moreover, teachers' colleges, publishing houses, educational accreditation organizations, and teacher-accreditation institutions have decisive impacts on education, and therefore have all become targets of infiltration.

The Role of Teachers' Unions

Chapter Nine of this book discussed how communism manipulates and utilizes unions. Teachers' unions have become one of the key reasons behind the failure of American education. These unions do not care about raising the quality of education, instead becoming professional organizations that reward failure, protect incompetence, and sacrifice conscientious teachers who aspire to make a contribution in their career and who truly dedicate themselves to teaching students.

In the article "How Teachers' Unions Handcuff Schools," *City Journal* editor and writer Sol Stern gives the example of Tracey Bailey, a former high school science teacher who won the National Teacher of the Year Award in 1993. At the time, the chief of the American Federation of Teachers called Bailey to say how he was pleased that a union member had won the honor. Bailey later dropped his membership and now believes that big teachers' unions are a primary reason for the failure of American public education. He holds that unions are simply special interest groups protecting the status quo and pillars of "a system that too often rewards mediocrity and incompetence." [49]

Major American teachers' unions are well funded and have immense influence; they are ranked among the most powerful political lobby groups in the country, and they have become the primary obstacle that hinders positive reform within the education system. For example, the California Teachers Association, under the American Federation of Teachers, uses its huge war chest collected from members to push for legislation and make political donations.

In 1991, California sought to add Proposition 174 to its state constitution, allowing families to use school vouchers provided by the state government to choose the best schools for their children. However, the California Teachers Association blocked the proposition and even threatened schools into revoking their contracts with a hamburger franchise that had donated $25,000 to support the proposition. [50]

The Exclusion of Family From Children's Education

Another key goal of communism is the removal of the child from his or her parents as soon as he or she is born, having the community or nation raise the child instead. This is not an easy feat, but things have been quietly moving in this direction.

In communist countries, students from the "bourgeoisie" class are encouraged to sever their relationships with their parents. In addition, exam-centric education extends the time that students must spend in school, thus reducing the impact parents can have on their children.

In Western countries, different approaches are used to exclude the influence of the family from children's education. These include maximizing students' school time, reducing the age requirement for children to attend school, preventing students from taking textbooks and study materials home, and discouraging students from sharing controversial topics they learned in class with their parents.

Courses such as "values clarification education" attempt to separate students from their parents. A parent of a student taking the Quest class commented: "It seemed as if the parents were always put in a bad light. The story would be about a father and his son, say; and the father was always overbearing, always too strict, always unfair." Oftentimes, the subtext of such courses is "your parents don't understand you, but we do." [51]

Sometimes, due to legal requirements, students must first obtain parental consent before they can participate in certain activities. On such occasions, teachers or administrative staff may use misleading and ambiguous words to make it very difficult for parents to know the details of what they're agreeing to. If parents complain, school authorities or the school district have methods of dealing with the complaint: procrastinating, shirking responsibility, or taking a superior stance. For example, they might say that parents do not have the professional knowledge of educators, that other school districts are doing the same thing, that only your family is complaining, and so on.

Most parents don't have the time or resources to engage in a prolonged argument with the school or school district. Moreover, in a few years, the student will graduate. Parents will generally choose to keep quiet. In the meantime, the child is almost held hostage by the school, and parents don't dare to offend the school authorities. When parents do protest against school practices, school authorities may label them as extremists, troublemakers, religious bigots, fanatics, fascists, and the like. By doing so, school authorities deter other parents from voicing an objection. [52]

Misleading and Obscure Education Jargon

In the preface to her book *The Deliberate Dumbing Down of America*, Iserbyt points out that America is engaged in a secret war, in which the wagers use sophisticated tools such as "Hegelian dialectic (common ground, consensus and compromise)," "gradualism (two steps forward; one step backward)," and "semantic deception (redefining terms to get agreement without understanding)." [53]

Schlafly also wrote about this phenomenon. In the foreword to her book *Child Abuse in the Classroom*, she said that psychotherapy classes use a set of special terms to prevent parents from understanding the true purpose and method of such courses. These terms include behavior modification, higher-order critical thinking, moral reasoning, and so on. [54]

For decades, American educators have created a dazzling array of terms such as constructivism, cooperative learning, experiential learning, deep understanding, problem-solving, inquiry-based and outcome-based education, personalized learning, conceptual understanding, procedural skills, lifelong learning, student–teacher interactive instruction, and so on. There are too many to list. Some concepts appear reasonable, but investigation into the context of the terms and where they lead to reveals that their purpose is to discredit traditional education and advance the dumbing down of education.[55]

Large-Scale Changes to Subjects and Textbooks

None Dare Call It Treason, published in 1964, analyzes the textbook reform program of the 1930s. This reform combined content from different disciplines, such as history, geography, sociology, economics, and political science, into a set of textbooks that abandoned the content, value system, and way of codifying found in traditional textbooks. "So pronounced was the anti-religious bias" and "so open was the propaganda for socialistic control of men's lives" that the textbooks downgraded American heroes and the US Constitution, author John A. Stormer writes. [56]

The set of textbooks was extensive and did not fall within the scope of any traditional discipline; therefore, experts in various disciplines did not pay much attention to it. Many years later, when the public realized the problem and began to oppose the materials, five million students had already been educated with them. By then, it was impossible to change the textbooks back to their traditional form.

If changes to textbooks had been implemented in a transparent way, they would have been questioned and met with resistance from experts and parents. The newly edited textbooks, which mixed several subjects together, didn't belong to any clear subject taxonomy, so experts had difficulty judging the content that went outside their professional knowledge. This made it relatively easy for the books to pass reviews and be accepted by a school district and society.

Similar changes to school curricula and teaching materials continued to take place throughout the century. While a minority of people may recognize and oppose these moves, their voices are ignored and have little chance of stopping the planned changes amid the presence of progressive lobbying. After several rounds of reforms, the new generation of students is then separated even further from tradition, making it almost impossible to go back.

American textbooks are constantly undergoing updates and revisions. Some say it's because knowledge has grown at an accelerating rate. However, the basic knowledge to be gained in primary and secondary school does not change much. So why have there been so many different textbooks published and continuously reprinted? The surface reason is that publishers compete with each other. Superficially, in order to pursue profits, they don't want students to repeatedly use the same set of textbooks for many years. But at a deeper level, just like the reorganization of textbook content, the process has been used to distort the teaching materials for the next generation.

Education Reform: A Dialectic Struggle

Since the 1950s and 1960s, American education has seen a series of reforms, but none brought the expected improvements. In 1981, American students' SAT scores reached a record low, triggering the publication of the 1983 report *A Nation at Risk* and the ensuing "back to basics" movement. In order to change the embarrassing condition of education in the United States, several administrations since the 1990s have successively launched large-scale reforms, to little effect. Not only did they not help, but they also brought problems that were more difficult to solve. [57]

Most people involved in education reform sincerely want to do good for students and society, but due to the influence of various communist ideas, their intentions often backfire. The results of many of these reforms end up promoting communist ideas. Just as in other fields, the infiltration through education reform doesn't need to win everything in one battle.

The success of a reform is not its true goal. In fact, every reform is designed to first fail in order to provide an excuse for the next reform. Every reform is a deeper deviation than the last, each further alienating people from tradition. This is the dialectic of struggle — one step back, then two steps forward. In this way, people will not only not regret the collapse of tradition — they won't even know what it is.

2. Communism in Western Universities

Four years of intensive indoctrination leave today's college graduates with a predisposition for liberalism and progressivism. They are more likely to accept atheism, the theory of evolution, and materialism without a second thought. Many become narrow-minded "snowflakes" who lack common sense and pursue hedonistic lifestyles without taking responsibility for their actions. They lack knowledge, have a narrow worldview, know very little or nothing about the history of America or the world, and have become the main target for communist deception.

Unlike the rebellious but eloquent student leaders of the 1960s, today's young protesters who are interviewed by television news reporters rarely articulate their demands clearly. They lack basic common sense and reason.

During the 2016 US presidential campaign, the mainstream media's longstanding vilification of conservative candidates, coupled with misleading polls, meant that many were left in shock — particularly young college students — when the results were announced. Following Donald Trump's victory, a ridiculous phenomenon appeared at universities around the United States. Some students felt such fear, exhaustion, or emotional trauma from the election that they demanded that classes be canceled and exams be rescheduled. In order to relieve students of their stress and anxiety, some prominent schools organized various "therapeutic" activities. These included playing with Play-Doh or building blocks, coloring, and blowing bubbles. Some even provided cats and dogs for petting in order to console students. A number of universities provided students with psychological counseling, organized support groups, or created "safe spaces" where students could seek help "recovering" from and processing the election results. [58] The absurdity of how a normal democratic process became more terrifying than a natural disaster or terrorist attack demonstrates the utter failure of the American education system. College students, who should be mature and rational, became intolerant and infantile when confronted with change and supposed adversity.

In the eyes of the world, the United States is still a leader in education. For over a century, the United States has been a political, economic, and military superpower. Its education spending far exceeds that of most countries. After World War II, American democracy and affluence attracted talented people from around the world. Its science, technology, engineering, and math (STEM) graduate programs and professional schools are second to none.

However, a crisis is unfolding within. The proportion of foreign students in graduate STEM programs far exceeds that of American students, and the gap is increasing each year. [59] This reflects the erosion of elementary, secondary, and post-secondary education across the United States. Students are purposefully being dumbed down and ruined.

It should be emphasized that nearly all people in the world, especially those who attended college after the 1960s, have been exposed to communist influences. The humanities and social sciences are the most affected. Only a few individuals set out to intentionally promote communist ideology, but the majority of people in these fields have been unknowingly indoctrinated. Here we expose communism's aims so that people can identify and distance themselves from them.

A. THE LEFTIST SLANT OF UNIVERSITY FACULTIES

One of the most important causes of students' embrace of socialist or communist ideology, and their acceptance of radical ideologies such as feminism and that of the environmental movement (see Chapter 16), is that a large proportion of staff at American universities leans to the left. Scholars with different ideas have been either marginalized in their teaching positions or barred from voicing their views.

In a 2007 study titled "The Social and Political Views of American Professors," among the 1,417 full-time college faculty members surveyed, 44.1 percent considered themselves liberal, 46.1 percent moderate, and only 9.2 percent conservative. At liberal arts colleges, 61 percent of faculty were liberal, while conservatives made up just 3.9 percent. [60]

Studies after 2007 also confirm the leftist trend among professors at four-year universities in the United States. A study published in *Econ Journal Watch* in 2016 surveyed the voter registration status of professors in the departments of history and social sciences at 40 leading US universities. Among 7,243 professors surveyed, there were 3,623 Democrats and 314 Republicans, or a ratio of 11.5 to 1. Among the five departments surveyed, the department of history was the most uneven, with a 35-to-1 ratio. Contrast this with a similar study published in 1968 that found that among history professors, the ratio of Democrats to Republicans was 2.7 to 1. [61]

Another study of four-year college and university faculties in 2016 found that the political inclination of professors was particularly uneven in New England. Based on 2014 data, the study found that the ratio of liberal to conservative professors at colleges and universities nationwide was 6 to 1. In New England, this ratio was 28 to 1. A 2016 study by the Pew Research Center found that among those who had studied in graduate schools, 31 percent held consistently liberal views, 23 percent tended to be mostly liberal, 10 percent held consistently conservative views, and 17 percent tended to be mostly conservative. The study found that since 1994, the number of those who had received graduate-level education and who held consistently liberal views had increased significantly. [62] Panelists at an American Enterprise Institute seminar in 2016 said that about 18 percent of social scientists in the United States considered themselves Marxists, while only 5 percent considered themselves conservative. [63]

Sen. Ted Cruz once commented, about the law school of a prestigious university he attended: "There were more self-declared communists [in the faculty] than there were Republicans. ... If you asked [them] to vote on whether this nation should become a socialist nation, 80 percent of the faculty would vote yes and 10 percent would think that was too conservative." [64]

Communism began its penetration of American education with the universities at the beginning of the twentieth century, when many American intellectuals began accepting communist ideas or its Fabian socialist variant. [65]

The 1960s counterculture movement produced a large number of young anti-traditional students. In these people's formative years, they were influenced greatly by cultural Marxism and Frankfurt School theory. In 1973, after President Richard Nixon withdrew American troops from Vietnam, student groups associated with the anti-war movement began to fade into obscurity, as the main reason for protest was gone. But the radicalism brewed by these large-scale student movements did not disappear.

Radical students went on to pursue graduate studies in the social and cultural fields — in journalism, literature, philosophy, sociology, education, cultural studies, and the like. After receiving their degrees, they began careers in the institutions with the most influence over society and culture, such as universities, news media, government agencies, and non-governmental organizations. What guided them at that time was mainly the theory of "the long march through the institutions" proposed by Italian Marxist Antonio Gramsci. This "long march" aimed to alter the most important traditions of Western civilization.

Marcuse was regarded as a "spiritual godfather" by rebellious Western students. In 1974, he asserted that the New Left did not die, "and it will resurrect in the universities." [66] In fact, the New Left has not only survived, but its long march through the institutions has been wildly successful.

As one radical professor wrote: "After the Vietnam War, a lot of us didn't just crawl back into our literary cubicles; we stepped into academic positions. With the war over, our visibility was lost, and it seemed for a while — to the unobservant — that we had disappeared. Now we have tenure, and the work of reshaping the universities has begun in earnest." [67]

The term "tenured radicals" was coined by Roger Kimball in his 1989 book of the same name, and referred to the radical students who had been active in the anti-war, civil rights, or feminist movements of the 1960s, later entered universities to teach, and obtained tenure in the 1980s. From there, they inculcated students with their system of political values and created a new generation of radicals. Some of these 1960s radicals became department heads and deans. The purpose of their scholarly work was not to explore the truth, but to use academia as a tool for undermining Western civilization and traditions. They aimed to subvert mainstream society and the political system by producing more revolutionaries like themselves.

Once tenured, professors can participate in various committees and have considerable say in recruiting new faculty members, setting academic standards, selecting topics for graduate theses, and determining the direction of research. They have ample means to use their power to exclude candidates who do not conform to their ideology. For this reason, more traditionally minded individuals who teach and do research according to traditional concepts are being steadily marginalized. As older professors retire, those who replace them are mostly leftist scholars who have been indoctrinated with communist ideas.

Gramsci divided intellectuals into two camps: "traditional" intellectuals and "organic" intellectuals. The former are the backbone of maintaining traditional culture and social order, while the latter belong to newly emerging classes or groups and play a creative role in the process of fighting for hegemony in their classes or groups. [68] In this view, the proletariat uses organic intellectuals on its path to seizing cultural and eventually political power. Many tenured radicals would define themselves as organic intellectuals who oppose the current system. Like Gramsci, they follow the Marxian axiom that "the philosophers have only interpreted the world in various ways; the point, however, is to change it." [69]

In this way, education for the Left is not about imparting the essence of knowledge and human civilization, but for priming students for radical politics, social activism, and "social justice." After graduation and upon joining society, they vent their dissatisfaction with the current system by rebelling against traditional culture and calling for destructive revolution.

B. RESHAPING TRADITIONAL ACADEMICS WITH COMMUNIST IDEOLOGY

While Marxism-Leninism is the guiding ideology for every subject in communist countries, academic freedom is a core focus in the West. Aside from ubiquitous moral standards and academic norms, there shouldn't be any bias in favor of particular intellectual trends. But since the 1930s, socialism, communism, Marxism, and the theories of the Frankfurt

School have entered American colleges in force, severely altering the humanities and social sciences.

Revolutionary Discourse Dominates the Humanities in America

Author Bruce Bawer once asked Alan Charles Kors, a historian at the University of Pennsylvania, about which three books he thought had had the deepest influence on the humanities in the United States. With hardly a pause, Kors named Gramsci's *Prison Notebooks*, Paulo Freire's *Pedagogy of the Oppressed*, and Frantz Fanon's *The Wretched of the Earth*. [70]

Gramsci, the Italian Marxist, needs no further introduction as his work has been described in previous chapters. Freire, a Brazilian educational theorist, adored Lenin, Mao Zedong, Fidel Castro, and Ernesto "Che" Guevara. His *Pedagogy of the Oppressed*, published in 1968 and reprinted in English two years later, has become mandatory reading at many academic institutions in the United States.

Freire's *Pedagogy* doesn't concern itself with any specific educational problems, but is rather "a utopian political tract calling for the overthrow of capitalist hegemony and the creation of classless societies," as described by *City Journal*'s Stern. [71] Freire's work does no more than repeat the Marxist view that there are only two kinds of people in the world: the oppressor and the oppressed. The oppressed should, then, reject their education, be awakened to their miserable circumstances, and be spurred to rebellion.

Fanon was born on Martinique Island in the Caribbean and joined the Algerian war against French colonial rule. His *The Wretched of the Earth* was published in 1961 with a preface by French existentialist and communist Jean-Paul Sartre, who summarized Fanon's theory as thus: Western colonizers are the embodiment of evil, whereas non-Westerners are inherently noble by virtue of their being colonized and exploited.

Fanon called on people in the colonies to engage in violent

revolt against the colonial ruling class. He said: "At the level of individuals, violence is a cleansing force. It frees the native from his inferiority complex and from his despair and inaction; it makes him fearless and restores his self-respect." [72]

Embracing Fanon's ideas, Sartre wrote in the preface: "For in the first days of the revolt you must kill: to shoot down a European is to kill two birds with one stone, to destroy an oppressor and the man he oppresses at the same time: there remain a dead man, and a free man; the survivor, for the first time, feels a national soil under his foot." [73]

The ideas of Gramsci, Freire, and Fanon are deceptive narratives that entice people to regard history and society through the lens of class struggle. Once the spark of class hatred enters their hearts, students learn to resent and oppose the normal structure and workings of society, for which the inevitable solution is rebellion and revolution.

Which particular theorist or school of thought has had the greatest influence on humanities and social sciences in American colleges is a matter of debate. What's clear, however, is that Marxism, the Frankfurt School, Freudian theory, and postmodernism (which worked alongside communism in destroying culture and morality) have come to dominate the field.

Communist Theory Permeates Academia

Since the 1960s, the discipline of literary research in the United States has experienced a fundamental paradigm shift across its various subfields. Traditionally, literary critics appreciated the moral and aesthetic values of classic works, considering literature an important resource for broadening readers' horizons, developing their moral character, and cultivating their intellectual taste. As a matter of principle, academic literary theory is secondary to the literature itself, serving as an aid to its comprehension and interpretation.

Following the popular trends in philosophy, psychology, and culture, various new literary theories emerged in the academic community during the height of the countercul-ture movement in the 1960s. The relationship between theory and literature was thrown in reverse as the actual works were reduced to material for validating modern interpretative approaches. [74]

What is the substance of these theories? Taken together, they make a mess of traditional academic disciplines, such as philosophy, psychology, sociology, and psychoanalysis, in their slanted depiction of society and culture. As literary theorist Jonathan Culler put it, "Theory is often a pugnacious critique of common-sense notions, and further, an attempt to show that what we take for granted as 'common sense' is, in fact, a historical construction, a particular theory that has come to seem so natural to us that we don't even see it as a theory." [75]

In other words, modern academic theories belittle, reverse, and destroy the understandings of right and wrong, good and evil, and beauty and ugliness that come from a traditional family upbringing, religious faith, and ethics, while replacing them with a sinister system devoid of positive values.

Peeling off their labyrinthine academic packaging, these so-called theories are no more than a jumbling of classical and neo-Marxism, the Frankfurt School, psychoanalysis, deconstructionism, post-structuralism, and postmodern-ism. Together they form an axis that aims to destroy the foun-dations of human civilization and serves as a camouflage for communism to burrow into Western academia. Since the 1960s, communism has made rapid breakthroughs in areas such as literature, history, and philosophy, establishing its dominance in the humanities and social sciences.

"Theory," as has been discussed, is more or less the same thing as "critical theory." Its permutations include the newly emerged critical studies of law, race, gender, society, science, medicine, and the like. Its pervasiveness is the result of communism's successful expansion into the academic and educational fields, corrupting youth with deviated thought and laying a path for the eventual destruction of humankind.

The Politicization of Literary Research

From the perspective of a Marxist literary critic, the significance of a literary text lies not in its intrinsic value, but rather in how it reflects the ideology of the ruling class, or its stance on issues emphasized by the Left, such as gender and race. From this perspective, the classics are said to have no intrinsic value at all. A prominent American Marxist literary theorist outright declared that the political interpretation of literature constitutes "the absolute horizon of all reading and all interpretation." [76] That is to say, all literary works should be treated as political allegories, and only when the deeper meanings of class, race, gender, or sexual oppression are uncovered can one's understanding be considered profound or qualified.

People from communist countries are familiar with this kind of dogmatic literary criticism. Chinese communist leader Mao Zedong summed up *Dream of the Red Chamber*, one of the four great Chinese classics, as "four families, fierce class struggle, and a few dozen human lives."

In communist countries, literary discourse is not always confined to civilized and sophisticated debates of the ivory tower. It can sometimes become the impetus for bloody struggle. The decadelong brutality of the Cultural Revolution in the 1960s and '70s was sparked by the official rebuke of a literary work.

In 1959, in response to Mao's call to learn from the honest and upright Ming Dynasty official Hai Rui, leading historian Wu Han was advised by a top propaganda official that he should begin studying the historic figure and write about him. In 1961, Wu finished penning the stage drama *Hai Rui Dismissed From Office*, depicting the life of the official who dared to criticize the emperor and was imprisoned for it. Several years later, on November 10, 1965, Shanghai's Wenhui News published a critical review of the play. The review had been jointly planned by Mao's wife, Jiang Qing, and radical theorist Zhang Chunqiao. It claimed that the play was an allusion to Peng Dehuai, a People's Liberation Army general who was purged for his opposition to the Communist Party's Three Red Flags — the General Line for Socialist Construction, the Great Leap Forward, and the People's Communes. In the 1950s, these policies led to the Great Famine, which starved tens of millions of people, and in the early 1960s weakened Mao's position in the regime. At a time when Mao and his supporters were looking for ways to restore his prestige, the criticism of *Hai Rui Dismissed From Office* became the fuse for the political decisions that led to the Cultural Revolution.

The Chinese communists' crude approach to interpreting all literary works in terms of class struggle can be contrasted with the much subtler literary criticism found in Western colleges over the last few decades.

Western neo-Marxist literary criticism is like a virus that becomes stronger and deadlier through endless mutation. It adapts other theories to become its weapons, dragging the great works of human culture — from the classics of Greece and Rome to Dante, Shakespeare, and Victorian novels — onto the literary operating table to be dismembered and reconfigured. Though this type of commentary makes use of arcane jargon to create the veneer of sophistication, the main arguments typically boil down to accusations of prejudice against disenfranchised classes, women, or ethnic minorities.

Modern critiques label these works as belonging to the superstructure of the ruling class, and describe them as having the effect of numbing the masses to their oppressive conditions and preventing them from achieving revolutionary class consciousness. As English philosopher Sir Roger Scruton said, "The methods of the new literary theorist are really weapons of subversion: an attempt to destroy humane education from within, to rupture the chain of sympathy that binds us to our culture." [77]

The Marxist Theory of Ideology

"Ideology" is a core concept in the Marxist-influenced humanities. Marx viewed morality, religion, and metaphysics collectively as ideology. He believed that the dominant ideology in a class-based society was the ideology of the ruling class, and that its values did not reflect reality, but rather its inverse. [78]

Twentieth-century neo-Marxism has made the destruction of culture a necessary stage of revolution and makes extensive reference to ideology in its literature. Lukács defined ideology as the "false consciousness" as opposed to the real "class consciousness." French Marxist Louis Althusser proposed the concept of the "ideological state apparatuses," which include religion, education, family, law, politics, trade unions, communication, and culture, that would work in conjunction with a brutal state apparatus.

The Marxist concept of ideology is a work of cunning sophistry. Every society or system has its shortcomings that should be articulated and corrected. However, Althusser and other Marxists do not concern themselves with specific problems. Instead, they reject the system in its entirety on the grounds that it is a structure set up and maintained by the ruling class to safeguard its own interests.

Poisoning the well is an important aspect of the Marxist fixation on ideology, and can be seen in Althusser's convoluted ideological critique. Instead of examining the factual merits of an argument, the ideological approach relies on accusing opponents of harboring ulterior motives or of being from the wrong background. Just as no one wants to drink from a poisoned well, subjecting a person to rumors or other forms of character assassination makes his opinion unacceptable to the public — no matter how reasonable or logical he may be. Althusser's concept of "ideological state apparatuses" reflects communism's extreme contempt for human society — nothing is acceptable short of complete rejection and destruction. This is a manifestation of communism's aim to eradicate human culture.

The Marxist concept of ideology rests on abstract, generalized, and false propositions that aim to purge traditional moral values. While masking their real intentions by expressing ostensible moral indignation, Marxists have deceived and influenced vast numbers of people.

Postmodern Marxism

In the wake of the 1960s, a group of French philosophers created what soon became the most powerful ideological weapon for Marxism and communism in the American academic community: deconstruction. These philosophers included Michel Foucault and Jacques Derrida. In 2007, Foucault was the most-cited author in the humanities, with 2,521 citations. Derrida ranked third, having been cited 1,874 times. [79] There are deep connections between postmodernism and Marxism, so we find it apt to refer to it broadly as postmodern Marxism. [80]

The fact that language possesses ambiguous and multifaceted layers of meaning, and that a text may have different interpretations, has been common knowledge since at least the time of the ancient Greeks and pre-imperial China. However, Derrida's theory of deconstruction, an elaborate deception that combines atheism and relativism, works by exaggerating the ambiguity of language to break down texts even where the meaning is clear and well-defined.

Unlike conventional atheists, Derrida expressed his views in the language of philosophers. As a result, his viewpoints are not only destructive to the idea of God, but also to the concepts of rationality, authority, and meaning as associated with traditional beliefs, as theorists aligned with Derrida carry out their deconstruction of these terms. Having deceived many people with its veneer of intellectual depth, deconstructionist theory ran rampant throughout the humanities and took its place as one of communism's most potent tools for destroying faith, tradition, and culture.

The essence of Foucault's theory revolves around the notion

that there is no truth, only power. Since power monopolizes the right to interpret truth, anything that purports truth is hypocritical and untrustworthy. In his book *Discipline and Punish: The Birth of the Prison,* Foucault, who once joined the French Communist Party, asked the question, "Is it surprising that prisons resemble factories, schools, barracks, hospitals, which all resemble prisons?" [81] In equating indispensable institutions of society with prisons and calling on people to overthrow these "prisons," Foucault lays bare the antisocial nature of his theory.

Armed with the weapons of deconstruction, Foucault's theory, and other critical theories, scholars have stigmatized tradition and morality by relativizing everything. They thrive on axioms like "all interpretation is misinterpretation," "there is no truth, only interpretations," or "there are no facts, only interpretations." They have relativized the understanding of basic concepts such as truth, kindness, beauty, justice, and so on, and then discarded them as trash.

Young students taking liberal arts courses dare not question the authority of their instructors. Staying clear-minded under the sustained ideological bombardment that follows is harder still. Once geared to the study of postmodern Marxist theory, it is difficult to get them to think in any other way. This is a major means by which communist ideology has been able to run amuck in the humanities and social sciences.

C. USING NEW ACADEMIC FIELDS FOR IDEOLOGICAL INFILTRATION

In a normal society, women's studies, research on racial minorities, and the study of foreign cultures reflect the prosperity and diversity of the academic community. Following the 1960s counterculture movement, however, some radicals made use of these new disciplines to spread their left-leaning ideas in universities and research institutes. In recent decades, academic disciplines such as feminist studies, queer studies, and various departments dedicated to non-white minorities became ubiquitous throughout American universities.

The basic premise of women's studies is that sex differences are not the result of biological differences, but rather are social constructs. Alleging that women have long been suppressed by men and patriarchy, the field of women's studies sets out to trigger feminist social consciousness and bring about social change and revolution.

One feminist professor at the University of California–Santa Cruz grew up in a famous communist family. She proudly displayed her credentials as a communist and a lesbian activist. Since the 1980s, she had been teaching feminism and regarded her sexual orientation as a way to arouse political consciousness. Her inspiration for becoming a professor was a fellow communist, who had told her it was her mission to do so. In a public statement, she said that "teaching became a form of political activism for me." [82] In one of her syllabi, she wrote that female homosexuality is "the highest state of feminism." [83]

The University of Missouri has designed its courses to prime students to see the issues of feminism, literature, gender, and peace from the position of the Left. For example, a course called Outlaw Gender saw the sexes as "artificial categories produced by a particular culture," rather than being naturally produced. Only one viewpoint was instilled in students — the narrative of gender-based oppression and discrimination against multiple-gender identities. [84]

As discussed in Chapter Five, the anti-war movement in the Western world following World War II was heavily influenced by communists. In recent decades, a new subject, Peace Studies, has emerged at American universities. Scholars David Horowitz and Jacob Laksin studied more than 250 organizations that had some connection to the new academic field. They concluded that these organizations were political, not academic, in nature, and their aim was to recruit students to the anti-war Left. [85]

Citing the popular textbook *Peace and Conflict Studies*, Horowitz and Laksin laid out the ideological motivations of the field. The textbook uses Marxist arguments to explain the problems of poverty and starvation. The author condemned landowners and agricultural merchants, claiming that their greed led to the starvation of hundreds of millions of people. Though the point is ostensibly against violence, there is one form of violence that the author does not oppose, and in fact praises: violence committed in the course of proletarian revolution.

A passage from *Peace and Conflict Studies* says the following: "While Cuba is far from an earthly paradise, and certain individual rights and civil liberties are not yet widely practiced, the case of Cuba indicates that violent revolutions can sometimes result in generally improved living conditions for many people." The book makes no mention of Castro's dictatorship or the catastrophic results of the Cuban Revolution.

Written after 9/11, *Peace and Conflict Studies* also touched on terrorism. Surprisingly, its authors seem to have so much sympathy for the terrorists that the term "terrorist" is in quotation marks. They defend their stance by saying: "Placing 'terrorist' in quotation marks may be jarring for some readers, who consider the designation self-evident. We do so, however, not to minimize the horror of such acts but to emphasize the value of qualifying righteous indignation by the recognition that often one person's 'terrorist' is another's 'freedom fighter.'" [86]

The Civil Rights Movement is rightfully noted for its supporters' peaceful advocacy of greater representation for African-Americans. However, not all activism at the time was carried out in good faith. In US colleges, the establishment of departments dedicated to African-American studies was in some cases the result of intimidation and political blackmail. In the late 1960s, student strikes and intimidation on the campuses of then-San Francisco State College, University of California–Santa Barabra, and Cornell University led to the establishment of the country's first black studies departments. At Cornell, faculty caved after more than one hundred black students showed up to demand the establishment of a black research department staffed solely by black people. Some of the protesters brandished shotguns and waved packs of ammunition. [87]

Shelby Steele, who became a senior fellow at Stanford University's Hoover Institution, voiced his opposition to affirmative action and the establishment of black research departments at universities. He said that university leaders had such a strong sense of "white guilt" that they would agree to any request from the representatives of black student unions. [88]

Academia should be objective and avoid harboring political agendas. However, these new academic fields have adopted an ideological stand: Professors of women's studies must embrace feminism, while professors involved in black studies must believe that the political, economic, and cultural hardships of African-Americans result from discrimination by whites. Their existence is not to explore the truth, but to promote an ideological narrative.

These new subjects are byproducts of the American cultural revolution. Having been established in universities, these new fields of study have expanded by demanding higher budgets and recruiting more students, who further strengthen them. These new fields, which are already deeply ingrained in academia, were created by people acting under the influence of communist ideology. Their aim is to foment and expand conflict among different groups and to incite hatred in preparation for violent revolution. They have little relation to the people (African-Americans, women, or others) they claim to stand for.

D. PROMOTING LEFTIST RADICALISM

In their book *One-Party Classroom: How Radical Professors at America's Top Colleges Indoctrinate Students and Undermine*

Our Democracy, Horowitz and Laksin listed about 150 leftist courses offered at twelve universities. These courses masked their political intent with scholarly language, but some of them neglected even basic academic principles, making them closely resemble political courses that are mandatory in communist countries. For example, the Community Studies Department at the University of California–Santa Cruz previously offered a seminar with a course description that read: "The goal of this seminar is to learn how to organize a revolution. We will learn what communities past and present have done and are doing to resist, challenge, and overcome systems of power including (but not limited to) global capitalism, state oppression, and racism." [89]

Bill Ayers, previously a distinguished professor at the University of Illinois–Chicago, is a 1960s-era radical and co-founder of Weather Underground, originally called Weatherman, which was a faction of the Students for a Democratic Society (SDS). In 1969, when SDS collapsed, Weather Underground stepped in, dedicating its efforts to organizing radical students, who took part in terrorist activities designed to inflame racial conflict. Weather Underground, which came to be designated as a domestic terrorist organization, perpetrated bombings at the Capitol, the New York City Police headquarters, the Pentagon, and offices of the National Guard. A well-known quote from Ayers says: "Kill all the rich people. Break up their cars and apartments. Bring the revolution home, kill your parents, that's where it's really at." Ayers's academic publications are consistent with his resumé.

A web of left-wing progressives successfully prevented the FBI from arresting Ayers. He reemerged in 1980 and became a faculty member at the University of Illinois–Chicago, where he researched early childhood education. His political views were unchanged, and he has shown no remorse for his terrorist attacks. Ayers successively became associate professor, professor, and eventually reached the standing of distinguished professor. He also received the title of senior university scholar, the institution's highest honor. [90]

Each title Ayers received was the result of a joint decision of his colleagues in the department. This itself reflects the university's tacit acknowledgment and support for his terrorist past.

E. DENYING AMERICA'S GREAT TRADITIONS

A group of politically engaged students on the campus of Texas Tech University conducted a survey in 2014 asking three questions: who won the Civil War; who is our vice president; and who did we gain our independence from? Many students had no idea of the answers. While ignorant of these basic facts about their country's politics and history, students were well-acquainted with the details of movie stars and their love affairs. [91]

In 2008, the Intercollegiate Studies Institute conducted a random survey of 2,508 Americans and found that only half could name all three branches of government. [92] Answering thirty-three straightforward civics questions, 71 percent of the respondents received an average score of 49 percent, a failing mark. [93]

Learning American history is not just the process of understanding how the nation was established, but it is also a process of understanding the values upon which the nation was built and what it takes to preserve those traditions. Only in this way will its people cherish what they have today, protect their national legacy, and pass it to the next generation. Forgetting history is the same as destroying tradition. When people don't know their civic duties, it's possible for a totalitarian government to form.

One can't help but wonder what happened to American history and civics education. The answers lie in the textbooks today's students use and in their teachers. The Marxist Howard Zinn is the author of a popular history book titled *A*

People's History of the United States. This book revolves around the premise that all the heroic deeds and inspiring episodes recounted as part of American history are shameless lies, and that the true history of the United States is a dark journey of suppression, deprivation, and genocide.

An economics professor at a university in Boston claimed that the terrorists who are enemies of the United States were the real freedom fighters against evil, that is, the United States. In an article published in 2004, he equated the terrorists who carried out the 9/11 attacks with the American rebels who, in 1775, fired the first shots in Lexington and started the American Revolutionary War. [94]

F. OPPOSING THE CLASSICS OF WESTERN CIVILIZATION

In 1988, radical students and teachers at Stanford University protested against a course called Western Civilization. They chanted, "Hey, hey, ho, ho! Western Civ has got to go!" Stanford conceded to the protesters' demands and replaced Western Civilization with a course called Cultures, Ideas, & Values (CIV). While the new class kept some of the Western cultural classics such as Homer, Plato, St. Augustine, Dante Alighieri, and Shakespeare, it did require that the course include works from several women, minority groups, and other groups of people deemed to have been subjected to oppression.

Then-US Secretary of Education William Bennett condemned the change as "an unfortunate capitulation to a campaign of pressure politics and intimidation." Despite the criticism, many prominent universities did the same, and lesser colleges followed suit so as to not be left behind. In a few years, liberal arts education in American universities had experienced a great transformation.

The "politically correct" drive to expel the classics from American universities has led to various deleterious results, including the following:

1. Low-quality writing with shallow content that contains revolutionary narratives or that passes as "victim literature" displaces classic works and their everlasting profundity.

2. Placing these average works on the same level as the classics trivializes and relativizes the classics.

3. The guiding themes behind the classics are now interpreted using critical theory, cultural studies, identity politics, and political correctness. Scholars enthusiastically research the "hidden racism and sexism" in Shakespeare's plays, for example, distorting and insulting classic works.

4. Students inculcated with this kind of mental attitude find the noble characters, great accomplishments, and moral lessons depicted in the classics hard to believe, and develop an instinct to instead see them in a negative and cynical light.

In traditional literary education, the main themes conveyed in the classics were universal love, justice, loyalty, courage, the spirit of self-sacrifice, and other moral values. Historical education revolved around major events concerning the establishment and development of the nation and its fundamental values.

Because the classics of Western literature are nearly all written by white European men, leftists take up the banners of multiculturalism and feminism to insist that people read literature by women, people of color, and so on. As for the teaching of history, modern education favors describing a country's historical path as entirely dark, filled with slavery and exploitation of women and other minority groups. The object is no longer to recall the traditional legacy, but to instill a feeling of guilt toward groups designated as the "oppressed."

Classic works embody the important experiences and

lessons of the past, and studying them is essential for students to learn about their culture. When schools focus on politically correct or modern works and de-emphasize the classics, students receive less exposure to the wisdom contained in the latter, or learn to view them in a superficial, critical light. As a result of this kind of education, entire generations are alienated from the origins of their civilization and its unique system of faith and values.

G. MONOPOLIZING TEXTBOOKS AND LIBERAL ARTS

Economist Paul Samuelson pointed to the power of textbooks when he said, "I don't care who writes a nation's laws — or crafts its advanced treaties — if I can write its economics textbooks." [95] Those textbooks that have a large circulation and carry an authoritative voice exert tremendous influence on students. Whoever writes the textbooks has the power to shape the impressionable minds of the young.

After radical scholars and professors received tenure and reputation, they gained control over university publication offices and committees. They used their authority to load teaching materials with their own ideologies and force-feed them to students. In some academic fields, the textbooks and required reading chosen by professors contain more works of Marxism than any other school of thought. *A People's History of the United States* is required reading for many history, economics, literature, and women's studies majors.

Once leftists enjoy strength in numbers, they can use the peer-review mechanism in the US academic community to suppress scholars with different opinions. A paper that challenges left-wing ideologies is bound to be rejected by leftists and their colleagues.

Many journals in the humanities are guided by critical theory and filled with obscure technical jargon, while the main theme is to reject the divine, reject traditional culture, and incite revolutions to overturn the current social, political, and economic order. One category of scholarship aims to prove that all traditional morals and standards, including even the scientific process, are social constructs whose purpose is to safeguard the power of the ruling class by forcing their norms on the whole society.

In 1996, New York University physics professor Alan Sokal had a paper published in *Social Text,* Duke University's cultural studies journal, titled "Transgressing the Boundaries: Towards a Transformative Hermeneutics of Quantum Gravity." Citing 109 footnotes and referencing 219 sources, the paper argued that "quantum gravity" is constructed by society and language. [96] Soon after, Sokal published a declaration in another magazine, *Lingua Franca*, stating that his original paper was a prank. [97]

During an interview on National Public Radio, Sokal said he found inspiration in the 1994 book *Higher Superstition: The Academic Left and Its Quarrels With Science.* The book's author said that some publications in the humanities will publish anything so long as it contains "the proper leftist thought" and quotes well-known leftist thinkers. Sokal tested this by filling his paper with leftist ideologies, pointless citations, and complete nonsense. [98] He later wrote: "The results of my little experiment demonstrate, at the very least, that some fashionable sectors of the American academic Left have been getting intellectually lazy. The editors of *Social Text* liked my article because they liked its conclusion: that 'the content and methodology of postmodern science provide powerful intellectual support for the progressive political project.' They apparently felt no need to analyze the quality of the evidence, the cogency of the arguments, or even the relevance of the arguments to the purported conclusion." [99] Sokal's satirical approach highlighted the dearth of academic principle or credibility in the fields of critical theory and cultural studies.

The extent to which communist thought has penetrated the social sciences becomes apparent when one takes a look at the titles of papers given at the annual meetings of major US academic bodies. The Modern Language Association is the largest of such societies, boasting twenty-five thousand members who consist mainly of professors and scholars in the fields of modern language research and education. Thousands join the association's annual conference.

A large portion of the papers listed on the association's website utilize the ideological framework of Marxism, the Frankfurt School, deconstruction, post-structuralism, and other deviant theories. Others use feminism, gay research, identity politics, and other radical trends. Similar organizations, including the American Sociological Association, reflect much the same slant, though to varying extents.

The American tradition of liberal arts education requires that students take a number of humanities courses, regardless of the students' majors. Today, these required courses are usually taught by leftist professors from the disciplines of literature, history, philosophy, and social sciences. American scholar Sowell has noted that required courses leave students with no alternative but to listen to these professors, who often use their classrooms as opportunities to spread their leftist ideologies, even using grades as an incentive to have students accept their views. At the University of Michigan, for example, students in an introductory biology course were required to watch films about politics. Students who dare to challenge a professor's views are often punished with lower grades. [100] The Marxist views of these humanities and social science professors not only corrupt students in their academic fields, but affect almost the entire student body.

College students wish to be respected as adults, but both their knowledge and practical experience is limited. In the relatively closed environment of the university, few of them suspect that their respected professors would take advantage of their innocence and trust to instill in them a set of damaging ideologies and values. Parents pay high tuition costs for their children to master the knowledge and skills they will use as a basis for finding their place in society. How could they imagine that their children are actually being robbed of their invaluable years, and instead being transformed into followers of radical ideologies that will affect them for the rest of their lives?

Generation after generation of youth has entered this education system that has been heavily infiltrated by communist ideologies. They study textbooks penned by leftists and internalize their deviated theories, hastening the decline of culture, morals, and humanity.

H. UNIVERSITY 'RE-EDUCATION': BRAINWASHING AND MORAL CORRUPTION

With the growth of Marxist ideology throughout universities, campus policy since the 1980s has increasingly focused on preventing "offensive" remarks, especially when it comes to offending women or ethnic minorities. According to American scholar Donald Alexander Downs, from 1987 to 1992, about three hundred US universities implemented policies for the regulation of speech, creating a paralegal system that forbids language deemed offensive regarding sensitive groups and topics. [101]

Those who support these prohibitions may mean well, but their actions lead to a ridiculous outcome, as ever greater numbers of people claim the right not to be offended for any reason. In fact, no such right exists according to law, but the prominence of cultural Marxism has allowed anyone to claim an association with oppressed groups, citing reasons such as culture, ancestry, skin color, gender, sexual orientation, and so on. Administrative staff at universities have consistently afforded privileged treatment to those who claim victimhood.

According to Marxist logic, the oppressed are morally correct in all circumstances, and many people do not dare to question the authenticity of their claims. This absurd logic is based on twisting the criteria for judging what is moral. As group identities and sentiments intensify (in Leninism and Stalinism, this is called a high level of class consciousness), people unconsciously abandon the traditional standards of good and evil, replacing them with groupthink. This has most markedly manifested in totalitarian communist states, where the "oppressed" proletariat was given a justification for killing the landowning and capitalist "oppressors."

The trend of making arbitrary claims regarding offensive or discriminatory language was started by cultural Marxist scholars who fabricated a series of new concepts for expanding the definition of discrimination. Among these are ideas like "microaggressions," "trigger warnings," "safe spaces," and so on. University administrators introduced corresponding policies and mandatory education, such as sensitivity training and diversity training.

Microaggression refers to an implicit nonverbal offense that one encounters in daily life, with the supposed offenders perhaps being completely unaware of its implications. This kind of unintentional offense or ignorance is labeled "insensitive" (Leninism or Stalinism would deem this to be low social consciousness). Sensitivity training has become a major aspect of acclimating incoming college freshmen. Students are told what can't be said and what clothes can't be worn, lest they commit a microaggression in violation of university regulations.

On some campuses, the phrase "welcome to America" cannot be said because it may constitute discrimination and is considered a microaggression: It could offend ethnic groups, such as Native Americans, Africans, Japanese, and Chinese, that have historically suffered unjust treatment in the United States.

The following are among a long list of statements deemed to be microaggressions by the University of California: "America is a melting pot" (racial discrimination), "America is the land of opportunity" and "Men and women have equal opportu-

nities for achievement" (denying gender or ethnic inequality).
[102] Microaggressions are cause for administrative discipline,
and they promote the establishment of "safe spaces."

In one incident of alleged microaggression on the India-
napolis campus of Indiana University–Purdue University, a
white student who worked as a janitor for the school was told
by the campus affirmative action office that he had violated a
racial harassment ordinance by reading the book *Notre Dame
vs. the Klan: How the Fighting Irish Defeated the Ku Klux Klan*
in a campus breakroom. Two of his student colleagues had felt
offended that the cover of the book featured a photo of a KKK
gathering and had filed complaints that his choice to read the
book in the breakroom constituted racial harassment. After
pressure from groups such as the Foundation for Individual
Rights in Education, the university conceded that the student
was not guilty and expunged any records about the incident
from his file. [103]

Sensitivity training and diversity training are compa-
rable in nature to the re-education programs in the former
Soviet Union and in China. The purpose of re-education is to
strengthen class concepts: The "bourgeoisie" and "landlord
class" (akin to white males) must recognize their original sin as
members of the oppressive class, and the supposedly oppressed
groups must have the "correct" understanding about "bourgeois" culture. Pressure is put on them to clear away their
"internalized oppression" so that they can come to recognize
their oppressive conditions. This is similar to how feminist
education teaches women to see traditional femininity as a
construct of the patriarchy.

According to the Marxist analysis of class, the personal
is political. It is considered wrong to understand a problem
from the standpoint of the designated oppressor. Therefore, to
reform people's worldview and ensure they completely follow
the Marxist program, any words and actions that deny class
oppression or class struggle are punished severely. Sensitivity

training is held to fully reveal "social injustice" and to reorient people to the standpoint of "oppressed" groups.

For example, in 2013, Northwestern University required all students to complete a course on diversity before graduating. According to the school's instructions, after the completion of the course, students would be able to "expand their ability to think critically" (learning to classify "class," in the Marxist sense), "recognize their own positionality in systems of inequality"(recognizing their "class component"), and "engage in self-reflection on power and privilege" (putting themselves in the shoes of the "oppressed" class). [104]

The University of Delaware began to implement a mandatory ideological re-education program in 2007 for seven thousand of its residential students. Referred to as "treatment" for incorrect attitudes and beliefs, its stated aim was to make students accept set perspectives concerning issues such as politics, race, gender, and environmentalism. Resident assistants at the university were required to personally conduct one-on-one interviews with the students, asking them questions about, for example, which races and genders they would date and when they discovered their "sexual identity." When a female student responded to the latter question by saying that it was none of the resident assistant's business, the assistant reported her to the university administration. [105] The program was disbanded after sustained backlash.

This mass political indoctrination not only mixes up the standards for discerning moral values, but also greatly strengthens egoism and individualism. What students learn is that they can use the highly politicized feelings of a group (identity politics) to pursue their own individual desires. Simply by claiming that one belongs to a group supposedly suffering from oppression, one can accuse and threaten others or use this identity for personal benefit.

Whether one is offended or not is a subjective feeling, but today, even feelings pass for objective evidence. It has gotten to the point where university professors must constantly beat around the bush. Recently, students at many universities demanded that before teaching certain content, professors must first issue trigger warnings, as some discussion topics or reading material might cause negative emotional reactions. In the last few years, even works such as Shakespeare's *The Merchant of Venice* and ancient Roman poet Ovid's *Metamorphoses* ended up on the list of literature that requires trigger warnings. Some universities even recommend that works deemed to trigger some students' emotions be avoided as much as possible. [106]

Many students growing up under this kind of atmosphere have egos that are easily hurt and try their utmost to avoid feeling offended. Group identity, promoted on campuses, is another version of the "class consciousness" preached by communism, and it leaves students ignorant of independent thought and personal responsibility. Like the radical students of the 1960s who are now their professors, these students are against tradition. They indulge in confused sexual promiscuity, alcohol addiction, and drug abuse. Yet beneath their contempt for worldly conventions are fragile hearts and souls, unable to bear the slightest blow or setback, let alone take on real responsibility.

Traditional education fosters self-restraint, independent thinking, a sense of responsibility, and understanding of others. The specter of communism wants nothing less than to have the next generation completely abandon its moral bearings and become its minions for its rule over the world.

3. How Communism Destroyed Education in China

When it comes to any goal, like that of corrupting education in the West, communism can take hundreds of years and gradually work over several generations, if necessary, to achieve its aims.

In China, the communists seized upon the country's instability from long periods of war to take power and impose their ideological program on the people. But even prior to the Chinese Communist Party's takeover in 1949, leftist Chinese scholars and activists were already attacking China's profound cultural heritage — starting with the traditional system of education.

At the beginning of the twentieth century, when Dewey's progressive education began to corrode the United States, his ethnic Chinese followers returned to China and became pioneers of modern Chinese education. The Opium Wars against the British had weakened the Chinese people's resolve, and the intellectuals were eager to find a way to strengthen the nation. The communists exploited these conditions to set off a so-called New Culture Movement that repudiated China's traditions and provided fertile ground for the development of the communist movement.

Starting in 1915 and lasting into the next decade, the New Culture Movement had three main representatives: Hu Shi, a disciple of Dewey; Chen Duxiu, a co-founder of the Chinese Communist Party (CCP); and Lu Xun, who was later praised by Mao Zedong as "the chief commander of China's Cultural Revolution." Li Dazhao, another CCP co-founder, also adopted an important role in the cultural movement of the later period.

Representatives of the New Culture Movement attributed China's national weakness over the past hundred years to traditional Confucian thought and advocated the abolition of this "old culture." Meanwhile, the movement saw all Western culture as advanced "new culture." The New Culture Movement used the words "science" and "democracy" as its chief slogans in criticizing "old" Chinese culture and beliefs.

Running concurrent to the New Culture Movement was the 1919 May Fourth student movement in Beijing. Sparked by patriotic outrage against Japanese imperialism, the movement was taken over by Li Dazhao and other communists, who used it to promote the New Culture Movement and amplify the rejection of the traditional Chinese worldview. In 1921, Li, Chen Duxiu, and a handful of others gathered in Shanghai and founded the CCP.

The New Culture Movement and the May Fourth Movement were instrumental in helping the CCP spread its ideas and organization throughout China. At a time of national crisis, the Party convinced many that China's only hope for survival was to break with "old culture" using the most radical methods. These early movements against traditional Chinese culture and civilization later served as the ideological inspiration for the Cultural Revolution.

Among the greatest harm wrought by the New Culture Movement was the campaign to promote the vernacularization of written Chinese. As advocated by Hu Shi, primary schools changed their teaching of the Chinese language to simplify written Chinese, while changing meanings and omitting many words. As a result, after one generation, the majority of Chinese people were hardly able to read and understand classical Chinese. This meant that *The Book of Changes*, the *Spring and Autumn Annals, Tao Te Ching, Yellow Emperor's Inner Classic (Huangdi Neijing)*, and other traditional books were now inaccessible to the ordinary student. Instead, they were treated as esoteric content for scholarly research. China's five thousand years' of glorious civilization became mere decoration.

In the development of the divinely arranged Chinese culture, the written classical language was purposely separated from the spoken language. In China, over the course of history, there have been many large-scale assimilations of different ethnic groups and multiple relocations of China's cultural center of gravity; thus, the spoken language was constantly changing. But, due to the separation between the spoken language and classical Chinese used in writing, classical Chinese remained largely unchanged. Students in the Qing Dynasty (1644–1911) could still read and understand classics from the Song and

Tang dynasties, or even those from the age prior to the Qin Dynasty (221–206 BC). This allowed traditional Chinese culture and literature to be transmitted unbroken over thousands of years.

However, communism caused the Chinese people to sever their cultural roots through the language. At the same time, by combining the written language with the spoken language, it became easier to mix in deviant words and phrases, thus pushing the Chinese people further from tradition.

The literacy campaigns and popularization of culture in elementary education undertaken by the CCP before and after its establishment subjected its captive audience to direct and explicit brainwashing. For instance, the first few phrases learned by students in literacy classes and the first year of primary school were propaganda like "long live Chairman Mao," "the evil old society," and "evil American imperialism" — phrases that fully exemplify the hate-based class struggle ethos the Party demanded.

Compared with deviant ideas that Western progressive education mixes into children's books (like *Heather Has Two Mommies*), the CCP's movements are also a potent form of ideological indoctrination imposed on the young. Chinese children who are educated in this way grow up to become fanatical defenders of the CCP's tyranny, vilifying and scorning those who dare talk about human rights or universal values. Meanwhile, in the progressive environment of the West, children grow up to be part of the angry student mobs that prevent speakers from talking about traditional values and accuse them of discrimination.

Not long after the CCP took power, it began its thought-reform campaign against intellectuals, focusing on university campuses and high schools. Its main objectives were to reform intellectuals' perspectives on life, force them to forsake traditional moral principles and give up the philosophy of first improving oneself before extending that to one's family, state, and the world. It used a Marxist class-based view of the world and life, from the perspective of the "proletariat" class.

Professors of the old generation, in particular, had to repeatedly criticize themselves, confess to wrongdoings, and acquiesce to being informed on, monitored, and criticized by their colleagues and students. They were even made to acknowledge and eliminate "counter-revolutionary thoughts" in their own subconscious minds, which were called "aggressions against the proletariat class." Of course, this was much more intense than the "sensitivity training" in the West today. Some were unable to take the humiliation and stress, and committed suicide. [107]

Subsequently, the CCP began adjusting faculties and departments in universities. It greatly diminished, merged, or eliminated departments like philosophy, sociology, and those related to the humanities, leaving many comprehensive universities with only Soviet-style science and engineering faculties. This was because the CCP was unable to tolerate the threat to its tyrannical rule from any independent ideological perspectives on politics and social issues. These were associated with the humanities-related faculties, which had enjoyed academic freedom in the days of the Republic of China.

The CCP also made the study of Marxist politics and philosophy mandatory for all students. The entire process was completed within two to three years. In the West, communism took an entire generation to establish new disciplines with the aim of ideological indoctrination and the injection of Marxist thought into universities. Although the speed differed between the two, they achieved similar results.

In 1958, the CCP started its education revolution, which had the following notable features:

Firstly, education was emphasized as a tool that should be used in service of the proletariat. Students, under the leadership of the Party Committee, were organized to prepare the curricula and teaching materials. At Peking University, sixty students in the Chinese language department wrote a 700,000-character treatise called the *History of Chinese Literature* in only thirty days. [108] This incident fully exemplified the core belief of progressive education that teaching methods should be "student-centric," focused on "exploratory learning" and "cooperative learning" — that is, what to learn and how to learn it were to be discussed and decided by the students themselves. The objective was clear: eliminating "superstitious beliefs" in authority figures (which was meant to instill an attitude opposed to tradition), magnifying students' self-centeredness, and laying the foundation for rebellion during the Cultural Revolution to come.

Secondly, education and productive labor were to be joined together. Every school had its own factory, and during the height of the Great Leap Forward, teachers and students smelted steel and tilled the land. Even Renmin University of China, which had previously focused on social disciplines, operated 108 factories. Supposedly, this was to have students "learn by doing."

In the subsequent Cultural Revolution, students were mobilized to destroy all forms of cultural heritage associated with traditional culture, including tangible artifacts and religious beliefs (see Chapter Six). This again echoes the counterculture movement that took place in the West.

After the Cultural Revolution began, Mao felt that "bourgeois intellectuals" should not run the schools. On June 13, 1966, the CCP issued a notice to reform university admissions and started the "corrective action campaign." University entrance exams were abolished and large numbers of "worker-peasant-soldier" students were enrolled.

The 1975 film *Breaking With Old Ideas*, produced during the Cultural Revolution, reflected the ideological spirit of this campaign: "A youth who grew up on a poor farm is not sufficiently literate, but the calluses on his hands from hard farm work qualify him for enrollment." A school principal said: "Can you blame us for their low level of literacy? No! This debt should be settled with the Nationalists, the landowners, and the capitalist class [the oppressors]!"

In the West, a professor published a paper claiming that mathematics leads to racial discrimination (because students of certain ethnic minority groups have lower math scores compared to white students). [109] Another professor published a paper that said math standards based on the higher scores achieved by male students leads to gender discrimination against females when they are held to the same standard. [110] Qualifying students for university based on the calluses they have or attributing lower math scores to racial and gender discrimination are methods that communism uses to dumb down students and stunt their intellectual growth.

After the Cultural Revolution, China resumed its university entrance examinations. From then on, preparing for this exam was the ultimate objective of primary and high school education. Under this utilitarian education system, many students became machines that learned only how to pass exams, without the ability to think independently or to distinguish right from wrong. At the same time, Marxist philosophy, politics, and economics have remained mandatory exam subjects.

In the minds of students who are cut off from tradition, the standards of right and wrong, and good and evil, are all evaluated according to communist standards. Thus after the 9/11 terrorist attack occurred, many Chinese students cheered. Primary school students declare that they want to become corrupt officials when they grow up. University students prostitute themselves and become surrogate mothers for cash.

4. Returning to Traditional Education

The education system shoulders the future of a country, a nation, and human civilization itself. It is a long-term endeavor whose impact extends through centuries or even millennia.

Looking back at the past one hundred years, the American

education system has all but been broken by the infiltration and influence of communist ideology. Parents and teachers have had their hands tied and cannot easily give students a good education. Schools, which should have cultivated students' talent, have instead indulged them and led them astray.

Much of society is deeply worried about students' lack of morality, low skill level, fragile psyches, and bad habits, as well as the chaotic, anti-traditional, and anti-social trends they're caught up in.

Nine of the forty-five goals listed in the 1958 classic *The Naked Communist*, relate to education, including "Get control of the schools. Use them as transmission belts for socialism and current Communist propaganda. Soften the curriculum. Get control of teachers' associations. Put the party line in textbooks." [111]

This has not only been achieved, but the situation has become worse. Due to the political and economic strength of the United States, American culture is the object of admiration and emulation by countries around the world. Many countries use the United States as a model for education reform and are influenced by American teaching concepts, teaching materials, teaching methods, and school-management practices. So, to a certain extent, changing American education is tantamount to changing education around the world.

Enlightened sages or saints appear both at the creation of human culture and in times when civilization has fallen into moral corruption. These sages and saints take the role of "teacher." For example, Socrates, the founder of the ancient Greek civilization, was an educator. In the Gospels, Jesus also called himself a teacher. Sakyamuni Buddha has ten names, one of which is "the teacher of heaven and man." Confucius was an educator, and Lao Zi was his teacher. They taught people how to be human, how to respect the divine, how to get along with others, and how to improve morality.

These enlightened beings and saints are the greatest educators of mankind. Their words have shaped major civilizations and become fundamental classics. The values they teach, and the ways they go about improving morality, allow each individual to achieve spiritual transcendence and health. Individuals with healthy minds are essential to social health. It is no wonder that these greatest educators have come to a similar conclusion: The purpose of education is the cultivation of good character.

Eastern and Western classical education, which have been practiced for thousands of years, inherit the culture that the divine has given to people and retain precious experiences and resources. According to the spirit of classical education, both talent and integrity are important criteria for judging the success of education. In the process of reviving the tradition of human education, the treasure of classical education is worthy of preservation, exploration, and learning.

People with high moral values are capable of self-governing. This is the social norm that the American Founding Fathers hoped for. Those who are morally noble will receive divine blessings, and through diligence and wisdom, will obtain material abundance and spiritual satisfaction. More importantly, people with high moral standards allow society to flourish and last for generations. These are the teachings of enlightened beings and saints, the greatest educators of humankind.

Chapter Thirteen

The Media – The Specter's Mouthpiece

THE INFLUENCE OF THE MEDIA in modern society is enormous and continues to grow. It permeates communities of all sizes, from the local to the global. With the rise of social media and user-generated content, the internet has greatly amplified the speed and reach of audiovisual communication.

People rely on the media for the latest news and analysis. In an ocean of information, the media — from newspapers and magazines, to radio, film, and television, to websites and social media — influence what information people see and how they interpret it. The media are in a position to influence people's first impressions on a particular topic, and thus carry considerable powers of psychological priming. For social elites, particularly politicians, the media can be used to determine the focus of public opinion and can serve as a rallying beacon for the public. Topics that the media cover become matters of grave social concern. Issues that go unreported are ignored and forgotten.

In the West, the media are traditionally regarded as the guardians of the truth and societies' core values. Journalists are respected for their expertise and sacrifices. Their duty is to report the truth of the world's major events in a fair, accurate, and timely manner. They must support justice and condemn wrongdoing, while promoting goodness. Their mission goes beyond the private interests of any one individual, company, or political party. Thomas Jefferson, father of the Declaration of Independence and third president of the United States, once said, "Were it left to me to decide whether we should have a government without newspapers or newspapers without a government, I should not hesitate a moment to prefer the latter." [1]

As the voice of a society, the media can act to safeguard morality or become instruments of evil. In the midst of mankind's moral decline, it's difficult for the media to protect their virtue and perform their duties under the pressure of power and the temptation of money.

Newspaper publisher Joseph Pulitzer, after whom the Pulitzer Prize is named, said: "Our Republic and its press will rise or fall together. An able, disinterested, public-spirited press, with trained intelligence to know the right and courage to do it, can preserve that public virtue without which popular government is a sham and a mockery. A cynical, mercenary, demagogic press will produce in time a people as base as itself. The power to mould the future of the Republic will be in the hands of the journalists of future generations." [2]

In communist countries, the media are controlled by the state. These regime mouthpieces brainwash the masses and act as accomplices to communist policies of terror and killing. In Western societies, the media have been heavily infiltrated by communist thought, becoming communism's main agents of anti-traditional, anti-moral, and demonic trends. They propagate lies and hatred, adding fuel to the flames of moral degeneration. Many media entities have abandoned their duties of reporting the truth and guarding society's moral conscience. It is imperative for us to awaken to the state that the media are in today and to bring responsibility back to this field.

1. Mass Indoctrination in Communist Countries

From the very beginning, communists have viewed the media as tools for brainwashing. The 1847 document "Rules of the Communist League," which Karl Marx and Friedrich Engels helped write, asked members to have "revolutionary energy and zeal in propaganda." [3] Marx and Engels often used terms like "party battlefield," "party mouthpiece," "political center," or "tool for public opinion" in their articles to express the character and function they desired of the media.

Vladimir Lenin used the media as tools to promote, incite, and organize the Russian Revolution. He helped run the official communist newspapers *Iskra* and *Pravda* to promote revolutionary propaganda and activism. Soon after the Communist Party of the Soviet Union seized power, it used the media for domestic political indoctrination and for spreading propaganda abroad to improve its image and export revolution.

The Chinese Communist Party (CCP) also regards the media as tools for controlling public opinion and as the mouthpiece of the Party. The CCP is highly conscious of the fact that "the guns and the pens are what it relies on for seizing and consolidating power." [4] As early as the Yan'an period (1935–1947), Mao Zedong's secretary Hu Qiaomu put forward the principle of "Party nature first," saying that the Party newspaper "has to carry through the Party's viewpoints and understandings in all articles, every essay, every news report, and every newsletter." [5]

Upon establishing its dictatorship, the CCP imposed strict control over the media and later the internet. It uses them as tools to indoctrinate the Chinese with communist ideology, suppress dissidents, intimidate the public, and conceal or distort the truth. Media workers are experts in self-censorship, constantly aware that a single error can result in a miserable outcome. Censorship not only permeates the official news channels, but also personal blogs and online communities, which are monitored and controlled by a vast network of internet police.

There is a contemporary Chinese phrase that vividly describes the role of the media under the CCP's rule: "I am the Party's dog, sitting by the Party's door. I'll bite whomever the Party tells me to bite and however many times I am told." This is no exaggeration. Every communist political movement starts with manipulating public opinion: The media spread lies to incite hatred, which cascades into violence and killing. The media play a crucial role in this deadly mechanism.

During the 1989 Tiananmen Square massacre, the CCP claimed that the students were violent thugs and so used the army to suppress the alleged "riot." Following the massacre, it claimed that the army didn't shoot anyone and that there were no casualties in the square. [6] In 2001, early on in the persecution of Falun Gong, the regime staged a self-immolation hoax in Tiananmen Square to frame the spiritual practice and kindle hatred toward Falun Gong practitioners across China and around the world. [7]

Leading cadres in committees at all levels of the CCP place great importance on propaganda work and field considerable personnel for this task. By the end of 2010, China had more than 1.3 million staff working in the national propaganda apparatus, including about 56,000 in propaganda departments at the provincial and county levels, 1.2 million in local propaganda units, and 52,000 people in the central propaganda work units. [8] This figure does not include a large number of staff who are responsible for monitoring and manipulating online opinion, such as internet police, moderators, Party-controlled commentators, and others employed in various forms of public relations.

Countries ruled by communist parties, without exception, use great amounts of resources to manipulate the media. Years of operation have honed communist state media into efficient mouthpieces for their totalitarian masters. They use any and all means to deceive and poison the people.

2. Communist Infiltration of Western Media and Hollywood

The last century was witness to great conflicts between the free world and the communist camp. All the while, communism has been successfully infiltrating and subverting the media in Western countries. This chapter focuses on the United States, in light of the extraordinary influence of American media throughout the world.

After the Soviet regime seized power in Russia, it attempted to establish control over public discourse in the West, dispatching its agents to infiltrate Western media and enticing local communist sympathizers. It used these people to great effect in eulogizing the Soviet Union and concealing the brutality of communist rule. Soviet propaganda efforts swayed large numbers of Westerners and even influenced government policy to favor the Soviet Union.

The Soviet KGB used its agents in the United States to work directly with prestigious American media organizations. Among these agents were John Scott, Richard Lauterbach, and Stephen Laird of *Time* magazine, who used their positions to mingle with politicians, celebrities, and heads of state. Aside from gathering a wide range of intelligence, they also influenced high-level decisions concerning matters of politics, economics, diplomacy, war, and more. Another *Time* editor and Soviet spy, Whittaker Chambers, later defected and wrote the book *Witness* detailing communist subversion in the United States. [9]

Walter Duranty, the Moscow correspondent for *The New York Times*, won the 1932 Pulitzer Prize for a series of articles on the Soviet Union. Former American communist Jay Love-stone and prominent journalist Joseph Alsop both believe Duranty acted as a Soviet agent. [10] During the 1932–1933 famine that ravaged Ukraine and other regions of the Soviet Union, Duranty denied that the famine even existed, let alone that millions of people were starving to death. He claimed that "any report of a famine in Russia is today an exaggeration or malignant propaganda." [11] Describing the consequences of Duranty's false reporting, Robert Conquest, a famous British historian and authoritative scholar on the history of the Soviet Union, wrote in his book *The Harvest of Sorrow: Soviet Collectivization and the Terror-Famine*: "As one of the best known correspondents in the world for one of the best known newspapers in the world, Mr. Duranty's denial that there was a famine was accepted as gospel. Thus Mr. Duranty gulled not only the readers of *The New York Times* but because of the newspaper's prestige, he influenced the thinking of countless thousands of other readers about the character of Josef Stalin and the Soviet regime. And he certainly influenced the newly-elected President [Franklin D.] Roosevelt to recognize the Soviet Union." [12]

At the same time, Hollywood was infiltrated by communist and leftist ideas. Willi Münzenberg, a German communist and member of the Third International, traveled to the United States and recognized that the American film industry could be used as a tool for propaganda, implementing Lenin's concepts of film development and production. He sent his trusted assistant Otto Katz and his associate Louis Gibarti to infiltrate the industry. Katz was highly successful in penetrating the social circles of the Hollywood elite and soon established a Communist Party branch organization, the Hollywood Anti-Nazi League.

Step by step, the Soviet Union's influence began to set in. Many filmmakers of the era idolized the Soviets, and these sentiments only grew during World War II, when the United States and the Soviet Union were briefly allied against Nazi

Germany. A famous playwright claimed that the German invasion of the Soviet Union was "an attack on our motherland." [13] A line in *Mission to Moscow*, a 1943 film intended to bolster support for the Soviet–American alliance, portrays the Soviet Union as being a country founded on the same fundamental principles as the United States. [14]

The Chinese communist regime also has greatly benefited from leftist media and journalists in the free world. Prominent among them were left-wing American journalists Edgar Snow, Agnes Smedley, and Anna Louise Strong. Snow's book *Red Star Over China* painted a glowing picture of Mao and other senior Chinese Communist Party leaders while hiding their crimes and the evil nature of communism from Western readers. Mao said, "Snow is the first person to clear the road for the friendly relations needed to establish a united front." [15] Smedley wrote many articles and books flattering the CCP and its leadership. There is strong evidence from the Soviet archives suggesting that she was a Comintern agent who worked to foster armed revolution in India and collect intelligence for the Soviets. [16] Strong also was an admirer of the Chinese communist movement. The CCP has acknowledged these three Americans by issuing postage stamps in honor of their "meritorious service."

3. Left-Wing Bias Among Media Professionals

The majority of Americans say the media have partisan biases. A 2017 Gallup poll showed that 64 percent of people felt that the media favor Democrats. By comparison, 22 percent believe the media favor Republicans. [17] A question then arises: With the news industry being so competitive, how can such an extreme bias exist?

Though reporters and editors have their own political and social views, their reporting should not be colored by personal opinion — objectivity and neutrality are key principles of journalism ethics. By normal market principles, any bias that exists should be offset by the emergence of new, more neutral competitors.

The reality is more complicated. American political scientist Tim Groseclose, in his 2011 book *Left Turn: How Liberal Media Bias Distorts the American Mind*, used rigorous scientific methods to analyze the political leanings of major American media. His findings revealed that the political leanings of American media on average trend dramatically toward liberalism and progressivism — far left of the typical voting citizen. The "mainstream" media are even further left of this average. [18] The book explains that the majority of media professionals, be they the owners of these organizations or the reporters and commentators, are liberal, which, objectively speaking, puts pressure on traditionalists in the field; the small number of conservatives working in liberal media companies may be seen as "mildly evil or subhuman," according to Groseclose. Even if these journalists aren't squeezed out of employment, they dare not air their political views publicly, much less promote conservative viewpoints in print or on television. [19] According to a 2013 *ABC News/Washington Post* poll, about 28 percent of journalists in the United States self-identified as Democrats compared to just 7.1 percent who identified as Republicans. [20]

The community of media professionals excludes views that do not align with its liberal bias, thus forming political echo chambers. Individuals in this community see themselves as the compassionate and intelligent elite at the forefront of societal development, while looking down on ordinary citizens as stubborn commoners. Left-wing bias discourages students with conservative viewpoints from picking journalism as their major or seeking a job in the media after graduation.

During the 2016 US presidential election, fifty-seven of the nation's one hundred biggest newspapers — with a combined circulation of thirteen million — endorsed the Democratic candidate. Just two of the top hundred, with a combined circulation of three hundred thousand, supported the Republican candidate. [21] But the mainstream media does not necessarily represent the opinions of the social mainstream. A 2016 poll conducted by Gallup found that 36 percent of American citizens identified as conservative, while liberals made up 25 percent. [22] That is to say, if the media accurately reflected the views of a majority of citizens, then the media as a whole wouldn't lean left.

The leftist bent of the media is evidently not the result of popular will. Rather, it comes from the behind-the-scenes pushing of a political agenda intended to shift the entire nation to the political left. The gap between conservatives and liberals in 1996 was 22 percent; in 2014, it was 14 percent; and in 2016, it was 11 percent. The proportion of conservatives has remained stable, but many in the middle have been converted to the Left. The mainstream media undeniably play a role in this demographic transformation, which, in turn, sustains the media's ideological bias.

Why does the media lean so far to the left? In the 1960s, the country was heavily influenced by communist ideology, with radical left-wing social movements taking the United States by storm. The radical students of that period later entered the media, the academic community, government agencies, and the arts scene, where they established control over public discourse. Today, the vast majority of university professors are leftists, and departments of journalism and literature have brought generations of graduates under leftist influence. Media workers are not paid high salaries, instead relying on their idealistic sense of purpose to persevere in the field. This idealism has become the tool for transforming the media into a left-wing base of operations.

Along with news media, the film industry also is under siege. Hollywood has become a bastion of left-wing propaganda. Using sophisticated production and narrative techniques, left-leaning producers promote leftist ideologies that have reached the entire world. The main theme of Hollywood films usually appears to be slandering capitalism and emphasizing class conflict, while praising immoral behavior or anti-American sentiment.

Author Ben Shapiro interviewed movie stars and producers in Hollywood for his book *Primetime Propaganda: The True Hollywood Story of How the Left Took Over Your TV*. According to Shapiro, a famous producer said that in his profession, liberalism is "100 percent dominant" and that "anyone who denies it is kidding or not telling the truth." When asked whether having a different political standpoint could hinder a person's ability to secure work in the film industry, the producer answered, "Absolutely." Another famous producer openly said that Hollywood has been selling liberal political views through its works: "Right now, there's only one perspective. And it's a very progressive perspective." [23] The producer of a television series about police said he intentionally portrays more whites as criminals because he doesn't "want to contribute to negative stereotypes." [24]

Shapiro argues that nepotism in Hollywood is ideological rather than familial: Friends hire friends with the same ideological views. The openness with which the Hollywood crowd admits its anti-conservative discrimination inside the industry is shocking. Those who talk about tolerance and diversity have no tolerance when it comes to respecting diversity of ideology. [25]

4. The Media Takeover by Liberalism and Progressivism

Walter Williams, the founder of journalism education and of the world's first journalism school at the University of Missouri, created "The Journalist's Creed" in 1914. It defined journalism as an independent profession that respects God and honors mankind. Journalists should be "unmoved by pride of opinion or greed of power." They must exercise self-control, patience, fearlessness, and constant respect for their readers. [26] After the 1960s, however, as progressivism became prevalent, advocacy replaced objectivity, and liberalism and progressivism replaced impartiality.

In the 1986 book *The Media Elite*, author Samuel Robert Lichter wrote that reporters tend to add their own opinions and educational background to their reports on controversial issues. Because the majority of the people in newsrooms are liberals, news reporting has shifted in favor of liberal politics. [27] Jim A. Kuypers, in his research on the evolution of American journalism over the past two hundred years, concluded that today's mainstream media are liberal and progressive in both their personnel and their reporting. He quoted a liberal editor of a major newspaper as saying: "Too often, we wear liberalism on our sleeve and are intolerant of other lifestyles and opinions. ... We're not very subtle about it at this paper: If you work here, you must be one of us. You must be liberal, progressive, a Democrat." [28] In a commentary piece published by *The Wall Street Journal* in 2001, former CBS reporter Bernard Goldberg wrote that mainstream news anchors are so biased that they "don't even know what liberal bias is." [29]

Despite polls suggesting that Americans are aware of media partisanship, many people still take it for granted that reports are written objectively and comprehensively, and that what is cited is serious expert analysis based on information from reliable sources. The leftist media make use of their consumers' trust to inculcate them with their ideological worldview. Because the free societies of the West have traditionally emphasized the need for a truthful, objective, and fair media, the left-wing media do not always spread fake news to deceive the public outright. Their methods are more subtle and elaborate, as described below.

Selective Coverage

Every day, thousands of newsworthy events occur around the world. But which events receive attention or quietly fade from view is almost completely determined by what the media chooses to cover.

Selective coverage can be divided into three categories. First, events are selected only or primarily for their utility in helping readers accept the ideological stand of the Left. Second, instead of reporting comprehensively on an event's context, the media report only the aspects that support the leftist point of view. Lastly, the media tend to give greater voice to those who lean left or whose statements agree with the Left, while other organizations and individuals are sidelined. Groseclose and Jeffrey Milyo wrote in their 2005 paper "A Measure of Media Bias" that "for every sin of commission ... we believe that there are hundreds, and maybe thousands, of sins of omission — cases where a journalist chose facts or stories that only one side of the political spectrum is likely to mention." [30]

Perhaps one of the most striking examples of selective coverage is the dearth of reporting on the largest persecution of faith in contemporary history. In China since 1999, the CCP has persecuted members of the spiritual practice of Falun Gong, which upholds the universal principles of truthfulness, compassion, and tolerance. This persecution has directly affected hundreds of millions of people in the world's most populous country for more than two decades, and it is being perpetrated to a degree of brutality that is hard to fathom. However, its coverage by the Western media has been disproportionately weak when placed next to the magnitude and severity of the actual events taking place. Most of the mainstream media outlets, influenced by the CCP's political clout, have exercised self-censorship or remained silent amid the CCP's monstrous assault on freedom of belief and the core values of human civilization. Some have even been complicit in helping the CCP spread its deceit.

At the same time, a trend has emerged that opposes communism and advocates a return to tradition. As of May 2020, more than 350 million people have withdrawn from the CCP and its affiliated organizations in the Tuidang ("Quit the Party") movement. Yet such a major phenomenon, which holds great significance for the future of China and the world, is rarely if ever mentioned in the Western media.

Agenda-Setting

In the 1960s, media researchers came up with the influential theory that the media determine which topics people find suitable for discussion. American political scientist Bernard Cohen articulated this well when he said that the press "may not be successful much of the time in telling people what to think, but it is stunningly successful in telling its readers what to think about." [31] That is to say, the press can determine the importance of events by the number of reports and follow-up reports that an event receives, while equally or more important issues can be dealt with more summarily or not at all. For example, though the issue of transgender rights concerns only a very small portion of the population, it has become a focal point of discussion and an example of the media successfully setting the agenda. In addition, a narrative about global warming became prominent in public discourse as the result of a long-term conspiracy between the media and other political forces.

Many progressive ideas — such as so-called social justice, equality, and feminism — have become mainstream, while the crimes of communism have been whitewashed. Former Speaker of the House Newt Gingrich once wrote in 2018, "The academic Left and its news media and Hollywood acolytes refuse to confront the horrifying record of Marxism's endless inhumanity." [32]

Framing

Many issues are too big to ignore, and in these cases, the media use the method of framing to influence the informational environment. The sexual liberation movement and state welfare policies of the 1960s resulted in the disintegration of the family, worsened poverty, and increased crime. However, leftists use the media and Hollywood to depict an image of the strong and independent single mother, hiding the real social issues behind this phenomenon. They get experts to blame systemic discrimination for the poor financial and social status of minority groups, thus obscuring the real causes — many of which have their roots in communism. The prevalence of such narratives is largely the result of collusion between the media and political forces.

The method of framing is seen mainly in the phenomenon of narratives preceding facts. In objective reporting, the writer summarizes the facts to form a narrative. But reporters and editors who hold prejudiced views on an issue shape the facts to fit the narrative that validates their biases.

Using Political Correctness to Enforce Self-Censorship

Political correctness, a potent communist tool, permeates the media. Whether written in the style guide or left implicit, many media outlets have policies of political correctness that affect what may or may not be reported and how it should be presented. Because of legislation on "hate crimes" in some European countries, many local media outlets dare not report on crimes committed by immigrants, despite that such crimes have become a severe social issue and are threatening the domestic security in those countries. American media organizations also self-censor when it comes to reporting crimes, often omitting the perpetrators' immigration status.

The Western media, along with leftist political groups and academia, have created a lexicon of politically correct language. It has been applied so frequently by the media that the language has become deeply rooted in the public consciousness, influencing the public on a subliminal level.

Labeling Conservative Sources to Neutralize Their Influence

In order to create the impression of balanced reporting, the liberal media have no choice but to report on the opinions of conservatives or conservative think tanks. But the media typically use labels like "far right," "right wing," or "religious right wing" when quoting these sources, subtly implying that their opinions are prejudiced or not trustworthy. By contrast, when quoting from liberals or liberal think tanks, the media usually use neutral titles such as "scholar" or "expert," suggesting that these opinions are impartial, objective, rational, and trustworthy.

Once the media validate a left-wing opinion, it manifests in all aspects of society. An October 2008 article by *The New York Times* headlined "Liberal Views Dominate Footlights" stated, "During this election season theatergoers in New York can see a dozen or so overtly political plays, about Iraq, Washington corruption, feminism, or immigration; what they won't see are any with a conservative perspective." [33]

The media's political colors are also reflected in their coverage of the democratic process. Liberal candidates are reported positively, while candidates who espouse traditional views receive more criticism. Such reports and "expert" analysis have great influence over the voting population.

Groseclose discovered that more than 90 percent of reporters in Washington voted for Democrats. According to Groseclose's calculation, in typical elections, media bias assists Democratic candidates by around 8 to 10 percentage points. For instance, if it weren't for media bias, John McCain would have defeated Barack Obama 56 percent to 42 percent, instead of losing 46 to 53. [34]

5. The Film Industry: A Vanguard Against Tradition

Hollywood, as an international symbol of American culture, has served to broadcast and amplify American values worldwide. But it also has become an instrument for exposing all of humanity to distorted, anti-traditional values.

Today it's hard for most Americans to imagine that families in the 1930s and '40s had no need to worry about the negative influence of movies on children, as the film industry at the time followed strict moral regulations. In 1930, with strong backing from churches, the film industry introduced the Motion Picture Production Code, commonly known as the Hays Code. Its first principle was that no film should be produced that would lower the moral standards of its viewers. The audience should never be made to sympathize with crime, wrongdoing, evil, or sin. The Hays Code principle on sex was to uphold the sanctity of marriage; motion pictures were not to imply that low forms of sexual relationships were acceptable norms. Adultery, while sometimes necessary as plot material, was not to be justified, nor depicted attractively or in an explicit manner.

After the 1950s, however, sexual liberation caused cultural and moral shock waves. The rise of television in the American household fostered enormous market pressure and rivalry among film producers. Hollywood increasingly ignored the Hays Code. For example, the 1962 Academy Award-nominated film *Lolita*, adapted from the novel of the same title, depicted an adulterous and pedophilic relationship between a man and his underage stepdaughter. Though the film received both negative and positive reviews after its release, today it holds a 91 percent rating on Rotten Tomatoes, a film and television review aggregator. This reflects the sea change in social morality that has occurred in recent decades.

The counterculture movements at the end of the 1960s marked the collapse of traditional morality and order in Hollywood productions. Several iconic films depicting themes of rebellion reflected the degeneracy that was growing in the American film industry. As discussed in previous chapters, a key tactic of communism is to cast criminal behavior in a noble or righteous light. *Bonnie and Clyde* is a 1967 crime film based on the real story of the Great Depression-era robbers. During the Great Depression, many families became homeless after banks foreclosed on their homes. The protagonists in the film are depicted as expressing righteous anger at this phenomenon and as fighting injustice when they commit bank robbery and murder. The film, which features some of Hollywood's first depictions of graphic violence, has a Robin Hood-like narrative. The criminal couple, played by a handsome actor and a beautiful actress, are portrayed as having an inherent sense of justice. The police, meanwhile, are cast as incompetent stooges rather than protectors of law and order. The deaths of Bonnie and Clyde as they are caught in a police trap in the film's finale had a profound impact on adolescent audience members. The two came to be regarded as martyrs, as though they had sacrificed themselves for the sake of some great cause.

The themes of crime and violence depicted in the film shocked the mainstream of American society, but found great resonance among rebellious students. Youth started to copy the titular characters' speech, style of dress, and contempt for tradition and custom. Some even sought to emulate the couple's manner of demise. [35] Though an initial review of the film in Time judged it as bawdy and full of plotholes, the lead actor and actress appeared on the magazine's cover several months later, with the cover story proclaiming, "Bonnie and Clyde is not only the sleeper of the decade but also, to a growing consensus of audiences and critics, the best movie of the year." [36] One film reviewer for a left-wing publication wrote an article comparing Bonnie and Clyde to Cuban guerrilla leader Ernesto "Che" Guevara and Viet Cong terrorist Nguyễn Văn Trỗi. [37] One radical group of young people claimed, "We are not potential Bonnie and Clydes, we are Bonnie and Clydes." [38]

In addition to glorifying crime, Bonnie and Clyde featured an unprecedented level of sexuality. However, the film still received critical acclaim, receiving ten Oscar nominations and winning two. Hollywood had deviated from its traditional principles.

The Graduate, released at the end of 1967, reflected the inner anxiety and conflicts of college students of the period. The film depicts a new graduate at a crossroads in his life, and the traditional values of his father's generation are presented as dull and hypocritical. Instead of entering mainstream American society, the graduate accepts the advances of an older married woman, only to fall in love with her daughter, who discovers the affair. At the end of the film, the protagonist storms the church where the daughter has just married someone else, and he and the young woman run off together. *The Graduate* features a jumble of adolescent rebellion, uncontrolled libido, and other themes reflecting the confused, anti-traditional milieu of rebellious youth. The film was phenomenally successful, generating high box-office sales, as well as seven Oscar nominations and one win.

Films like *Bonnie and Clyde* and *The Graduate* kickstarted the New Hollywood era. At the end of 1968, the Hays Code was replaced with the modern film-rating system. That is, films with all kinds of content could be screened as long as they were labeled with a rating. This loosened the moral self-discipline of the entertainment industry considerably and blurred the standards of right and wrong. In this way, entertainers and media staff separated morality from their creations, giving them free rein to feature amoral and evil content. Degenerate entertainment hooked audiences with cheap, exciting, and readily available stimulation. Meanwhile, producers gave in to greed as they reeled in prodigious commercial profits.

Film is a special medium with the power to depict compelling atmospheres and realistic personalities. Skillful direction can alter the viewpoints of audience members, especially the young and impressionable, on many levels, shaping their feelings and worldviews. A well-known film producer once said: "Documentaries convert the already converted. Fictional films convert the unconverted." [39] In other words, documentaries strengthen the values that viewers already hold, while fictional films use fascinating stories to prime their unwitting audiences with a new set of values.

The producer and male lead of *Bonnie and Clyde* is a supporter of socialism. His 1981 historical drama *Reds* won him Academy and Golden Globe awards. At the height of the Cold War, the film changed the stereotype of a radical communist into that of a calm and sympathetic idealist. [40] In another of his Oscar-nominated movies, *Bulworth,* he played a liberal senatorial candidate who takes drugs, raps about socialized health care and class inequities, rages against corporate America, and hires an assassin to kill him so his daughter can cash in on his life insurance policy. [41] The film was such a success that some urged him to run for president of the United States.

After the introduction of the new movie-rating system, Hollywood began to mass-produce films that cast a positive glow on degenerate behaviors such as sexual promiscuity, violence, illicit drugs, and organized crime. A study found that up to 58 percent of the Hollywood movies produced between 1968 and 2005 were rated R. [42] One of the first R-rated movies, 1969's *Easy Rider,* became an instant hit and contributed to the popularity of drug abuse. The film follows the adventures of two cocaine-dealing hippie motorcyclists as they practice "free love" at a commune, visit a brothel, and indulge in hallucinogenic drugs on their way to Mardi Gras. Real drugs were used during the film's production. The characters' lifestyle of antisocial indulgence free from conventional values became the dream of numerous youth. The director said: "The cocaine problem in the United States is really because of me. ... There was no cocaine before *Easy Rider* on the street. After *Easy Rider* it was everywhere." [43]

American scholar Victor B. Cline did an analysis in the 1970s of thirty-seven movies that were shown in the Salt Lake City area. He found that 57 percent of the movies presented dishonesty as heroic or as justified by the circumstances and that 38 percent portrayed crime as something that pays off or as an exciting pastime without negative consequences. In 59 percent of the movies, the heroes killed at least one person. He also found that 72 percent of the heroines were shown as promiscuous to some extent and that only one of the films suggested normal sexual relations between a married couple. Only 22 percent of the movies portrayed any principal characters as having healthy and satisfying marriages. [44]

A common argument against criticizing violence and sexuality in films is that such things exist in real life and that films only reflect the nature of reality, rather than causing any negative impact. But from the figures above and more, this is demonstrably false. Moreover, numerous films produced by Hollywood leftists naturally reflect their values and, in turn, have changed the values of society. According to film critic and former Hollywood screenwriter Michael Medved, the liberal-minded social revolutionaries in Hollywood are attacking the values of society by assaulting the legitimacy of the family, promoting sexual perversion, and glorifying ugliness. [45]

Others argue that the profusion of morally degenerate content in the film industry is merely driven by market forces. But whatever the means, diabolical goals are being achieved to frightening effect. The speed and power with which the film industry has been used to take down public morality are astounding. Some movies glorify beasts or monsters. Those that depict man transforming into a beast or even engaging in bestiality are approved of and praised by the Hollywood mainstream. In a spiritual sense, this may be understood as a manifestation of the specter's control in our world, as humankind has come to fetishize the demonic and the monstrous.

Although these anti-tradition movies probe into social

issues with an air of sophistication, their critiques of society are superficial at best. Ugly deeds that conventional society disapproves of are rationalized, given sympathetic treatment, or even made to appear positive. Audiences immersed in such movies are led to regard moral standards as circumstantial. The ultimate message, implanted in the minds of the audience, is that there isn't a clear divide between right and wrong or good and evil, that traditions are boring and oppressive, and that morality is relative.

6. Television: Corruption in Every Household

Television has become a ubiquitous part of everyday life, and watching it frequently can change people's worldviews without their noticing. Research conducted by the Media Research Center has found that the more people watch television, the less committed they are to the traditional values of honesty, reliability, and fairness, and the more lenient their attitudes are likely to be toward issues related to sexual morality, such as sex outside of marriage, abortion, and homosexuality. [46]

The research compared two sets of people: light TV viewers who said they believed in God, and heavy TV viewers who said they believed in God. Although the percentages of the two sets who believed in God were almost the same (85 percent and 88 percent, respectively), the study found that the more one watched television, the less likely it was for the person to value religious principles. For example, when asked on a questionnaire to choose whether people should always live by God's teachings and principles or should combine their personal set of morals and values with God's teachings, those who watched more television tended to choose the latter. From figures like these, it can be generally concluded that television predisposes people to moral relativism.

Television has been an integral part of daily life since the 1950s. Not only do TV series and movies achieve a similar effect in molding people's values, but talk shows, sitcoms, and documentaries also quietly inculcate their audiences with all sorts of distorted ideas.

Take talk shows, for example. Television studios are especially keen to invite guests whose opinions or behavior contradict traditional values or whose lives are fraught with conflict, or to invite "experts" to discuss some controversial issues of morality. The guests are encouraged to disclose the "deep" or "complex" problems in their personal lives. The host, experts, or even audience members then suggest solutions to the problems. To ensure the popularity of such programs, usually no moral judgment is made about the guests' choices. In this way, many programs become a venue for displaying corrupt and distorted behaviors and perspectives. People have gradually come to believe that the values they used to uphold should not apply under some special circumstances. This perspective negates the existence of universal principles.

Many television programs are filled with despicable and distasteful content that is hard to watch. Some program hosts take pride in swearing profusely. Quite a number of programs indoctrinate people with vulgar taste and anti-culture or anti-tradition content via entertainment — while the audience is in a state of relaxation and thus more vulnerable to suggestion. As time passes, people do not feel alarmed at all and even come to accept and appreciate this material, thus eroding their moral thinking.

Sitcoms, in particular, serve to normalize deviated values and behaviors that are rarely seen in people's daily lives, by airing such content repeatedly and encouraging audiences to feel amused by it. Shapiro gave the example of a scene from the episode "The One With the Birth" from the popular US sitcom *Friends*. Ross's lesbian ex-wife, Carol, is having his baby. Ross is perturbed that Carol's lesbian lover will play a bigger role in his child's life than he will. Phoebe says to him: "When I was growing up, you know, my dad left, and my mother died, and my stepfather went to jail, so I barely had enough pieces of parents to make one whole one. And here's this little baby who has like three whole parents who care about it so much that they're fighting over who gets to love it the most. And it's not even born yet. It's just, it's just the luckiest baby in the whole world." [47] As Shapiro writes, the episode portrays "pregnant lesbians and three-parent households as not only normal, but admirable."

Modern medicine has discovered that human brains experience five different types of electrical patterns, or brain waves. The two that occur most often while one is in a state of wakeful consciousness are alpha and beta waves. When people are busy working, their dominant brain waves are beta waves. They exhibit an enhanced ability to analyze and tend to use logical thinking. A person having a debate would exhibit predominantly beta brainwaves. In other words, people in a state of beta-wave dominance are more alert and less gullible. When people are relaxed and alpha waves dominate — as is the case while one is watching television — their emotions take the lead and their analytical ability weakens. Under such circumstances, people tend to be subliminally persuaded by the themes and views represented in the television program.

Television programs begin polluting people at very young ages. Research shows that close to two-thirds of TV programming, including children's programs, contain scenes of violence. Further research shows that viewing such content desensitizes young people and increases their chances of committing violent acts later in life. Some children's programs are loaded with hidden themes of progressivism and liberalism, such as teaching homosexuality under the name of "cultural diversity." They use sayings like "there's only one person in this whole world like you" to foster unearned self-esteem and the concept of welcoming all people regardless of their immoral behaviors.

Television and movies have had a very negative influence on youth, increasing the tendency for violence, underage sexual activity, and teen pregnancy. Young people list the media as the second-most important source for learning about sexual activity, after sex education classes. Two studies found that teenage girls who often watched programs containing depictions of sexual activity were twice as likely to be pregnant within three years compared to girls who more rarely watched such programs. Such media programs also increased the risk of sexual assault and engagement in dangerous behavior. [48] As one academic pointed out: "The media are so compelling and so filled with sex, it's hard for any kid, even a critic, to resist. ... I think of the media as our true sex educators." [49] Due to media influence, sex outside of marriage, adultery, and other behaviors are regarded as normal lifestyle choices; as long as all parties are willing, such behaviors are thought to be acceptable.

In the book *Primetime Propaganda*, Shapiro studied nearly one hundred influential American TV series. He found that over time, these programs increasingly promoted liberalism and leftist viewpoints, including atheism, disdain for faith, the rejection of morality, the admiration of promiscuity, violence, feminism, homosexuality, and transsexuality, and the rejection of the traditional relationships between husband and wife, and parent and child. Such programs also established ruthless antiheroes devoid of sympathy as the protagonists. The evolution of this kind of programming has been a process of continuous moral decay. The promotion of these anti-traditional lifestyles has had a major influence on the mindset of the general public, and of young people in particular. [50] A show running five nights a week on the channel MTV in the early 2000s, for example, unreservedly promoted perverse sexual behavior and content similar to softcore porn to young audiences. [51]

After the film-rating system was implemented, many pornographic films could be sold as long as they were labeled with an X or NC-17 rating. As technology developed, these indecent programs went from underground to general consumption and could easily be obtained at movie-rental stores, through paid TV channels, and in hotels. Certainly, few Hollywood producers had a formal agenda to instill their audiences with corrupt ideologies. But when the producers themselves agree with the concepts of progressivism and liberalism, then these corrupt ideologies will inevitably end up on the screen. The real plan is moral subversion, and producers who stray too far from the divine become pawns of evil.

7. The Media: A Key Battleground in a Total War

The communist philosophy of struggle spares no means and respects no moral bottom line in achieving its political objectives. In the 2016 US presidential campaign, candidate Donald Trump opposed "political correctness" and supported measures to shift America away from the far left in order to return to traditional values and rule of law, renew the nation's spiritual faith, cut taxes to revitalize the economy, secure the borders, and correct the skewed trade relationship with communist China. Trump's outspokenness threw liberals into a frenzy. Armed with the mainstream media, they lashed out in a full-scale assault against him, abandoning virtually all pretense of balanced journalism.

During the campaign, left-wing media used various methods to willfully demonize and denigrate Trump while ostracizing his supporters, who were described as racists, sexists, anti-immigrant xenophobes, and uneducated whites. That is, the media tried to influence the results of the election by manipulating public opinion. Almost 95 percent of the media repeatedly predicted that Trump would lose the election in a landslide. Against all expectations, Trump was elected.

Under normal circumstances, no matter how fierce the rhetoric on the campaign trail may be, the different parties and their supporters should return to normal operations after the election is over. More importantly, the media should uphold the principle of fairness, put national interests first, and maintain neutrality. However, after the 2016 presidential election in the United States, the media have continued their campaign-trail frenzy, even at the risk of their public image. Most media outlets have since deliberately ignored the achievements of the Trump administration, such as record-low unemployment rates, the stock market's soar to record highs, American diplomatic successes, and the near-total eradication of the ISIS terrorist group.

In 2017, 90 percent of coverage on Trump was negative, according to a study by Newsbusters, the analytical arm of the Media Research Center. In the beginning of 2018, negative coverage reached 91 percent. Rich Noyes, a senior editor from Newsbusters, concluded, "Without question, no President has ever been on the receiving end of such hostile coverage, for such a sustained period of time, as has Trump." Furthermore, the media is doing everything possible to undermine the Trump administration by making groundless accusations. For example, the media stirred up a conspiracy theory of collusion between Trump and Russia, with two prominent newspapers even winning the coveted Pulitzer Prize for such coverage. According to the study, the Russia-collusion investigation was the main focus of Trump-related evening news broadcasts by the three main US media networks over the previous two months, taking up nearly one-fourth of those networks' Trump-related airtime. [52] However, a two-year special counsel investigation found no evidence to support the allegations. [53]

The media have been known to fabricate some news stories. In 2017, a TV news giant suspended a senior journalist for four weeks without pay and issued a correction of his work because he had created a fake report that Trump had ordered Lt. Gen. Michael Flynn to make contact with Russia when Trump was a presidential candidate. [54] The reporter and the producer who had worked with the journalist ended up leaving the TV station. This particular team had previously achieved outstanding success, winning four Peabody Awards and seventeen Emmy Awards.

When Trump condemned the violent MS-13 gang, especially those members who had committed brutal murders after entering the United States illegally, he said: "They're not people. These are animals, and we have to be very, very tough." However, media outlets immediately took his statement out of context, claiming that Trump said that illegal immigrants were animals.

In June 2018, a photo of a crying Honduran girl was widely circulated in the media and on the internet. This little girl and her mother were stopped by Border Patrol while trying to sneak into the United States. The media claimed that the girl was forcibly separated from her mother and used this opportunity to criticize Trump's border policies and zero-tolerance stance toward illegal immigration. Later, *Time* combined the photo of the little girl with a photo of Trump on the magazine cover, adding the caption "Welcome to America" to ridicule Trump. However, the girl's father later told the media that border officials had not separated her from her mother and that the mother had taken his daughter against his wishes. [55]

Fortunately, the American public is becoming more aware of fake news. From a poll conducted by Monmouth University in March 2018, the percentage of Americans who thought that the major media outlets were reporting fake news at least occasionally had increased from 63 percent in the previous year to 77 percent. [56] In 2016, a Gallup poll found that Americans' trust in the media had sunk to a new low, with only 32 percent of people having "a great deal" or "a fair amount" of trust in the media, down 8 percentage points from the previous year. [57] Unsurprisingly, the owner of a large media company lamented that "fake news is the cancer of our times." [58]

Judging from the results of the US election, half of Americans support Trump, but the attitude taken by the media is one-sided. Under these abnormal circumstances, Trump is attacked and demonized because he adopts a conservative political stance and supports traditional American values, ideals that cannot coexist with the anti-traditional ideology of the Left. If the media's attacks on Trump are able to cause the public to lose their confidence in him, the attacks will achieve their underlying objective: to prevent society from returning to tradition.

More worrisome, however, is that many media outlets have become catalysts for magnifying radical rhetoric, provoking animosity and hatred, and polarizing the population, thereby further widening the cracks in society. Basic ethics have been thrown out, and consequences are ignored to the point that destroying oneself so as to bring about the demise of an opponent has become acceptable. The country has been pushed to a state of extreme chaos and danger.

8. Restoring the Integrity of the 'Fourth Branch'

Because of the role it plays in shaping and guiding public opinion, the media is often referred to as the "fourth branch" alongside the executive, legislative, and judicial branches of government. Under the communist specter's influence, the media has been used effectively to sway and deceive billions of people, corrupting their traditions and morality.

In Western countries, many liberal media establishments have become tools for concealing the truth and deceiving people. Many have forsaken basic professional ethics and now resort to all sorts of unscrupulous attacks, abuse, and slander, regardless of the impact on their reputation or on society.

Communism has been successful because it has exploited human failings: the pursuit of fame and gain, ignorance, laziness, selfishness, misapplied sympathy, competitiveness, and the like. Some journalists self-righteously rebel against traditional values under a facade of knowing the truth. Some conform to the already morally debased "public demand" in order to get views. Some conform to the lowered standards for the sake of their careers. Some fabricate fake news out of jealousy and hostility. Some believe fake news because of their ignorance and laziness. Some exploit the kindness and sympathy of others in advocating social justice and thus tilt the entire society toward the Left, resorting to unscrupulous tactics to achieve their political and economic goals.

The mission of the media is a lofty one. They are meant to be the lifeline by which people obtain their information about public events, and they are also an important force in maintaining the healthy development of society. Objectivity and impartiality are the basic ethical requirements of the media and are key to the trust people place in it. But in the media today, chaos reigns, severely affecting the confidence people have in it. Reclaiming the mission of the media and re-establishing the glory of the news profession is the noble responsibility of people employed in this field.

Restoring the media's mission means that the media need to pursue truth. The media's coverage of the truth must be comprehensive and come from a place of sincerity. When reporting social phenomena, many media outlets present only part of reality in ways that are often misleading and can do more harm than outright lies.

The media will be good if they can help society value and uphold morality, for good and evil are both present in human society. It is the responsibility of the media to spread truth, to extol virtue, and to expose and restrain evil.

In returning to this mission, the media must pay more attention to the major events that affect the future of humankind. The last century has seen many battles between the free world and communism. While it appears to be an ideological confrontation, it is, in fact, a life-and-death struggle between righteousness and evil, for communism is ruining the morals that hold civilization together. Even after the collapse of the communist regimes in Eastern Europe, the specter of communism persists.

As the world undergoes great changes, truth and traditional values are more important than ever. The world needs media that can distinguish between right and wrong, do good deeds, and maintain public morality. Transcending the interests of individuals, companies, and political parties to present the real world to the people is the duty of every media professional.

Today, when facing the moral decline in the media profession, it is imperative that readers and audiences make a conscious distinction between right and wrong, and scrutinize rationally the information produced by the media. People must judge issues in line with the moral tradition, regard social phenomena through the lens of universal values, and, in doing so, push the media to fulfill their historic mission. This is also the key for humankind to stave off the influence of the communist specter and find the path to a better future.

Chapter Fourteen

Popular Culture —
A Decadent Indulgence

THE DIVINE CREATED HUMANKIND, and over the long course of history, laid down an orthodox culture for humankind to live by. Although the nations of the world have different cultures, they share a strikingly similar set of core values. All ethnic groups in the East and the West attach importance to the virtues of sincerity, kindness, generosity, justice, moderation, humility, courage, selflessness, and the like — virtues that every nation has paid tribute to and taught their descendants through their classics. Common among all groups is the paying of homage to the divine and adhering to divine law — because the divine handed down the culture and code of conduct that humankind should possess and embody. This is the origin of universal values.

The Founding Fathers of the United States attached great importance to morality and etiquette. In his early years,

George Washington copied by hand *110 Rules of Civility & Decent Behavior in Company and Conversation,* which were based on rules composed by French Jesuits in 1595. [1] Although some of the specifics may change over time, the rules contain many universal principles: One must be reverent when talking about God and related matters, treat others with respect, be modest, uphold public morality, not harm others' feelings and interests, behave decently on all occasions, dress neatly and exemplify good taste, refrain from retaliating, refrain from speaking ill of others behind their backs, learn from the wise and good, listen to one's conscience, and so on.

Similarly, Benjamin Franklin's thirteen virtues were temperance, silence, order, resolution, frugality, industry, sincerity, justice, moderation, cleanliness, tranquility, chastity, and humility. [2]

Before the 1950s, the moral values of most people generally met a common, respectable standard. People in the East and the West retained many of the traditions and customs that humans should have. In China, despite that the Chinese Communist Party (CCP) had begun to ruin China's cultural heritage and morality, the public retained many of the traditional virtues that held sway before the Party usurped power.

But as communism expanded its power and influence, especially after the 1960s, people in the East and the West went further and further down the road of moral corruption.

The CCP's Cultural Revolution began in 1966, starting a decadelong campaign to eradicate the "four olds" (old customs, old culture, old habits, and old ideas). It was soon matched with the fierce counterculture movement in the United States and other anti-traditional movements in other parts of the world. All these were global events that unfolded in line with the communist specter's aim of destroying tradition and bringing about humanity's moral collapse.

These political and cultural movements have left deep scars in today's world. Since that time, the traditional cultural foundations of Chinese society have been completely destroyed and morality has been in rapid decline. In Western society, drug abuse, sexual liberation and promiscuity, rock 'n' roll and hippie culture, and spiritual emptiness have taken hold, seriously damaging the foundation of Western tradition.

After the young radicals of the counterculture found themselves pulling the levers of society, they continued their movement by other means. Avant-garde art and literature, modern ideologies, and deviant concepts were all brought together. With the help of technology, including the internet, mobile phones, and various mass media, the entire human race rapidly deviated from traditional culture and ways of life toward the abyss of aberrance and degradation.

If we look at the world today, the decline of human morality and the corruption of almost every aspect of popular culture and social life are shocking to behold. After the CCP destroyed the profound traditional Chinese culture through incessant political campaigns, it created a malicious system of Party culture. The younger generations grew up in this Party culture and know nothing about traditional, divinely inspired culture. With the exception of some segments of society in the West that held onto tradition and refused to be tempted and suborned, it would be fair to say that communism has almost succeeded in achieving its goal of ruining human culture across the world.

1. Communist Party Culture

After the Communist Party's "reform and opening up" in the 1980s, the Chinese people shocked citizens of other countries with their conduct when they traveled abroad. At the time, many Westerners retained the impression of the traditional Chinese people as gentle, courteous, modest, kind, hardworking, and simple.

However, after decades of brainwashing and transformation by the Communist Party, the Chinese people had completely changed. They were rude and spoke loudly. They wouldn't stand in lines or be respectful and quiet in public. They smoked in front of no-smoking signs. They dressed in a slovenly manner, spit on the sidewalk, and tossed litter. They readily took advantage of others' courtesy and kindness.

Today, the behavior of some Chinese tourists is even more pronounced. They climb on and damage cultural relics and historic sites, let their children urinate in public, fail to flush the toilet after using it, snatch up free goods, grab and waste food in cafeterias, get into brawls over slight disagreements, and create trouble in airports, causing flight delays.

What happened to the Chinese people?

The answer is simple. The CCP destroyed traditional Chinese culture and replaced it with Communist Party culture, an important component in the corruption of humankind.

The term "Party culture" refers to the way of thinking, speaking, and behaving that arises from the characteristics of the Communist Party, which can be summed up as deceit, malice, and struggle. The guiding ideology of Party culture is atheism and materialism, including the communist concepts that the Party instills in those under its rule, which include all manner of deviant cultural elements, the philosophy of struggle, and the worst aspects of ancient times repackaged. The CCP has effectively used Party culture to transform the thoughts of the Chinese people.

The CCP's proletarian revolution slapped the label of "the exploiting classes" on those who upheld traditional morality, civilization, and manners. The CCP described the habits of the proletariat (working class) as revolutionary and good, called on the Chinese intellectuals to roll in the mud and grow calluses on their hands, and described lice on the body as "revolutionary bugs." From the Party leader to ordinary cadres, all became proud of swearing because it showed their class consciousness, commitment to the revolution, and supposed closeness to the masses.

Thus the Party forces people to abandon whatever is elegant and civilized and instead accept the rough lifestyle of proletarian hooligans. A country with such a long history, famous for its good manners, is thus reduced to a state of turmoil, with everyone competing for fame and fortune. The Party turned China into an exhibition hall for vulgar communist culture.

Under the control and infiltration of Party culture, all areas of cultural life — including literature, the arts, and education — have degenerated.

The Party wants to fight with heaven, earth, and man. It instills a set of wicked standards of good and evil and distorts how people think. This indoctrination is backed with state violence. The Party's subjects are then imperceptibly influenced by what they constantly see and hear, from the day they are born, because the Party monopolizes all social resources. A constantly whirring propaganda machine forces people to read the works of communist leaders, while the elite are co-opted to produce textbooks, literature, film, news, and so on, that all exist to further instill Party culture.

It took only a few decades for communism to make the Chinese people think with the Party's thoughts, talk with the Party's language, stop believing in the divine, act without regard to the consequences, and dare to do just about anything. Nearly every interpersonal interaction may involve deception, and there are no bottom lines for conduct. The zombie-like language of the Party and its ready-made lies are overwhelming.

Due to Party culture, today's Chinese people are far removed from universal values. Their minds, thoughts, and behaviors have undergone profound changes and deviation. Their family, social, educational, and work relationships are abnormal, and their ways are often incompatible with those of people from non-communist societies, who find their behavior difficult to understand.

During the Cultural Revolution, the Red Guards were immersed in Party culture, and they have since brought vicious habits to the younger generations. Children and adolescents brought up in Party culture are crafty and mature beyond their years. They know everything bad at a young age.

Members of the younger generations often lack spiritual beliefs and are immoral and arrogant. When they're provoked or angered, they are prone to reacting with irrational viciousness. Sexual restraint and morality have collapsed. Having lost their traditional roots, today's Chinese people are adopting all the worst parts of the counterculture movement of the West.

Manifestations of Communist Party Culture

The CCP now talks about restoring traditional culture, but what it's restoring is not true traditional culture. It's simply Party culture with a traditional appearance, missing the most important aspect of China's tradition: faith in the divine.

Under the influence of Party culture, people even use so-called gods to make a fortune. The Grandma Temple in Hebei Province is very popular, and it's said that people can find all the "gods" they want to worship there. If one wants to be a government official, there's a "god of officials" to worship. Similarly, there's a "god of wealth" composed of banknotes, a "god of study," and even a "god of cars" that holds a steering wheel. The administrator of the Grandma Temple has boasted, "Whichever god is lacking, just make a new one." [3]

It is impossible to revive traditional culture without simultaneously cleaning out the moral corruption created by the CCP. Although many contemporary literary and artistic works offer retellings of ancient stories, the content is sullied by modern ideas. Actors don traditional dress but engage in contemporary drama; thus traditional culture becomes a façade, and its true meaning is further obscured. For example, palace dramas set in imperial China have been popular in recent years, but they revolve around jealousy and intrigue — a display of the struggle and hatred inherent in communism rather than a reflection of historical realities.

Arbitrary adaptations of *Journey to the West* even have Sun Wukong (the Monkey King) embrace and be seduced by the demons that he vanquished in the classic novel. What is even more frightening is that many — especially the young who know nothing of China's traditional culture — regard all this as somehow traditional, or close enough. This is the consequence of the Party's having ravaged divinely inspired genuine Chinese culture and indoctrinating the public for decades. The Chinese people have come to think that the ethos of struggle is traditional, and that art, literature, and drama imbued with Party-culture ideas, but dressed in traditional garb, are the real thing.

Party culture destroys faith in the divine and replaces it with atheism. The most direct consequence of this is a loss of social trust: Fraud, counterfeit goods, toxic food, corruption, and more have all become common phenomena. The so-called "shanzhai culture" is a typical example of this integrity crisis. Shanzhai culture refers to the counterfeiting of well-known, particularly foreign, products or brands. It amounts to both theft and deception. The term has become so well-known that the Oxford Chinese-English Dictionary included it as a neologism. [4]

Shanzhai behavior not only counterfeits products, but also entire stores. Fake Apple stores have been documented repeatedly in China. The stores are carefully furnished with all the trappings of real Apple stores: glass frontage, light-wood display tables, a winding staircase, posters of Apple products, neatly arranged accessory walls, and white Apple logos. Staff wear the characteristic dark-blue T-shirts with the Apple logo and even appear to believe they work in a real Apple store. [5]

In a social atmosphere characterized by such deception, some Chinese stop at nothing to further their own interests and fear no punishment from heaven or man. Lying and falsification become part of mainstream culture. Those who refuse to counterfeit are considered the odd ones out.

Party culture also has ruined the Chinese language, as can be seen in the constant use of hyperbolic words and phrases. Restaurants are given names like Heaven Beyond Heaven, Emperor Above All Emperors, or King of Kings. Literary styles and propaganda have also become pompous. Official propaganda regularly uses phrases like "the world's first," "the most formidable in history," "the United States is afraid," "Japan is aghast," "Europe regrets," and the like.

News stories are full of headlines such as "China's scientific and technological strength surpasses the United States and ranks first in the world," "China has won the world's first place again, personally defeating US blue chips and utterly routing Apple," "Something big will happen. A magic weapon in China again makes the US afraid, the world stunned, Japan completely scared," "China is the world's No. 1 in another field! Completing a historical great change in just thirty years, making the US, Japan, and South Korea amazed," and "Huawei announced that it has created the world's first 5G chip, which shocked the world!"

The propaganda movie *Awesome, My Country!* and the special series of television programs called *Great, My Country!* are also full of exaggerations in tone and meaning. They make it seem as though the whole world is surrendering to China, conveying an attitude redolent of the propaganda used during the Great Leap Forward, when the Party claimed China would surpass Britain and catch up with the United States.

The new wave of exaggeration is the concrete manifestation of the "fake, exaggerated, empty ethos" (as it's known in China) of Party culture in the online age. The fundamental question is still one of integrity. Reform and opening up through the 1980s and 1990s brought change to China in the form of the worst aspects of contemporary Western culture, such as sexual liberation, drug abuse, homosexuality, computer games, and the like. The entertainment programs on television have become vulgar. The entire society has become a pleasure palace for the indulgence of material and carnal desires.

Communism has turned China, a country that was once civilized, magnificent, and beautiful, into an uncivilized nation.

2. *Communism's Subversion of Western Mass Culture*

Western countries of the free world have been known for their civilized societies, where men are genteel and women virtuous and graceful, and where people treat each other with honesty and friendship. Communism has implemented arrangements in Western countries to subvert and sabotage this civilization. Although it can't use violence and totalitarianism to directly damage Western civilization as it did in China, it has provoked people's negative and rebellious thoughts and behaviors in order to undermine tradition, destroy public morals, and ruin individual morality.

As the public rejoiced over the Allies' triumph in World War II, some were already hard at work in the fields of ideology and culture. While reflecting on the war and the new waves of ideology to come, they helped to bring about a systematic departure from the traditions that connected humans to the divine.

In the United States, the post-war American writers of the Beat Generation, which appeared in the 1950s, were the progenitors of an art and literary movement whose goal was to redefine culture. While they rightly despised some of the hypocrisy of moral corruption in society at the time, their response was to cynically reject and overturn all traditional morality. They advocated unrestrained freedom; delved into pseudo-mysticism, drugs, and crime; and pursued undisciplined, willful lifestyles. Their attempt at a radical critique of bourgeois, capitalist society coincided with the ideological thrust of communism in the West, making them a natural tool for the leftist movement.

Many members of the Beat Generation were indeed deeply influenced by communist and socialist ideology. For example, before the movement's co-founder Jack Kerouac became famous, he wrote the short story "The Birth of a Socialist" about his rebellion against capitalist society. [6] Another representative of the movement, Allen Ginsberg, said he had no regrets about the communist beliefs he once held. He also supported pedophilia (see Chapter Eleven). The group's works rejected traditional conventions, were deliberately disorganized, and used vulgar language. They represented the counterculture movement that would engulf the West in the 1960s — the first major departure from the rules and principles of tradition.

The 1960s saw the elaboration and extension of what the Beats had proposed, with subcultures like the hippie, punk, goth, and more. These countercultural trends found an eager audience in the urban areas of the West, tempting one young generation after another toward violence, drug abuse, sexual liberation, nonconformist attire, and cultural alienation, and ultimately giving them an inclination toward darkness and death.

In what is known as the Summer of Love, in 1967, thousands of hippies gathered in San Francisco's Haight-Ashbury Park and Golden Gate Park for several days, expressing their resistance to society with bizarre behavior, drug use, nudity, singalongs, poetry, and rock 'n' roll music. This movement reached its climax around the time of the assassinations of Martin Luther King Jr. and Robert Kennedy and the escalation of the Vietnam War.

In the summer of 1969, more than four hundred thousand people gathered in the same way at the Woodstock festival, held on a farm northwest of New York City. Hundreds of thousands indulged in debauchery while shouting about "love," "freedom," and "peace." Woodstock was a significant cultural event in the 1960s, and over the following decades, New York's Central Park, San Francisco's Golden Gate Park, and Woodstock all became symbols of the American counterculture.

Just as the counterculture in the United States was taking off, turmoil involving millions broke out in France in what is now known as the events of May '68. It began with angry students rebelling against traditional morality and culture. At that time, schools imposed strict separation between male and female student dormitories, and the two sexes were forbidden from freely coming and going from each others' bedrooms. The abolition of this provision and the demand for the right to sexual activity in student dorms were the major goals of the initial protests. The students' rebellion then found support among both the socialist and communist parties in France.

There is a saying that in the late 1960s, there were two centers for revolution: One was Beijing, where the Cultural Revolution was in full swing; the other was Paris, where the events of May '68 shook the world. This was called by many the Cultural Revolution of the West. At the time, Chinese students marched with slogans and banners in support of the French student rebels, while in Paris, the "Western Red Guards" wore green military caps and uniforms with red armbands in support of the Maoists in China. They held up huge portraits of Mao Zedong in their parades, and the "three M's" — Marx, Mao, and Marcuse — became their ideological mainstay. [7]

Japan also began its own counterculture movement in the 1960s. The All-Japan League of Student Self-Government, associated with the Japanese Communist Party, had extensive influence among students at the time. They were in turn organized by the Japanese Communist Party in reaction to the activities of the Red Guards in China. The league organized numerous counterculture demonstrations in Japan in conjunction with other left-wing student organizations, such as the Japanese Red Army and the All-Campus Joint Struggle Councils, and went so far as to advocate and commit acts of terror against Japanese society. [8]

Similar chaos unfolded in some Latin American countries. For instance, under the influence of the Cuban Communist

Party, Mexico's student movement mobilized for protests, such as gathering in the Plaza de las Tres Culturas, and other left-wing student groups sent telegrams to students in Paris supporting the May '68 rebellion.

Seen as a global whole, the counterculture movements erupting simultaneously in multiple countries formed a massive communist assault on traditional society. The age-old moral traditions and values that the divine left to humankind had been developed over thousands of years, but suffered enormous damage under the impact of this global communist movement.

Western rock 'n' roll culture, drug abuse, sexual liberation, abortion, iconoclastic clothing, and modern art were all departures from traditional norms and orthodox faith. As in communist China, where the country's ancient culture was actively destroyed by the totalitarian CCP regime, the counterculture movements of the free world largely succeeded in banishing the treasures of Western civilization and uprooting faith in the divine.

3. Pop Culture and Social Chaos

With traditional culture under attack from within and without, the negative elements of anti-traditional ideology began to take root in society. Given its global influence, America is the de facto leader in setting the tone of popular culture worldwide, and the corruption of American popular culture has thus affected the entire world. As mentioned, some traditionally conservative countries with profound traditional cultures, like China and Japan, found the deviated trends coming from the United States irresistible and have gone about emulating them. The same holds true for virtually every country and region exposed to globalization; unrestrained, amoral, anti-social, and self-indulgent popular culture has spread throughout the whole world.

A. HIP-HOP AND ROCK 'N' ROLL

The focus of traditional music was on civilizing humans, culti-vating virtue, and helping people to be mentally and physically healthy. Its effect was social harmony, and harmony between humans and nature. Beautiful music that celebrated the glory of the divine was promoted, while atonal, chaotic, or licen-tious music was anathema. But today, popular culture is full of shockingly corrupt musical productions, with hip-hop and rock 'n' roll being striking examples.

Hip-hop emerged in New York in the 1970s. Over the past several decades, hip-hop, rap, and breakdance have been exported from New York to become a global craze, with hip-hop becoming part of popular culture in Asia, Europe, and many African regions. Despite the obvious moral corruption of this music, with its focus on promiscuity, murder, violence, and drugs, it has gained worldwide recognition and is even celebrated in world-famous theaters.

Rock 'n' roll traces its roots back to the 1940s. In the 1960s, it had become the theme music of the counterculture movement. The genre's hysterical vocals, violent drumming, and distorted electric guitar riffs can transport listeners to a mad, irrational state of mind. With reason cast aside, demon nature, which is typically kept at bay due to the demands of civilization, is unleashed. Nihilism and other dark modes of thought became the predominant theme of many rock subgenres. Psychedelic rock encouraged the use of drugs, while some psychedelic and other, darker forms of rock called for rebellion, suicide, and violence, or encouraged promiscuity, adultery, homosexuality, and rejection of marriage. Lyrics suggested the lewd or obscene, or delighted in praising evil and condemning the divine. Some rock superstars justified the sexual harassment of underage girls in their popular lyrics, which desensitized audiences to a culture of sexual abuse and promiscuity.

Some lyrics were full of strife, such as, "Hey! Said my name is called Disturbance/ I'll shout and scream/ I'll kill the King,

I'll rail at all his servants." One song was titled "Sympathy for the Devil." One psychedelic album was called "Their Satanic Majesties Request." An iconic rock lyric goes, "Hey Satan, payin' my dues .../ I'm on the highway to hell."

Some rock songs praised socialism and communism. The song "Imagine" challenged its listeners to imagine a communist society free of religion, country, and private property.

Even religious groups have found it hard to resist the negative impact of rock 'n' roll. Christian church music was meant to praise God, yet the modern music of Christian churches has taken on rock elements to appeal to young people, which gave rise to so-called contemporary Christian music. [9]

Accompanying rock 'n' roll are adultery, violence, decadence, drug abuse, corruption, and opposition to belief in the divine. Corrupt behaviors forbidden by traditional morality and beliefs have all accompanied the genre's rise.

B. DRUG ABUSE

Drug abuse has become a global issue over the last several decades. In the early stages, the root of large-scale drug abuse in the West was the counterculture. In their campaign against bourgeois morality, hippies sought to deconstruct and undermine all tradition and to erect their own beliefs, moral standards, and lifestyle. LSD and psilocybin mushroom trips counted as spiritual explorations, while they used amphetamines or cocaine as uppers and heroin and barbiturates as downers, all intended to remove them from the world and take them to another state.

Many young members of the counterculture movement had a keen interest in Eastern philosophy and spiritual cultivation. However, psychedelics became a shortcut for those seeking insight without the challenges of cultivating the mind and enduring the physical pain of meditation. Instead, they would simply take a tab of acid, which would deliver them a pseudo-spiritual experience, though it did not connect them to anything real. Such drugs simply put their bodies in the control of demonic elements, not at all related to true, orthodox cultivation practices. These experiences led many with true spiritual aspirations down a crooked path.

Many pop singers and rock stars have died in their twenties and thirties, often due to drug overdoses. In the contemporary United States, the longest and sorriest war has been the war on drugs. The country has dedicated itself to arresting and monitoring thousands of drug traffickers over decades. Government officials have given repeated warnings against illegal drug use, yet it still prevails. From 2000 to 2018, at least three hundred thousand Americans died of opioid overdoses. On October 26, 2017, President Donald Trump declared the opioid crisis a public health emergency and outlined ways to combat the problem. [10]

According to a 2017 report by the National Institute on Drug Abuse for Teens, marijuana use among students is rampant: 45 percent of twelfth-graders said they had used marijuana at least once, and 37.1 percent of them had used it in the past year; 71 percent of seniors in high school did not believe that frequent use of marijuana was very harmful. [11]

Using ecstasy and smoking marijuana have become standard among young people, while newer and stronger drugs, including fentanyl, continue to emerge. Fentanyl is a synthetic opioid that is fifty times more potent than heroin and 100 times stronger than morphine. It is so deadly that it has been called a chemical weapon; two milligrams can be fatal. [12] Yet such destructive drugs are flooding American streets at a terrifying pace, killing many more people than other opioids, simply because it's so easy to overdose on them.

According to the National Institute on Drug Abuse, among the approximately sixty-seven thousand deaths from drug overdoses in 2018, about thirty-one thousand were due to fentanyl and its analogs. [13] The trafficking of fentanyl from China has been widely reported. In 2018, authorities performing a routine inspection at the Port of Philadelphia discovered and seized 110 pounds of fentanyl in a shipment of iron oxide from China. The street value of the drugs discovered was $1.7 million. [14]

In China, drug abuse is also spreading like a cancer through society. The production and abuse of drugs, especially synthetic drugs, is rampant and internet drug sales are out of control. According to the 2015 China National Narcotic Control Commission (CNNCC) report, the number of illegal drug users exceeds fourteen million. The real number is probably higher since drug users increasingly include white-collar workers, freelancers, entertainers, and public servants. [15]

The 2017 China Narcotics Situation Report from the CNNCC shows that China's narcotics departments have cracked 140,000 drug cases, destroyed 5,534 drug-trafficking groups, arrested 169,000 trafficking suspects, seized 89.2 tons of drugs, and carried out 870,000 raids, which uncovered 340,000 new drug users. [16]

Drugs are often highly addictive, leading people to destroy their families, ruin their careers, sabotage their reputations and relationships, commit crimes, and even lose their lives through overdose. Using and trafficking drugs harms individuals, families, and the entire nation, and it has thus become yet one more of the dark phenomena plaguing modern society.

C. PORNOGRAPHY AND PROSTITUTION

Of all the forms of revolution called for by communists, the most complete is probably the sexual revolution. If the seizure of political power marks a revolution against the external components of society, then sexual liberation is the communist revolution instigated internally.

Freud's pansexualism, a theory that regards all desire and interests as originating from the sex instinct, provided the theoretical basis for sexual liberation, while the emergence of oral contraceptives began to separate sex from reproduction. The sexual revolution struck at traditional morality and brought about and promoted radical feminism, abortion, premarital sex, and the gay movement. Sexual liberation established the distorted idea that participating in recreational sex and the sex trade are basic human rights. It destroyed traditional sexual ethics and restraints, and allowed sex to become a form of entertainment. It turned humans into mere sex tools and opened the floodgates for pornography to infiltrate and sabotage society.

In the 1950s, *Playboy* magazine played an exceptionally significant role in assisting in sexual indulgence as it made a business out of pornography. While the slogan "make love, not war" was in the air during the anti-war era, the sexually explicit film *Blue Movie* became the first of its kind to be released widely in theaters in the United States. A fifteen-year-long era (1969–1984) of "porno chic," accompanied by rock music and the overall rejection of tradition, emerged in the West.

In the 1970s, porn films were generally available only in seedy adult movie theaters. By the early 1980s, VHS brought pornography into millions of households, while the spread of the internet in the late 1990s, and later the smartphone era, brought pornography on demand. Worldwide, the pornography industry was worth $97 billion annually as of 2015, and in the United States alone, $10 billion to $12 billion. [17]

The introduction of the internet and smartphones has brought major changes to the porn industry. The total amount of pornographic content that a typical adult in the 1980s might have been exposed to over the course of years can now be accessed by a child in just minutes. On average, children are now exposed to pornography by the age of eight. One twelve-year-old British boy became so addicted to online porn that he raped his sister. A prosecutor involved in the case said, "Cases of this nature will increasingly come before the court because of the access young people now have to hard core pornography." [18]

There are many consequences of exposing children to porn, such as early sexual activity and an increased incidence of sex crimes. Pornography reinforces the impression that sex is a kind of entertainment or transactional service, rather than a part of private marital life, and the belief that the behavior seen in porn is common. It also promotes the normalization of sexual depravity and perversion.

In Japan, the porn industry has already been normalized as part of society, with supermarket racks full of adult magazines and comics and late-night television programs featuring porn actors. Pornographic actresses are packaged as teen idols and openly appear in the media. The Japanese porn industry has had a profoundly negative influence on all of Asia.

Even in predominantly Muslim countries, such as Egypt and Tunisia, the porn industry — forbidden by Islam — is in full swing, operating underground.

In many European countries, prostitution is legal, and many Europeans consider it a normal form of work. In 1969, Denmark became the first country to legalize pictorial pornography. Norway, which had some of the strictest limitations on pornography in Europe, legalized hardcore pornography in 2006. [19] The purchase of sex in Denmark can sometimes even be subsidized by the government. For instance, in order to protect "equal rights," eligible disabled individuals can visit a brothel while the taxpayer foots the bill. [20] This type of thinking was advocated for early on by utopian socialist Charles Fourier in the nineteenth century.

China, with a society long characterized by its conservative family ethics and moral restraint, where even the discussion of sex was taboo, has also gotten caught up in the global wave of sexual degeneracy in recent decades. Of all the CCP's policies, the most "successful" — far beyond the opening of the economy or political system — must be that of sexual liberation. In the space of thirty years, there has been a total transformation from "revolutionary discipline" to "sexual liberation." Prostitution is rampant in China, with an estimate from the late 2000s claiming that the country had between twenty million and thirty million sex workers. [21] The more mistresses a wealthy businessman or corrupt official has, the higher his social status. China is thought of as the world's factory, but it also exports a large number of prostitutes to countries and regions including Japan, Malaysia, the Middle East, the United States, Europe, and Africa. Estimates in 2018 suggest that there were 13,000 to 18,500 Chinese prostitutes in sub-Saharan Africa. [22]

Southeast Asian and South American countries are no different. Many cities have become major destinations for sex tourism, a practice that, while illegal, has become so rampant it's contributing to economic growth.

The most direct consequence of a society flooded with pornography and prostitution is the destruction of the family and marriage. Porn in particular has come to be called "the quiet family killer." [23] Viewing pornography causes disinterest in healthy family relationships while feeding desire and lust, which creates sexual urges that often can only be satisfied through extramarital affairs or other means, including violent or criminal acts.

During a 2005 Senate hearing, Jill Manning presented a poll of divorce and matrimonial lawyers that showed 56 percent of divorce cases included one partner who had "an obsessive interest in pornographic websites." [24] During the annual meeting of the American Sociological Association in 2016, a research paper that was presented showed a doubling in instances of divorce among marriages in which one party started watching pornography versus marriages of non-porn-consumers. The research showed that if the husband started watching porn, the divorce rate increased from 5 percent to 10 percent, while if the wife started watching porn, the divorce rate increased from 6 percent to 18 percent. The younger the individual, the more likely the divorce. [25]

Before the 1950s, virtually all traditional cultures of the world viewed sex before marriage as indecent and in contravention of the commandments that the divine left to mankind. Both social pressure and public opinion acted to suppress such activities. If a young man and woman conceived a child before marriage, they would be expected to take responsibility, get married, and raise the child together as a family. At the time, the majority of people believed that if a man got a woman pregnant, the decent thing to do was to marry her. [26] If one made a mistake, one would be expected to take responsibility for it.

However, with moral decay and the rise of sexual liberation since the 1960s, out-of-wedlock pregnancies have drastically increased. All this took place right as the porn industry began to have a greater impact on public consciousness. In 1964, in most countries in the Organisation for Economic Co-operation and Development, birth outside of marriage was typically less than 10 percent; by 2014, it was more than a third. In the United States, out-of-wedlock births averaged 40 percent in 2014, reaching 71 percent among African-Americans. Among the world's 140 million newborns in the year 2016, around 15 percent, or 21 million, were born outside of marriage. [27]

Single-parent families, out-of-wedlock pregnancies, and divorce are often closely associated with poverty. Such families, in turn, increase the burden on the social welfare system.

D. VIDEO GAMES

Many children today spend countless hours playing video games. Game developers make the games increasingly realistic, dynamic, and interactive. They're also increasingly violent and erotic. Children and adults alike are easily addicted to gaming, which has become a major issue for parents, schools, and even the government.

Video games are now a form of popular culture that follows people from childhood to adulthood, but what sort of culture is it? It is a culture of destruction, no different from drugs. Those who are addicted to video games can't see the drawbacks in a sober and objective manner. They simply think of the games as fun and interesting and won't give up as long as there is another level to advance to, another kill to make, or a new high score to set.

In addition, almost all video games today, from their gameplay and plot to aesthetic atmosphere, are about violence and killing, or contain erotic content or cold-bloodedness. Simply put, the messages conveyed appeal to the demon nature in humankind. All of this is inappropriate and harmful for teenagers and young people. Delivering a sense of excitement from killing, destruction, violence, and fighting can desensitize young people by introducing them to unhealthy thoughts and behaviors, and can even contribute to some committing crimes.

Online games are even more addictive. In the past, games were used to pass the time when people were alone and felt bored. Nowadays, online gaming has become a competitive sport and a social activity in and of itself, especially for children. Because a large number of players interact in a game, they can quickly become enthralled in the game's virtual world.

Huge amounts of effort and capital are invested in such games, and kids who don't play them may be the odd ones out among their peers. Thus, almost against their will, parents feel forced to allow their children to join the online gaming community, then witness their children develop an addiction. Video games take up time that should have been used for study, outdoor activities, and normal socialization. Instead, children are turned into captives of video games.

Scholar Erik Hurst said he allowed his twelve-year-old son to play video games for only a couple of hours on weekends after finishing his homework. But if the child had been left to his own devices, he would have played almost nonstop, skipping showers and meals to keep gaming. [28]

Scholarly research has shown that video games come to occupy and dominate the leisure time of young people. Data suggests that young adults, especially those in lower income brackets and with lower levels of education, increasingly find happiness in video games, reducing the time they spend on their jobs and in the real world. [29] This is a common phenom-enon in the United States and other developed countries.

Hurst has observed a trend in today's society in which video games lead young adults to refuse to enter the job market and instead rely on their parents to support them financially. It's unlikely that video games will help them earn a living, or that they'll be able to improve their skills or find better jobs. When these young people become parents, their children won't be able to rely on them for guidance. Video games have thus reached the point of undermining normal human life.

Video games are spiritual drugs. Unlike the manufacture of hard drugs such as heroin, which is illegal in most countries, video game development is a major industry. What are the consequences of this? As the companies produce these drugs that destroy the next generation, the countries that embrace gaming are sabotaging their own futures.

The emergence of the internet and mobile phones has opened up an even broader market for the video game industry. Research firm Newzoo, in its April 2018 Global Games Market Report, forecast that gamers around the world would spend $137.9 billion on games in 2018, representing an increase of 13.3 percent from the previous year. More than half of all gaming revenue was projected to come from the mobile segment. Digital game revenues would make up 91 percent of the global market.

The report also predicted that the games market would maintain double-digit growth in the following several years. While the GDP growth rate in many countries is struggling in the single digits, the games industry continues to advance. Mobile gaming alone was expected to reach $100 billion by 2021. The top three countries in the global games market, according to the report, would be China, the United States, and Japan, with China accounting for more than 25 percent of the total market. [30]

Traditional games, including sports and other outdoor activities, are limited by the natural environment, the weather, equipment, and physical strength, and players don't typically develop an addiction to them. Video games have no such restrictions. Players are invited and lured to immerse themselves in the virtual world of the game nonstop, going without sleep or breaks. This, on top of the fact that such games rarely have anything edifying to recommend them, means that those who play them come increasingly under the influence of negative factors.

E. THE CULTURE OF VIOLENCE

In America, from 1960 to 2016, the total population increased by 1.8 times, while the total number of crimes grew 2.7 times, and the number of violent crimes grew 4.5 times. [31]

According to author and criminologist Grant Duwe, in the fifty years before the 1966 University of Texas tower shooting incident took place, there were only twenty-five public mass shootings in which four or more people died. Since then, mass shootings have become more deadly. [32] From the Killeen mass shooting in Texas in 1991 that killed twenty-three, to the 2017 Las Vegas mass shooting that killed fifty-eight, the incidents have grown more shocking.

Terrorist incidents worldwide increased from 651 per year in 1970 to 13,626 in 2016, a twenty-fold increase. Since the September 11 terrorist attacks in 2001, the number of annual terrorist attacks had increased by about five times as of 2018. [33]

Many violent acts in the real world are manifestations of people's immersion in a culture of violence via mass media. Not only is the intense music of heavy metal full of violence, but the majority of entertainment, including film, television, and video games, depicts or is centered around violence. Many film and television productions portray the mafia, gangs, and pirates in a positive light, making these negative stereotypes look attractive and respectable, such that people not only no longer feel repulsed by them, but start to see crime and criminals as glorious.

The advent of video games gave people yet another channel for the glorification of violence, one that is interactive and allows the players themselves to employ violence within the virtual world. Instead of the unidirectional indoctrination of violence via film and television, players experience violence for themselves through these games, many of which contain scenes of decapitated heads, dismembered bodies, and blood spraying everywhere — all in excess of the normal boundaries of film and television.

In a study published in 2013, researchers analyzed movies that were produced between 1985 and 2012 and found that the amount of gun violence in PG-13 movies had tripled. [34] A follow-up study of films from 2013 through 2015 showed that this trend had continued. [35] In 2008, the Pew Research Center reported that 97 percent of young people between the ages of twelve and seventeen played video games, and that two-thirds of them played the categories of games that tended to contain violence. [36]

Faced with the problem of increasing violence in society, experts, scholars, and the general public continue to propose theories and solutions, from stricter restrictions via laws and stronger law enforcement, to providing the public with psychological counseling. But such solutions are simply akin to cutting off the branches of a poisonous tree without tearing it out by the roots.

F. DECADENT FASHION

On the surface of today's society, the various forms of strange attire, behavior, and other commonplace elements of popular culture all appear to be part of "freedom of expression" or the current "fashion trend," but, in fact, there is more to it. Tracing these phenomena to their source reveals their connections to the communist push against tradition and faith. Though these trends may encounter initial resistance from society, people simply become accustomed to them as time goes on and no longer find them strange, allowing these negative factors to become an accepted part of everyday life and culture.

For example, today's society is accustomed to women having short hairstyles. This was popularized by flappers in the West during the 1920s. Influenced by first-wave feminism and the sexual liberation movement (see Chapter Seven), flappers wore short dresses, cut their hair short, listened to jazz, wore thick make-up, drank alcohol, smoked cigarettes, and were casual about sex. Wearing their hair short was a way for them to express their disdain for traditional gender roles and their pursuit of female "emancipation."

After the hairstyle became popular, a well-known opera singer wrote: "Bobbed hair is a state of mind and not merely a new manner of dressing my head. ... I consider getting rid of our long hair one of the many little shackles that women have cast aside in their passage to freedom." [37]

During the Great Depression in the 1930s, this short hair for women gradually fell out of favor. However, in the 1960s, when rebellion from traditional norms became trendy again, short hairstyles for women made a comeback. Similarly, long hairstyles among men in contemporary times originated from the beatniks and hippies. [38] Although long hair for men can be traced back to ancient times, men in the West had worn their hair short in the decades since World War I, and the counterculture movement of the 1960s promoted long hair for men as a form of rebellion.

At first, mainstream society was highly resistant to young people dressing in an anti-traditional manner. Over time, people have become accustomed to anti-traditional trends, and in the views of progressives, this is due to an increase in social tolerance. In the traditions of the East and the West, however, differences between men and women were reflected not only in their physicality and in their different roles in society and the family, but also in their dress, hairstyle, speech, and mannerisms.

Along with disintegrating class distinctions in society, communism aims to eliminate the sexual distinctions between men and women. Similarly, the LGBT and feminist movements use the slogan of "equality" to blur gender differences in social and familial roles. Androgynous fashion trends further blur and reverse the differences in dress. These factors serve to pave the way for a wider social acceptance of what have traditionally been considered deviant sexual practices and lifestyles, and further contribute to undermining traditional morality.

For thousands of years, moral standards in both the East and the West have clarified the difference between men and women, and the idea that male and female, like yin and yang, each have their respective roles. Communism reverses yin and yang, hoping to overturn traditional morality and pit individuals against each other in the name of liberation.

Given this agenda, it can be seen that although the various deviations in dress and fashion may superficially seem like mere developments and shifts in popular taste, they are actually meant to undermine human society. Much of modern fashion emphasizes lewdness, having originated in the counterculture movement of the 1960s. [39]

Another sign of cultural decadence is the groupie phenomenon, which was popular among young people and another byproduct of the counterculture. In the 1960s, as rock 'n' roll became popular in the West, groups of young girls obsessed with rock stars followed their performances and provided personal and sexual services for band members. These young women became victims of a fad. [40] Today, young people admire stars who promote confused sexual identities, including male celebrities who behave effeminately, and vice versa.

There is also the supposedly fashionable punk subculture. Similar to those in the hippie movement, punks rebel against tradition and promote nihilism. Most hippies were rebellious young people from traditional middle-class families, while punk is more typically the rebellion of lower classes against social traditions. [41] In order to express their thorough anti-traditionalist attitudes, punks often exhibit bizarre hairstyles and wear tattered clothes full of spikes and buckles. They dye their hair, get tattoos, pierce their bodies all over, and sometimes expose body parts that the average person would be inclined to keep hidden. Punk style provides inspiration for many of today's fashion trends.

Punks advocate hedonism, which is why one popular punk slogan is "live fast, die young, and leave a pretty corpse." This fully reflects the tragedy of lost faith in the divine and of being deceived into falling into the abyss of hedonism and materialism. Though such self-destructive nihilism ought to elicit alarm among individuals and society, most are too deeply immersed in contemporary pop culture to see it for what it is.

Deviant and twisted contemporary culture fills everyday life: the display of ghostly or demonic images on popular clothing or in music; the choice of ugly images for tattoos; grotesque children's toys and ornaments; literature, film, and television works full of demons, ghosts, and supernatural horror — media that are widely consumed by the public — and the destructive and nihilistic content found on the internet.

4. Recovering the Moral Foundations of Human Culture

Everyone has the right to pursue happiness — but with the right comes the responsibility to remain within moral parameters. Excessive pursuit of pleasure inevitably brings suffering, calamity, and sorrow.

The traditional culture of humanity doesn't forbid the reasonable satisfaction of desire. However, traditional culture teaches people to control their desires and choose a healthy lifestyle. It values harmony with nature, traditional labor, harmonious family relationships, a healthy civil society, and participation in self-rule and state management, as well as traditional arts, literature, sports, and entertainment. All of this brings happiness and satisfaction, benefiting the individual in body and mind, as well as society at large.

The ultimate goal of communism, however, is to destroy humankind. One of the steps in this process is the corruption of morality and the removal of the divine from human culture. Therefore, the goal is for popular culture and lifestyles to be infused with negativity and darkness. In the past few decades, just such a popular culture has been created in the East and the West. Self-centeredness, hedonism, and nihilism have become common, accepted, and even fashionable.

Sex, drugs, rock 'n' roll, and video games stimulate and magnify desires. Many indulge in these things to escape the misery and disappointment of life, but they never stop to reflect. These addictions only bring momentary satisfaction, followed by more pain and disaster. Drug abuse causes disease, death, and personality disorders; chaotic sexual relationships destroy the family, making people lose trust and warmth; and video games make people lose themselves in a false world. Addicts feel that they're in a carnival of fun, but in fact, they are simply being exploited by outside forces, as the only thing waiting for them is spiritual decay and physical death.

The same is true of societies and nations. When a large number of people are addicted to desire and pleasure, disaster is at hand.

The divine created humankind and gave every individual free will. People should not abuse their freedoms and continue walking the path of degeneracy. Instead, they should make good use of that freedom and choose to return to a traditional culture and way of life. The divine has always looked after and protected humankind. But whether people can return to the right path depends entirely on the choice of each individual.

Notes

Chapter Nine:
The Communist Economic Trap

1. THOMAS JEFFERSON et al., "United States Declaration of Independence," July 4, 1776, National Archives, accessed April 20, 2020, https://www.archives.gov/founding-docs/declaration-transcript.

2. KARL MARX AND FRIEDRICH ENGELS, "Manifesto of the Communist Party," in *Marx & Engels Selected Works*, vol. 1, trans. Samuel Moore, ed. Andy Blunden (Moscow: Progress Publishers, 1969), Marxists Internet Archive, accessed April 20, 2020, https://www.marxists.org/archive/marx/works/1848/communist-manifesto/cho4.htm.

3. FRED SCHWARZ, *You Can Trust the Communists (to Be Communists)* (New Jersey: Prentice-Hall, 1960), 26–27.

4. FRIEDRICH A. HAYEK, *The Fatal Conceit: The Errors of Socialism,* W. W. Bartley III, ed. (Chicago: University of Chicago Press, 1991).

5. THOMAS SOWELL, *Intellectuals and Society,* Revised and Expanded Edition (New York: Basic Books, 2012), chap. 2.

6. LUDWIG VON MISES, "Economic Calculation in the Socialist Commonwealth," Mises Institute, accessed April 20, 2020, https://mises.org/library/economic-calculation-socialist-commonwealth.

7. SHI SHAN 石山, "Zhongguo guoqi gaige de kunjing" 中国国企改革的困境 ["Quagmire in the Reform of China's State-Owned Enterprises"], Radio Free Asia, September 22, 2015, https://www.rfa.org/mandarin/yataibaodao/jingmao/xql-09222015103826.html. [In Chinese]

8. LINETTE LOPEZ, "Zombie Companies Are Holding China's Economy Hostage," *Business Insider*, May 24, 2016, https://www.businessinsider.com/chinas-economy-is-being-held-hostage-2016-5.

9. MARX AND ENGELS, "Manifesto."

10. MAX GALKA, "The History of US Government Spending, Revenue, and Debt (1790–2015)," Metrocosm (blog), February 16, 2016, http://metrocosm.com/history-of-us-taxes.

11. ORGANIZATION FOR ECONOMIC COOPERATION AND DEVELOPMENT, "OECD Tax Rates on Labour Income Continued Decreasing Slowly in 2016," November 4, 2017, http://www.oecd.org/newsroom/oecd-tax-rates-on-labour-income-continued-decreasing-slowly-in-2016.htm.

12. RACHEL SHEFFIELD AND ROBERT RECTOR, "The War on Poverty After 50 Years," The Heritage Foundation, September 15, 2014, https://www.heritage.org/poverty-and-inequality/report/the-war-poverty-after-50-years.

13. ROBERT RECTOR, "The War on Poverty: 50 Years of Failure," The Heritage Foundation, September 23, 2014, https://www.heritage.org/marriage-and-family/commentary/the-war-poverty-50-years-failure.

14. ALEXIS DE TOCQUEVILLE, Memoir on Pauperism, trans. Seymour Drescher (London: Civitas, 1997).

15. SHEFFIELD AND RECTOR, "The War on Poverty."

16. NIMA SANANDAJI, Scandinavian Unexceptionalism: Culture, Markets, and the Failure of Third-Way Socialism (London: Institute for Economic Affairs, 2015), Kindle edition, 75.

17. TOCQUEVILLE, Memoir.

18. Ibid, 31.

19. "A National Sport No More," The Economist, November 3, 2012, https://www.economist.com/europe/2012/11/03/a-national-sport-no-more.

20. MARTIN HALLA, MARIO LACKNER, AND FRIEDRICH G. SCHNEIDER, "An Empirical Analysis of the Dynamics of the Welfare State: The Case of Benefit Morale," Kyklos 63, no.1 (2010): 55–74, Wiley Online Library, accessed April 20, 2020, https://onlinelibrary.wiley.com/doi/abs/10.1111/j.1467-6435.2010.00460.x.

21. NICHOLAS KRISTOF, "Profiting From a Child's Illiteracy," The New York Times, December 7, 2012, https://www.nytimes.com/2012/12/09/opinion/sunday/kristof-profiting-from-a-childs-illiteracy.html.

22. Ibid.

23. Ibid.

24. WILLIAM A. NISKANEN, "Welfare and the Culture of Poverty," The Cato Journal 16, no. 1 (1996), https://www.cato.org/sites/cato.org/files/serials/files/cato-journal/1996/5/cj16n1-1.pdf.

25. WALTER E. WILLIAMS, "The True Black Tragedy: Illegitimacy Rate of Nearly 75%," CNSNews.com, May 19, 2015, https://www.cnsnews.com/commentary/walter-e-williams/true-black-tragedy.

26. ORGANIZATION FOR ECONOMIC COOPERATION AND DEVELOPMENT, "General

Government Debt (Indicator),"
2019, accessed April 27, 2020,
https://data.oecd.org/gga/
general-government-debt.htm.

27. RONALD COASE, as quoted in
Thomas W. Hazlett, "Looking
for Results: An Interview
With Ronald Coase," *Reason*,
January 1997, https://reason.
com/archives/1997/01/01/
looking-for-results.

28. FRIEDRICH A. HAYEK, *The
Road to Serfdom* (Chicago:
University of Chicago Press,
1944).

29. M. SZMIGIERA, "Direct
Investment Position of the
United States in China from
2000 to 2018," Statistica.
com, September 2, 2019,
https://www.statista.com/
statistics/188629/united-states-
direct-investments-in-china-
since-2000.

30. "Zhongguo waishang touzi
baogao, 2016" 中国外商投
资报告, ["Report on Foreign
Investments in China, 2016"],
in *Zhongguo washang zhijie
touzi linian gaikuang* 中国
外商直接投资历年概况 [*A
General Summary of Direct
Foreign Investments in China*],
The Ministry of Commerce of
China. [In Chinese]

31. US COMMISSION ON THE
THEFT OF AMERICAN
INTELLECTUAL PROPERTY,
"Update to the IP Commission
Report: The Theft of American
Intellectual Property:
Reassessments of the
Challenge and United States
Policy," (Washington DC:

The National Bureau of Asian
Research, February 2017),
http://www.ipcommission.
org/report/IP_Commission_
Report_Update_2017.pdf.

32. CHRIS STROHM, "No Sign
China Has Stopped Hacking
US Companies, Official Says,"
Bloomberg, November 18,
2015, https://www.bloomberg.
com/news/articles/2015-11-18/
no-sign-china-has-stopped-
hacking-u-s-companies-
official-says.

33. KURT BIRAY, "Communist
Nostalgia in Eastern Europe:
Longing for the Past," Open
Democracy, November 10, 2015,
https://www.opendemocracy.
net/can-europe-make-it/
kurt-biray/communist-
nostalgia-in-eastern-europe-
longing-for-past.

34. JOHN POLGA-HECIMOVICH,
"The Roots of Venezuela's
Failing State," *Origins* 10, no. 9
(June 2017), http://origins.osu.
edu/article/roots-venezuelas-
failing-state.

35. JOSÉ NIÑO, "Venezuela Before
Chavez: A Prelude to Socialist
Failure," Mises Wire, May 4,
2017, https://mises.org/wire/
venezuela-chavez-prelude-
socialist-failure.

36. JOHN BISSETT, "Hugo Chavez:
Revolutionary Socialist
or Leftwing Reformist?"
Socialist Standard 101, no.
1215 (November 2005), http://
socialiststandardmyspace.
blogspot.com/2015/05/
hugo-chavez-revolutionary-
socialist-or.html.

37. JULIAN ADORNEY, "Socialism Set Fire to Venezuela's Oil Crisis," Real Clear World, August 29, 2017, https://www.realclearworld.com/articles/2017/08/29/socialism_set_fire_to_venezuelas_oil_crisis_112520.html.

38. JOSÉ NIÑO, "John Oliver is Wrong About Venezuela — It's a Socialist Country," Mises Institute, May 30, 2018, https://mises.org/wire/john-oliver-wrong-about-venezuela-%E2%80%94-its-socialist-country.

39. CHRIS MCGREAL, "Zimbabwe's Inflation Rate Surges to 231,000,000%," The Guardian, October 9, 2008, https://www.theguardian.com/world/2008/oct/09/zimbabwe.

40. JASON LONG, "The Surprising Social Mobility of Victorian Britain," European Review of Economic History 17, no. 1 (February 1, 2013): 1–23, https://doi.org/10.1093/ereh/hes020.

41. MICHAEL ROTHSCHILD, Bionomics: Economy as Ecosystem (Washington, DC: Beard Books, 2004), 115.

42. ADAM SMITH, The Theory of Moral Sentiments (Malta: Gutenberg Publishers, 2011).

43. LAWRENCE KUDLOW, American Abundance: The New Economic and Moral Prosperity (New York: HarperCollins Publishers, 1997).

44. THOMAS SOWELL, Economic Facts and Fallacies (New York: Basic Books, 2008), 174.

45. FRIEDRICH ENGELS, "Trades Unions," The Labour Standard, May 28, 1881, Marxists Internet Archive, accessed April 20, 2020, https://www.marxists.org/archive/marx/works/1881/05/28.htm.

46. VLADIMIR LENIN, "The Trade Unions, The Present Situation and Trotsky's Mistakes," in Lenin's Collected Works, trans. Yuri Sdobnikov (Moscow: Progress Publishers, 1965), 32:19–42, Marxists Internet Archive, accessed April 20, 2020, https://www.marxists.org/archive/lenin/works/1920/dec/30.htm.

47. LÜ JIAMIN 吕嘉民, "Liening gonghuixueshuo shi" 列寧工會學說史 ["A History of Leninist Theory on Unions"], (Liaoning People's Press, 1987). [In Chinese]

48. JAMES SHERK, "What Unions Do: How Labor Unions Affect Jobs and the Economy," The Heritage Foundation, May 21, 2009, https://www.heritage.org/jobs-and-labor/report/what-unions-do-how-labor-unions-affect-jobs-and-the-economy.

49. Ibid.

50. EDWIN J. FEULNER, "Taking Down Twinkies," The Heritage Foundation, November 19, 2012, https://www.heritage.org/jobs-and-labor/commentary/taking-down-twinkies.

51. SHERK, "What Unions Do."

52. Ibid.

53. STEVE INSKEEP, "Solidarity for Sale: Corruption in Labor Unions," National Public Radio, February 6, 2007, https://www.npr.org/templates/story/story.php?storyId=5181842.

54. KARL MARX, "Critique of the Gotha Programme," in *Marx & Engels Selected Works* (Moscow: Progress Publishers, 1970), 3:13–30, via Marxists Internet Archive, April 20, 2020, https://www.marxists.org/archive/marx/works/1875/gotha/ch01.htm.

55. KEITH WOOTTON, dir., *Children on the Titanic* (Marina Del Rey, CA: Vision Films, 2014).

56. WALTER LORD, *A Night to Remember: The Classic Account of the Final Hours of the Titanic* (United States: Henry Holt and Company, 2005), 50.

57. LI HONGZHI, "Wealth With Virtue," in *Essentials for Further Advancement*, January 27, 1995, https://www.falundafa.org/eng/eng/jjyz02.htm.

Chapter Ten: Corrupting the Legal System

1. HAROLD J. BERMAN, *The Interaction of Law and Religion* (Nashville: Abingdon Press, 1974), 51–55.

2. DONG ZHONGSHU 董仲舒, as quoted in Ban Gu 班固, "Dong Zhongshu zhuan" 董仲舒傳 ["Chronicle of Dong Zhongshu"] in *Han Shu* 漢書 [*The Book of Han*]. [In Chinese]

3. BERMAN, *The Interaction.*

4. KARL MARX, as quoted in W. Cleon Skousen, *The Naked Communist* (Salt Lake City: The Ensign Publishing Co., 1962), 13.

5. SERGEY NECHAYEV, *The Revolutionary Catechism* (1869), Marxists Internet Archive, accessed on April 20, 2020, https://www.marxists.org/subject/anarchism/nechayev/catechism.htm.

6. VLADIMIR LENIN, "The Proletarian Revolution and the Renegade Kautsky: How Kautsky Turned Marx Into A Common Liberal," in *Lenin Collected Works*, trans. Jim Riordan (Moscow: Progress Publishers, 1974), 28:227–325, Marxists Internet Archive, accessed on April 20, 2020, https://www.marxists.org/archive/lenin/works/1918/prrk/common_liberal.htm.

7. LI YUZHEN 李玉貞, *Yi bu dianfuxing zhuzhuo: Ershi shiji Eguoshi* 一部顛覆性著作：二十世紀俄國史 [*Work of Insurrection: 20th-Century Russian History*], (Beijing: Yanhuang Chunqiu, 2010). [In Chinese]

8. ALEXANDER NIKOLAEVICH YAKOVLEV, "Zhi Zhongguo Duzhe" 致中國讀者 ["To

Chinese Readers"], in *Yibei kujiu—Eluosi de Buershiweikezhuyi he gaige yundong* 一杯苦酒——俄羅斯的布爾什維克主義和改革運動 [*A Bitter Cup: Bolshevism and the Reformation of Russia*], trans. Xu Kui 徐葵 et al., (Beijing: Xinhua chubanshe, 1999), 10. [In Chinese] The cited text is a preface written for the Chinese-language edition of Yakovlev's book.

9. AN LINXIAN 安霖贤, *Xianfa yuanze yu yi fa zhiguo* 宪法原则与依法治国 [*Constitutional Principles and Governing the Country by Law*], *People. com.cn,* November 2, 2006, http://legal.people.com.cn/GB/43027/73487/73490/4990833.html. [In Chinese]

10. OUYANG FEI 歐陽非, "Hongse huangtang huangyan lun" 紅色荒唐言論 ["Red Nonsense"], Minghui.org, January 8, 2015, http://www.minghui.org/mh/articles/2015/1/8/302850.html. [In Chinese]

11. FRANCIS BACON, "Of Judicature," in *The Essays or Counsels, Civil and Moral of Francis Bacon,* ed. Samuel Harvey Reynolds (Oxford: Clarendon Press, 1890), Internet Archive, accessed on April 20, 2020, https://archive.org/stream/essaysorcounseloobacouoft/essaysorcounseloobacouoft_djvu.txt.

12. *Planned Parenthood of Southeastern Pennsylvania v. Casey (Nos. 91–744, 91–902),* Legal Information Institute, accessed on April 20, 2020, https://www.law.cornell.edu/supct/html/91-744.ZO.html.

13. NEIL EGGLESTON, "President Obama Has Now Granted More Commutations Than Any President in This Nation's History," The White House, January 17, 2017, https://obamawhitehouse.archives.gov/blog/2017/01/17/president-obama-has-now-granted-more-commutations-any-president-nations-history.

14. GREGORY KORTE, "Obama Commutes Sentence of Chelsea Manning in Last-Minute Clemency Push," *USA TODAY,* January 17, 2017, https://www.usatoday.com/story/news/politics/2017/01/17/obama-commutes-sentence-chelsea-manning/96678814.

15. PAIGE ST. JOHN AND ABBIE VANSICKLE, "Here's Why George Soros, Liberal Groups Are Spending Big to Help Decide Who's Your Next DA," *Los Angeles Times*, May 23, 2018, http://www.latimes.com/local/california/la-me-prosecutor-campaign-20180523-story.html.

16. US CONGRESS, HOUSE, Affidavit of Roger N. Baldwin, *Investigation of Un-American Propaganda Activities in the United States: Hearings before a Special Committee on Un-American Activities*, December 31, 1938, 3081–3082, Internet Archive, accessed on April 20, 2020, https://archive.org/details/

investigationofu193804unit/
page/2448/mode/2up/search/
Baldwin.

17. MYRON H. THOMPSON, as
quoted in Phyllis Schlafly, *The
Supremacists: The Tyranny
of Judges and How to Stop It*
(Minneapolis, MN: Richard
Vigilante Books, 2006), 26–27.

18. PHYLLIS SCHLAFLY, "Pots
of Gold Behind Crosses and
Ten Commandments," Eagle
Forum, June 23, 2004, http://
eagleforum.org/column/2004/
june04/04-06-23.html.

19. *Elk Grove Unified School
District v. Newdow*, 542 US 1
(2004).

20. US CONGRESS, HOUSE,
*Expressing the Sense of the
House of Representatives that
Newdow v. US Congress Was
Erroneously Decided, and for
Other Purposes*, HR 459, 107th
Cong., 1st sess., introduced and
agreed in House June 27, 2002,
https://www.congress.gov/
bill/107th-congress/house-
resolution/459.

21. US CONGRESS, SENATE,
*A Resolution Expressing
Support for the Pledge of
Allegiance*, S. 292, 107th Cong.,
1st sess., introduced and
agreed in Senate June 26, 2002,
https://www.congress.gov/
bill/107th-congress/senate-
resolution/292.

22. SCHLAFLY,
The Supremacists, 30.

23. Ibid., 58.

24. Ibid., 60–61.

25. "CNN Revels in Pot Smoke
During New Year's Eve
Report From Denver," Fox
News, January 1, 2018,
http://www.foxnews.com/
entertainment/2018/01/01/
cnn-revels-in-pot-smoke-
during-new-years-eve-report-
from-denver.html.

26. PATRICK MCGREEVY,
"Billionaire Activists like
Sean Parker and George
Soros Are Fueling the
Campaign to Legalize Pot,"
Los Angeles Times, November
2, 2016, http://www.latimes.
com/politics/la-pol-ca-
proposition64-cash-snap-
20161102-story.html.

27. SEN. MIKE LEE, "GOP
Senators Call on Sec.
Tillerson to Investigate State
Department Meddling,"
March 14, 2017, https://
www.lee.senate.gov/
public/index.cfm/press-
releases?ID=B5BD5596-25C8-
495F-A8B1-A4D248649C04.

28. SCHLAFLY, *The Supremacists*.

29. *Obergefell v. Hodges*, 576 US
644 (2015).

30. TODD STARNES, "Kentucky
Clerk: 'This is a fight worth
fighting," Fox News,
September 3, 2015, http://
www.foxnews.com/
opinion/2015/09/03/kentucky-
clerk-am-prepared-to-go-to-
jail.html.

31. MIKE HUCKABEE, as quoted
in "Attorney for Kim Davis
Speaks Out, Huckabee
Blasts 'Judicial Overreach'

in Case," interview by Sean Hannity, *Fox News*, September 8, 2015, http://www.foxnews. com/transcript/2015/09/08/ attorney-for-kim-davis- speaks-out-huckabee-blasts- judicial-overreach-in-case. html.

32. STOP THE KINSEY INSTITUTE COALITION, "Kinsey Helped Undermine Laws Protecting Women & Children," accessed on April 20, 2020, http:// stopthekinseyinstitute.org/ more/undermining-laws.

33. PAUL RUBIN, et al., "Does Capital Punishment Have a Deterrent Effect? New Evidence From Post-Moratorium Panel Data," Clemson University and Emory University (October 2003), https:// cjlf.org/deathpenalty/ DezRubShepDeterFinal.pdf.

34. *Lawrence v. Texas*, 539 US 558 (2003).

35. BERMAN, *The Interaction*.

36. SKOUSEN, *The Naked Communist*.

Chapter Eleven: Desecrating the Arts

1. "Record of Music," in *Classic of Rites*, trans. James Legge, Chinese Text Project, accessed May 8, 2020, https://ctext.org/ liji/yue-ji?filter =435370&searchmode =showall#result.

2. CONFUCIUS 孔子, *Lun Yu* 論 語 [*The Analects of Confucius*] (New York: Ballantine Books, 1999), 3.14. [In Chinese]

3. SIMA QIAN, "A Treatise on Music," in *Records of the Grand Historian*, trans. Burton Watson, vol. 24, 3rd ed. (New York: Columbia University Press, 1995).

4. OUYANG XIU 歐陽脩 and SONG QI 宋祁, *Xin Tang Shu* 新 唐書 [*New Book of Tang*], vol. 237 (1060). [In Chinese]

5. ROBERT MCKEE, *Story: Style, Structure, Substance, and the Principles of Screenwriting* (New York: ReganBooks, 1997), 129–130.

6. YINGSHOU XING et al., "Mozart, Mozart Rhythm and Retrograde Mozart Effects: Evidences from Behaviours and Neurobiology Bases," in *Scientific Reports*, vol. 6 (January 21, 2016), https://www. nature.com/articles/srep18744.

7. DAVID NOEBEL, *The Marxist Minstrels: A Handbook on Communist Subversion of Music* (Tulsa, OK: American Christian College Press, 1974), 58–59.

8. DAVID CLOUD, "Rock Music and Suicide," Way of Life Literature, December 20, 2000, https://www.wayoflife.org/ reports/rock_music_and_ suicide.html.

9. VAL WILLIAMS, "Leni Riefenstahl: Film-maker Who Became Notorious as Hitler's Propagandist," *The*

Independent, September 10, 2003, https://web.archive.org/web/20090830045819/http://www.independent.co.uk/news/obituaries/leni-riefenstahl-548728.html.

10. MAO ZEDONG, "Talks at the Yenan Forum on Literature and Art," in *Selected Works of Mao Tse-Tung* (Beijing: Foreign Languages Press), Marxists Internet Archive, accessed on April 23, 2020, https://www.marxists.org/reference/archive/mao/selected-works/volume-3/mswv3_08.htm.

11. PRAGERU, "Why Is Modern Art So Bad?", YouTube, September 1, 2014, https://www.youtube.com/watch?v=lNI07egoefc.

12. HERBERT MARCUSE, *The Aesthetic Dimension: Toward a Critique of Marxist Aesthetics* (Boston: Beacon Press, 1978), ix.

13. JACKSON SPIELVOGEL, *Western Civilization: Volume C: Since 1789* (United States: Cengage Learning, 2010), 698.

14. PABLO PICASSO, "Why I Became a Communist" (1945), as quoted in "Picasso, the FBI, and Why He Became a Communist," Meyer Schapiro Collection at Columbia University's Rare Book & Manuscript Library, February 24, 2010, accessed July 11, 2018, https://blogs.cul.columbia.edu/schapiro/2010/02/24/picasso-and-communism.

15. ROBERT HUGHES, *The Shock of the New: The Hundred-Year History of Modern Art—Its Rise, Its Dazzling Achievement, Its Fall* (London: Knopf, 1991), 24.

16. RICHARD HUELSENBECK AND RAOUL HAUSMANN, "What Is Dadaism and What Does It Want in Germany?", in Charles Harrison and Paul Wood, *Art in Theory, 1900–2000: An Anthology of Changing Ideas*, 2nd ed. (Malden, Mass, Oxford: Blackwell Pub, 2003).

17. JOSEPH BEUYS, as quoted in "Joseph Beuys: The Revolution Is Us," Tate.org, February 23, 1993, https://www.tate.org.uk/whats-on/tate-liverpool/exhibition/joseph-beuys-revolution-us.

18. WALDEMAR JANUSZCZAK, as quoted in Ben Cade, "Zhu Yu: China's Baby-Eating Shock Artist Goes Hyperreal," Culture Trip, October 5, 2016, https://theculturetrip.com/asia/china/articles/zhu-yu-china-s-baby-eating-shock-artist-goes-hyperreal.

19. JOHN WIILIAM GODWARD, as quoted in Brad Smithfield, "'The World Is Not Big Enough for Me and a Picasso': The Life and Artwork of John William Godward," The Vintage News, January 10, 2017, https://www.thevintagenews.com/2017/01/10/world-not-big-enough-picasso-life-artwork-john-william-godward.

20. WALTER FRISCH, ed., *Schoenberg and His World* (Princeton, NJ: Princeton University Press, 1999), 94.

21. NORMAN LEBRECHT, "Why We're Still Afraid of Schoenberg," *The Lebrecht Weekly,* July 8, 2001, http://www.scena.org/columns/lebrecht/010708-NL-Schoenberg.html.

22. GOLAN GUR, "Arnold Schoenberg and the Ideology of Progress in Twentieth-Century Musical Thinking," *Search: Journal for New Music and Culture,* 5 (Summer 2009), http://www.searchnewmusic.org/gur.pdf.

23. JULIA MICKENBERG, *American Girls in Red Russia: Chasing the Soviet Dream* (United States: University of Chicago Press, 2017), 216–217.

24. MICHAEL MINNICINO, "The New Dark Age: The Frankfurt School and 'Political Correctness,'" in *Fidelio Magazine* 1, no.1 (Winter 1992), accessed April 24, 2020, http://archive.schillerinstitute.org/fid_91-96/921_frankfurt.html.

25. MAO ZEDONG, "Talks at the Yenan Forum."

26. MAO ZEDONG, "On New Democracy," in *Selected Works of Mao Tse-Tung* (Beijing: Foreign Languages Press, 1942), Marxists Internet Archive, accessed on April 24, 2020, https://www.marxists.org/reference/archive/mao/selected-works/volume-2/mswv2_26.htm.

27. ANDRÉ BRETON, *Manifestoes of Surrealism,* trans. Richard Seaver and Helen Lane (Ann Arbor, MI: University of Michigan Press, 1969), 26.

28. ALLEN GINSBERG, "America," *Selected Poems 1947–1995* (New York: HarperCollins Publishers Inc., 2001).

29. IRVING BABBITT, *Rousseau and Romanticism* (Oxford, UK: Routledge, 1991), 104.

Chapter Twelve: Sabotaging Education

1. YURI BEZMENOV, as quoted in G. Edward Griffin, *Deception Was My Job: A Conversation with Yuri Bezmenov, Former Propagandist for the KGB* (New York: American Media Inc., 1985).

2. NATIONAL COMMISSION ON EXCELLENCE IN EDUCATION, *A Nation at Risk* (Washington DC: US Department of Education, 1983), https://www2.ed.gov/pubs/NatAtRisk/risk.html.

3. Ibid.

4. MARK BAUERLEIN, *The Dumbest Generation: How the Digital Age Stupefies Young Americans and Jeopardizes Our Future* (New York: Tarcher, 2008), chap. 1.

5. JOHN TAYLOR GATTO, *Dumbing Us Down: The Hidden Curriculum of Compulsory Schooling* (Gabriola Island, BC, Canada: New Society Publishers, 2005), 12.

6. CHARLES J. SYKES, *Dumbing Down Our Kids: Why American Children Feel Good About Themselves but Can't Read, Write, or Add* (New York: St. Martin's Press, 1995), 148–9.

7. THOMAS SOWELL, *Inside American Education: The Decline, the Deception, the Dogmas* (New York: The Free Press, 1993), 4.

8. CHARLOTTE THOMSON ISERBYT, *The Deliberate Dumbing Down of America: A Chronological Paper Trail* (Ravenna, OH: Conscience Press, 1999), xvii.

9. SIDNEY HOOK, as quoted in Robin S. Eubanks, *Credentialed to Destroy: How and Why Education Became a Weapon* (Scotts Valley, CA: Createspace Independent Publishing Platform, 2013), 48.

10. ALBERT P. PINKEVICH, as quoted in Eubanks, *Credentialed,* 49.

11. ALAN RYAN, as quoted in Eubanks, *Credentialed,* 45–46.

12. "Ten Most Harmful Books of the 19th and 20th Centuries," *Human Events,* May 31, 2005, http://humanevents. com/2005/05/31/ten-most-harmful-books-of-the-19th-and-20th-centuries/.

13. MORTIMER SMITH, *And Madly Teach: A Layman Looks at Public School Education* (Chicago: Henry Regnery Company, 1949).

14. JOHN A. STORMER, *None Dare Call It Treason* (Florissant, MO: Liberty Bell Press, 1964), 99.

15. SAMUEL TAYLOR COLERIDGE, as quoted in I. L. Kandel, "Prejudice the Garden Toward Roses?", *The American Scholar* 8, no. 1 (Winter 1938–1939): 77.

16. CHRISTOPHER TURNER, "A Conversation About Happiness, Review – a Childhood at Summerhill," *The Guardian,* March 28, 2014, https://www.theguardian. com/books/2014/mar/28/ conversation-happiness-summerhill-school-review-mikey-cuddihy.

17. A. S. NEILL, *Summerhill: A Radical Approach to Child Rearing* (New York: Hart Publishing Company, 1960), chap. 3.

18. JOANNE LIPMAN, "Why Tough Teachers Get Good Results," *The Wall Street Journal,* September 27, 2013, https://www.wsj.com/articles/ why-tough-teachers-get-good-results-1380323772.

19. DAISY CHRISTODOULOU, *Seven Myths About Education* (London: Routledge, 2014).

20. DIANA WEST, *The Death of the Grown-Up: How America's Arrested Development Is Bringing Down Western Civilization* (New York: St. Martin's Press, 2008), Kindle Edition.

21. FRED SCHWARZ AND DAVID NOEBEL, *You Can Still Trust*

the Communists ... to Be Communists (Socialists, Statists, and Progressives Too) (Manitou Springs, CO: Christian Anti-Communism Crusade, 2010), http://www.schwarzreport.org/resources/you-can-trust-the-communists-to-be-communists.

22. *Stein v. Oshinsky*, 348 F.2d 999 (2nd Cir. 1965); *Collins v. Chandler Unified School District* et al., 644 F.2d 759 (9th Cir. 1981).

23. JOHN TAYLOR GATTO, *The Underground History of American Education: A Schoolteacher's Intimate Investigation Into the Problem of Modern Schooling* (Baltimore: Odysseus Group, 2000), chap. 14.

24. DIANE RAVITCH, "Education after the Culture Wars," *Daedalus* 131, no. 3 (Summer 2002), 5–21.

25. E. MERRILL ROOT, *Brainwashing in the High Schools: An Examination of Eleven American History Textbooks* (Papamoa Press, 2018), Kindle edition.

26. KATHERINE KERSTEN, "Inside a Public School Social Justice Factory," *Washington Examiner*, February 1, 2018, https://www.washingtonexaminer.com/weekly-standard/inside-a-public-school-social-justice-factory.

27. *History Social Science Framework*, adopted by the California State Board of Education July 2016 (Sacramento: California Department of Education, 2017), 431, https://www.cde.ca.gov/ci/hs/cf/documents/hssfwchapter16.pdf.

28. Ibid., 391.

29. PHYLLIS SCHLAFLY, ed., *Child Abuse in the Classroom* (Wheaton, IL: Crossway Books, 1984), 13.

30. HERBERT MARCUSE, *Eros and Civilization: A Philosophical Inquiry Into Freud* (Boston: Beacon Press, 1966), 35.

31. BROCK CHISHOLM, as quoted in B. K. Eakman, *Cloning of the American Mind: Eradicating Morality through Education* (Lafayette, LA: Huntington House Publishers, 1998), 109.

32. WILLIAM KILPATRICK, *Why Johnny Can't Tell Right from Wrong and What We Can Do About It* (New York: Simon & Schuster, 1993), 16–17.

33. SOWELL, *Inside American Education*, 36.

34. Ibid., 48.

35. 20/20, "Death in the Classroom," ABC, August 30, 1991, https://www.youtube.com/watch?v=vbiY6Fz6Few.

36. SOWELL, *Inside American Education*, 38.

37. 20/20, "Death in the Classroom."

38. KILPATRICK, *Why Johnny*, 32.

39. JUDITH A. REISMAN et al., *Kinsey, Sex and Fraud: The Indoctrination of a People* (Lafayette, LA: Lochinvar-Huntington House, 1990).

40. ROBERT RECTOR, "When Sex Ed Becomes Porn 101," The Heritage Foundation, August 27, 2003, https://www.heritage.org/education/commentary/when-sex-ed-becomes-porn-101.

41. Ibid.

42. MARGARET SANGER, as quoted in Norman K. Risjord, *Representative Americans: Populists and Progressives* (Lanham, MD: Rowman & Littlefield Publishers, 2004), 267.

43. MARGARET SANGER, as quoted in Madeline Gray, *Margaret Sanger* (New York: Penguin Adult Hc/Tr, 1979), 227–228.

44. REBECCA HERSHER, "It May Be 'Perfectly Normal,' but It's Also Frequently Banned," National Public Radio, September 21, 2014, https://www.npr.org/2014/09/21/350366435/it-may-be-perfectly-normal-but-its-also-frequently-banned.

45. KILPATRICK, *Why Johnny*, 53.

46. MAUREEN STOUT, *The Feel-Good Curriculum: The Dumbing Down of America's Kids in the Name of Self-Esteem* (Cambridge, MA: Da Capo Lifelong Books, 2000), 1–3.

47. Ibid., 17.

48. B. K. EAKMAN, *Educating for the 'New World Order'* (Portland, OR: Halcyon House, 1991), 129.

49. SOL STERN, "How Teachers' Unions Handcuff Schools," *City Journal*, Spring 1997, https://www.city-journal.org/html/how-teachers%E2%80%99-unions-handcuff-schools-12102.html.

50. TROY SENIK, "The Worst Union in America: How the California Teachers Association Betrayed the Schools and Crippled the State," *City Journal*, Spring 2012, https://www.city-journal.org/html/worst-union-america-13470.html.

51. KILPATRICK, *Why Johnny*, 39.

52. SAMUEL BLUMENFELD AND ALEX NEWMAN, *Crimes of the Educators: How Utopians Are Using Government Schools to Destroy America's Children* (Washington DC: WND Books, 2015), chap. 14.

53. ISERBYT, *The Deliberate Dumbing Down*, xvii.

54. SCHLAFLY, *Child Abuse*, 14.

55. VALERIE STRAUSS, "A Serious Rant about Education Jargon and How It Hurts Efforts to Improve Schools," *The Washington Post*, November 11, 2015, https://www.washingtonpost.com/news/answer-sheet/wp/2015/11/11/a-serious-rant-about-education-jargon-and-how-it-hurts-efforts-

to-improve-schools/?utm_term=.8ab3d85e9e45.

56. STORMER, *None Dare*, 104–106.

57. DIANE RAVITCH, "The Common Core Costs Billions and Hurts Students," *The New York Times*, July 23, 2016, https://www.nytimes.com/2016/07/24/opinion/sunday/the-common-core-costs-billions-and-hurts-students.html.

58. ROBBY SOAVE, "Elite Campuses Offer Students Coloring Books, Puppies to Get Over Trump," *Daily Beast*, last updated April 13, 2017, accessed on April 20, 2020, https://www.thedailybeast.com/elite-campuses-offer-students-coloring-books-puppies-to-get-over-trump.

59. ELIZABETH REDDEN, "Foreign Students and Graduate STEM Enrollment," Inside Higher Ed, October 11, 2017, accessed on April 20, 2020, https://www.insidehighered.com/quicktakes/2017/10/11/foreign-students-and-graduate-stem-enrollment.

60. SCOTT JASCHIK, "Professors and Politics: What the Research Says," Inside Higher Ed, February 27, 2017, https://www.insidehighered.com/news/2017/02/27/research-confirms-professors-lean-left-questions-assumptions-about-what-means.

61. MITCHELL LANGBERT, Anthony J. Quain, and Daniel B. Klein, "Faculty Voter Registration in Economics, History, Journalism, Law, and Psychology," *Econ Journal Watch* 13, issue 3, September 2016, 422–51, https://econjwatch.org/articles/faculty-voter-registration-in-economics-history-journalism-communications-law-and-psychology.

62. JASCHIK, "Professors and Politics."

63. "The Close-Minded Campus? The Stifling of Ideas in American Universities," American Enterprise Institute, June 8, 2016, https://www.aei.org/events/the-close-minded-campus-the-stifling-of-ideas-in-american-universities.

64. TED CRUZ, as quoted in Fred Schwarz and David A. Noebel, *You Can Still Trust the Communists ... to Be Communists (Socialists, Statists, and Progressives Too)*, revised edition (Manitou Springs, CO: Christian Anti-Communism Crusade, 2010), 2–3.

65. ZYGMUND DOBBS, "Chapter III: American Fabianism," in *Keynes at Harvard: Economic Deception as a Political Credo* (Web version, 2009, transcribed from revised edition 1969), Keynes at Harvard, accessed on April 20, 2020, http://keynesatharvard.org/book/KeynesatHarvard-ch03.html.

66. HERBERT MARCUSE, as quoted in Robin S. Eubanks, *Credentialed to Destroy: How*

and *Why Education Became a Weapon* (CreateSpace Independent Publishing Platform, 2013), 26.

67. JAY PARINI, as quoted in Walter E. Williams, *More Liberty Means Less Government: Our Founders Knew This Well* (Stanford, CA: Hoover Press, 1999), 126.

68. DAVID MACEY, "Organic Intellectual," in *The Penguin Dictionary of Critical Theory* (London: Penguin Books, 2000), 282.

69. KARL MARX, "Theses on Feuerbach," in *Marx/Engels Selected Works*, vol. 1, 13–15, accessed via Marxists Internet Archive on April 20, 2020, https://www.marxists.org/archive/marx/works/1845/theses/theses.pdf.

70. BRUCE BAWER, *The Victims' Revolution: The Rise of Identity Studies and the Closing of the Liberal Mind* (New York: Broadside Books, 2012), chap. 1.

71. SOL STERN, as quoted in Bawer, *The Victims' Revolution.*

72. FRANTZ FANON, *The Wretched of the Earth*, trans. Constance Farrington (New York: Grove Press, 1966), 94.

73. JEAN-PAUL SARTRE, "Preface," in Frantz Fanon, *The Wretched of the Earth*, trans. Constance Farrington (New York: Grove Press, 1966), https://www.marxists.org/reference/archive/sartre/1961/preface.htm.

74. ROGER KIMBALL, *Tenured Radicals: How Politics Has Corrupted Our Higher Education* (Chicago: Ivan R. Dee, 1998), 25–29.

75. JONATHAN CULLER, *Literary Theory: A Very Short Introduction* (Oxford: Oxford University Press, 1997), 4.

76. FREDRIC JAMESON, *The Political Unconscious: Narrative as a Socially Symbolic Act* (Ithaca, NY: Cornell University Press, 1981), chap. 1.

77. SIR ROGER SCRUTON, as quoted in Kimball, *Tenured Radicals*, xviii.

78. KARL MARX, "The German Ideology" in Marx-Engels Collected Works, vol. 5 (New York: International Publishers Co., 1976), Marxists Internet Archive, accessed on April 21, 2020, https://www.marxists.org/archive/marx/works/1845/german-ideology.

79. THOMSON REUTERS' ISI WEB OF SCIENCE, "Most Cited Authors of Books in the Humanities, 2007," *Times Higher Education*, March 26, 2009, accessed on April 21, 2020, https://www.uky.edu/~eushe2/Bandura/BanduraTopHumanities.pdf.

80. JOSHUA PHILLIP, "Jordan Peterson Exposes the Postmodernist Agenda," *The Epoch Times*, June 21, 2017, https://www.theepochtimes.com/jordan-peterson-explains-how-communism-

came-under-the-guise-of-identity-politics_2259668.html.

81. MICHEL FOUCAULT, as quoted in Roger Kimball, "The Perversions of M. Foucault," *The New Criterion*, March 1993, https://www.newcriterion.com/issues/1993/3/the-perversions-of-m-foucault.

82. DAVID HOROWITZ AND JACOB LAKSIN, *One Party Classroom: How Radical Professors at America's Top Colleges Indoctrinate Students and Undermine Our Democracy* (New York: Crown Forum, 2009), 3.

83. DAVID HOROWITZ, *The Professors: The 101 Most Dangerous Academics in America* (Washington DC: Regnery Publishing, Inc., 2013), Kindle Edition.

84. HOROWITZ AND LAKSIN, *One Party Classroom*, 212.

85. DAVID HOROWITZ, *Indoctrination U.: The Left's War Against Academic Freedom* (New York: Encounter Books, 2009).

86. DAVID P. BARASH AND CHARLES P. WEBEL, *Peace and Conflict Studies* (New York: SAGE Publications Inc., 2008), as quoted in Ibid.

87. HOROWITZ AND LAKSIN, *One Party Classroom*, 51–52.

88. BAWER, *The Victims' Revolution*, 121–180.

89. HOROWITZ AND LAKSIN, *One Party Classroom*, 1–2.

90. DINITIA SMITH, "No Regrets for a Love of Explosives; In a Memoir of Sorts, a War Protester Talks of Life With the Weathermen," *The New York Times,* September 11, 2001, https://www.nytimes.com/2001/09/11/books/no-regrets-for-love-explosives-memoir-sorts-war-protester-talks-life-with.html.

91. LINTON WEEKS, "Who Won the Civil War? Tough Question," National Public Radio, November 18, 2014, https://www.npr.org/sections/theprotojournalist/2014/11/18/364675234/who-won-the-civil-war-tough-question.

92. ISI ARCHIVE, "Our Fading Heritage: Americans Fail a Basic Test on Their History and Institutions," Intercollegiate Studies Institute, November 19, 2008, https://isi.org/lectures/press-conference-our-fading-heritage-americans-fail-a-basic-test-on-their-history-and-institutions/.

93. "Study: Americans Don't Know Much About History," NBC News, November 20, 2008, https://www.nbclosangeles.com/news/local/Study-Americans-Dont-Know-About-Much-About-History.html.

94. HOROWITZ, *The Professors*, 74.

95. PAUL SAMUELSON, as quoted in foreword to Phillips Saunders and William B. Walstad, eds., *The Principles of Economics Course* (New York: McGraw-Hill Companies, 1989).

96. ALAN D. SOKAL, "Transgressing the Boundaries: Toward a Transformative Hermeneutics of Quantum Gravity," *Social Text*, no. 46/47 (Spring–Summer 1996): 217–252, https://physics.nyu. edu/faculty/sokal/transgress_ v2/transgress_v2_singlefile. html.

97. ALAN D. SOKAL, "A Physicist Experiments with Cultural Studies," *Lingua Franca,* June 5, 1996, http://www.physics. nyu.edu/faculty/sokal/lingua_ franca_v4/lingua_franca_ v4.html.

98. ALAN D. SOKAL, "Parody," National Public Radio, May 15, 1996, https://www.npr. org/templates/story/story. php?storyId=1043441.

99. ALAN D. SOKAL, "Revelation: A Physicist Experiments with Cultural Studies," in *Sokal Hoax: The Sham That Shook the Academy*, ed. Editors of Lingua Franca (Lincoln, NE: Bison Books, 2000), 52. https:// physics.nyu.edu/faculty/sokal/ lingua_franca_v4/lingua_ franca_v4.html.

100. SOWELL, *Inside*, 212–213.

101. DONALD ALEXANDER DOWNS, *Restoring Free Speech and Liberty on Campus* (Oakland, CA: Independent Institute, 2004), 51.

102. EUGENE VOLOKH, "UC Teaching Faculty Members Not to Criticize Race-Based Affirmative Action, Call America 'Melting Pot,' and More," *The Washington Post*, June 16, 2015, https:// www.washingtonpost. com/news/volokh- conspiracy/wp/2015/06/16/ uc-teaching-faculty- members-not-to-criticize- race-based-affirmative- action-call-america-melting- pot-and-more/?utm_term=. c9a452fdb00f.

103. "Victory at IUPUI: Student- Employee Found Guilty of Racial Harassment for Reading a Book Now Cleared of All Charges," Foundation for Individual Rights in Education, May 1, 2008, https://www. thefire.org/victory-at-iupui- student-employee-found- guilty-of-racial-harassment- for-reading-a-book-now- cleared-of-all-charges/.

104. "Colleges Become Re-Education Camps in Age of Diversity," *Investor's Business Daily*, April 22, 2013, https://www.investors.com/ politics/editorials/students- indoctrinated-in-leftist- politics/.

105. "University of Delaware: Students Required to Undergo Ideological Reeducation," Foundation for Individual Rights in Education, 2007, https://www.thefire.org/ cases/university-of-delaware- students-required-to-undergo- ideological-reeducation/.

106. ALISON FLOOD, "US Students Request 'Trigger Warnings' on Literature," *The Guardian*, May 19, 2014, https://www. theguardian.com/books/2014/

may/19/us-students-request-trigger-warnings-in-literature.

107. ZHOU JINGWEN 周鯨文, *Fengbao shinian: Zhongguo hongse zhengquan de zhen mianmao* 風暴十年：中國紅色政權的真面貌 [*Ten Years of Storm: The True Face of China's Red Regime*], (Hong Kong: Shidai piping she, 1962), https://www.marxists.org/chinese/reference-books/zjw1959/06.htm#2. [In Chinese]

108. LUO PINGHAN 罗平汉, "1958 nian de jiaoyu geming" 1958年的教育革命 ["The Educational Revolution of 1958"], in *Dangshi xijie* 党史细节 [*Details in the History of the Communist Party*], vol. 34. [In Chinese]

109. ROBERT GEARTY, "White Privilege Bolstered by Teaching Math, University Professor Says," Fox News, October 24, 2017, http://www.foxnews.com/us/2017/10/24/white-privilege-bolstered-by-teaching-math-university-professor-says.html.

110. TONI AIRAKSINEN, "Prof Complains About 'Masculinization of Mathematics,'" Campus Reform, August 24, 2017, https://www.campusreform.org/?ID=9544.

111. W. CLEON SKOUSEN, *The Naked Communist* (Salt Lake City: The Ensign Publishing Co., 1962), chap. 12.

Chapter Thirteen:
The Media —
The Specter's Mouthpiece

1. THOMAS JEFFERSON, *The Works*, vol. 5 (Correspondence 1786–1789), as quoted in Online Library of Liberty, accessed on April 24, 2020, http://oll.libertyfund.org/quote/302.

2. JOSEPH PULITZER, as quoted in Michael Lewis, "J-School Confidential," *The New Republic*, April 18, 1993, https://newrepublic.com/article/72485/j-school-confidential.

3. KARL MARX AND FRIEDRICH ENGELS, "Rules of the Communist League," in *The Communist League (1847)*, Marx/Engels Internet Archive, accessed April 26, 2020, https://www.marxists.org/archive/marx/works/1847/communist-league/index.htm.

4. LIN BIAO 林彪, "Zai Zhongyangzhengzhiju kuodahuiyi shang de jianghua" 在中央政治局擴大會議上的講話 ["Speech at the Enlarged Meeting of the Politburo"], in *Zhongguo Wenhuadageming wenku* 中國文化大革命文庫 [*Collection of Documents From China's Cultural Revolution*], May 18, 1966. [In Chinese]

5. HU QIAOMU 胡喬木, "Baozhi shi jiaokeshu" 報紙是教科書 ["Newspapers Are Textbooks"], in *Hu Qiaomu wenku* 胡喬木文集 [*The Collected Works of Hu Qiaomu*], (Beijing: People's

Daily Publishing House, 1994), 3:303. [In Chinese]

6. HAN MEI 韩梅, "Ying jiemi dang'an baoguang 'liu si' siwang renshu: shiti duiji zai dixiatongdao 英解密档案曝光"六四"死亡人数：尸体堆积在地下通道 ["UK Declassifies Files on Casualties at Tiananmen; Bodies Stored Underground in Heaps"], Sound of Hope Radio, December 20, 2017, http://www.soundofhope.org/gb/2017/12/20/n1378413.html. [In Chinese]

7. "Self-Immolation Hoax on Tiananmen Square," Minghui.org, http://en.minghui.org/cc/88/.

8. "Zongshu: Chuangxinjizhi qianghua peiyang – goujian gaosuzhi xuanchuanwenhuaduiwu" 综述:创新机制强化培养构建高素质宣传文化队伍 ["General Overview: Intensify the Fostering of a Mechanism for Innovation, Construct a High-Grade Propaganda Cultural Team"], Xinhua News Network, September 28, 2011, http://www.gov.cn/jrzg/2011-09/28/content_1958774.htm. [In Chinese]

9. MATTHEW VADUM, "Journalistic Treachery," *Canada Free Press*, July 1, 2015, https://canadafreepress.com/article/journalistic-treachery.

10. MARCO CARYNNYK, "The New York Times and the Great Famine," *Ukrainian Weekly,* vol. LI, no. 37,

published September 11, 1983, accessed April 26, 2020, http://www.ukrweekly.com/old/archive/1983/378320.shtml.

11. WALTER DURANTY, as quoted in Robert Conquest, *The Harvest of Sorrow: Soviet Collectivization and the Terror-Famine* (New York: Oxford University Press, 1986), 319.

12. ROBERT CONQUEST, as quoted in Arnold Beichman, "Pulitzer-Winning Lies," *The Weekly Standard*, June 12, 2003, https://www.washingtonexaminer.com/weekly-standard/pulitzer-winning-lies.

13. RONALD RADOSH AND ALLIS RADOSH, *Red Star Over Hollywood: The Film Colony's Long Romance With the Left* (San Francisco: Encounter Books, 2005), 80.

14. Ibid., 105.

15. MAO ZEDONG, as quoted in Edgar Snow, *Random Notes on Red China, 1936–1945* (Montana: Literary Licensing, LLC, 2011).

16. RUTH PRICE, *The Lives of Agnes Smedley* (New York: Oxford University Press, 2004), 5–9.

17. ART SWIFT, "Six in 10 in US See Partisan Bias in News Media," Gallup, April 5, 2017, https://news.gallup.com/poll/207794/six-partisan-bias-news-media.aspx.

18. TIM GROSECLOSE, *Left Turn: How Liberal Media Bias*

Distorts the American Mind (New York: St. Martin's Press, 2011).

19. Ibid., 111–122.

20. CHRIS CILLIZZA, "Just 7 Percent of Journalists Are Republicans. That's Far Fewer than Even a Decade Ago," *The Washington Post*, May 6, 2014, https://www.washingtonpost.com/news/the-fix/wp/2014/05/06/just-7-percent-of-journalists-are-republicans-thats-far-less-than-even-a-decade-ago/?noredirect=on&utm_term=.3d0109901e1e.

21. "2016 General Election Editorial Endorsements by Major Newspapers," The American Presidency Project, last updated November 8, 2016, http://www.presidency.ucsb.edu/data/2016_newspaper_endorsements.php.

22. LYDIA SAAD, "US Conservatives Outnumber Liberals by Narrowing Margin," Gallup, January 3, 2017, https://news.gallup.com/poll/201152/conservative-liberal-gap-continues-narrow-tuesday.aspx.

23. BEN SHAPIRO, *Primetime Propaganda: The True Hollywood Story of How the Left Took Over Your TV* (New York: Broadside Books, 2012), 55–85.

24. Ibid., 161–223.

25. Ibid., 55–85.

26. RONALD FARRAR, *A Creed for My Profession: Walter Williams, Journalist to the World* (Missouri: University of Missouri, 1999).

27. S. ROBERT LICHTER et. al., *The Media Elite: America's New Powerbrokers* (Castle Rock, CO: Adler Publishing Co., 1986).

28. JIM KUYPERS, *Partisan Journalism: A History of Media Bias in the United States* (Lanham, MD: Rowman & Littlefield, 2013).

29. BERNARD GOLDBERG, "On Media Bias, Network Stars Are Rather Clueless," *The Wall Street Journal,* May 24, 2001, https://www.wsj.com/articles/SB990662606943995140.

30. TIM GROSECLOSE AND JEFF MILYO, "A Measure of Media Bias," *The Quarterly Journal of Economics* 120, no. 4 (November 2005), 1205.

31. BERNARD COHEN, as quoted in Maxwell E. McCombs and Donald L. Shaw, "The Agenda-Setting Function of Mass Media," *The Public Opinion Quarterly* 36, no. 2 (Summer 1972): 177.

32. NEWT GINGRICH, "China's Embrace of Marxism Is Bad News for Its People," Fox News, June 2, 2018, http://www.foxnews.com/opinion/2018/06/02/newt-gingrich-chinas-embrace-marxism-is-bad-news-for-its-people.html.

33. PATRICIA COHEN, "Liberal Views Dominate Footlights,"

The New York Times, October 14, 2008, https://www.nytimes.com/2008/10/15/theater/15thea.html.

34. GROSECLOSE, *Left Turn*, ix.

35. JOHN BELTON, *American Cinema/American Culture*, 2nd Edition (New York: McGraw-Hill Publishing Company, 2004), chap. 14.

36. "Hollywood: The Shock of Freedom in Films," *Time*, Dec. 8, 1967, http://content.time.com/time/magazine/article/0,9171,844256,00.html.

37. TODD GITLIN, *The Whole World Is Watching: Mass Media in the Making and Unmaking of the New Left* (Berkeley, CA: University of California Press, 2003), 199.

38. STEVEN ROSS, *Hollywood Left and Right: How Movie Stars Shaped American Politics* (New York: Oxford University Press, 2011), 322.

39. Ibid., 338.

40. Ibid., 338–39.

41. Ibid., 352.

42. ASHLEY HAYGOOD, "The Climb of Controversial Film Content," (master's thesis, Liberty University, May 2007), accessed October 5, 2018, https://digitalcommons.liberty.edu/cgi/viewcontent.cgi?&httpsredir=1&article=1007&context=masters&sei-re.

43. DENNIS HOPPER, as quoted in Peter Biskind, *Easy Riders, Raging Bulls: How the Sex-Drugs-and-Rock 'n' Roll Generation Saved Hollywood* (New York: Simon and Schuster, 1999), 74.

44. VICTOR CLINE, "How the Mass Media Affects Our Values and Behavior," *Issues in Religion and Psychotherapy* 1, no. 1 (October 1, 1975), https://scholarsarchive.byu.edu/cgi/viewcontent.cgi?article=1004&context=irp.

45. MICHAEL MEDVED, *Hollywood vs. America* (New York: Harper Perennial, 1993), 4.

46. "The Media Assault on American Values," Media Research Center, accessed April 26, 2020, https://www.mrc.org/special-reports/media-assault-american-values.

47. SHAPIRO, *Primetime Propaganda*.

48. JANE ANDERSON, "The Impact of Media Use and Screen Time on Children, Adolescents, and Families," American College of Pediatricians, November 2016, https://www.acpeds.org/wordpress/wp-content/uploads/11.9.16-The-Impact-of-Media-Use-and-Screen-Time-on-Children-updated-with-ref-64.pdf.

49. JANE BROWN, as quoted in Marc Silver, "Sex and Violence on TV," *Congressional Record Online* 141, no. 146 (September 19, 1995): S 13810-13812, https://www.gpo.gov/fdsys/pkg/CREC-1995-09-19/html/CREC-1995-09-19-pt1-PgS13810.htm.

50. SHAPIRO, *Primetime Propaganda*.

51. LIBBY COPELAND, "MTV's Provocative 'Undressed': Is It Rotten to the (Soft) Core?", *Los Angeles Times*, February 12, 2001, http://articles. latimes.com/2001/feb/12/ entertainment/ca-24264.

52. RICH NOYES, "TV vs. Trump in 2018: Lots of Russia, and 91% Negative Coverage (Again!)," NewsBusters, March 6, 2018, https://www. newsbusters.org/blogs/nb/ rich-noyes/2018/03/06/tv-vs- trump-2018-lots-russia-and- 91-negative-coverage.

53. ROBERT MUELLER III, "Report on the Investigation Into Russian Interference in the 2016 Presidential Election," Department of Justice, March 2019, https://www.justice.gov/ storage/report.pdf.

54. JULIA MANCHESTER, "Trump: ABC Should Have Fired 'Fraudster' Brian Ross," *The Hill*, December 8, 2017, http:// thehill.com/homenews/ administration/364061- trump-abc-should-have-fired- fraudster-brian-ross.

55. SAMANTHA SCHMIDT AND KRISTINE PHILLIPS, "The Crying Honduran Girl on the Cover of Time Was Not Separated From Her Mother," *The Washington Post*, June 22, 2018, https:// www.washingtonpost. com/news/morning-mix/ wp/2018/06/22/the-crying- honduran-girl-on-the-cover- of-time-was-not-separated- from-her-mother-father- says/?noredirect=on&utm_ term=.bd08dbdaf5bc.

56. "'Fake News' Threat to Media; Editorial Decisions, Outside Actors at Fault," Monmouth University Polling Institute, April 2, 2018, https://www.monmouth.edu/ polling-institute/reports/ monmouthpoll_us_040218/.

57. ART SWIFT, "Americans' Trust in Mass Media Sinks to New Low," Gallup, September 14, 2016, https://news.gallup.com/ poll/195542/americans-trust- mass-media-sinks-new-low. aspx.

58. POLINA MARINOVA, "New LA Times Owner Tells Readers: 'Fake News Is the Cancer of Our Times,'" *Fortune*, June 18, 2018, https://fortune. com/2018/06/18/los-angeles- times-owner.

Chapter Fourteen: Popular Culture — A Decadent Indulgence

1. GEORGE WASHINGTON, as quoted in "George Washington's Rules of Civility and Decent Behavior in Company and Conversation," *Foundations Magazine*, http:// www.foundationsmag.com/ civility.html.

2. BENJAMIN FRANKLIN, *The Autobiography and Other Writings on Politics, Economics, and Virtue,* ed. Alan Houston

(Cambridge, UK: Cambridge University Press, 2004), 68–69.

3. XUE FEI 薛飞, "'Que nage shen jiu zao yige': Hebei nainai miao luanxiang" "缺哪个神就造一个" 河北奶奶庙乱象 ["'If a god is missing, just make one': Chaos at the grandmother temple, Hebei"], *The Epoch Times*, August 10, 2017, http://www.epochtimes.com/gb/17/8/9/n9513251.htm. [In Chinese]

4. "Oxford Dictionary Adds Popular Chinese Terms," *China Daily*, September 6, 2010, http://www.chinadaily.com.cn/business/2010-09/06/content_11259791.htm.

5. LORETTA CHAO, "The Ultimate Knock-Off: A Fake Apple Store," *The Wall Street Journal*, July 21, 2011, https://blogs.wsj.com/chinarealtime/2011/07/21/the-ultimate-knock-off-a-fake-apple-store/.

6. JACK KEROUAC, "The Birth of a Socialist," in *Atop an Underwood: Early Stories and Other Writings,* ed. Paul Marion (New York: Penguin, 2000).

7. ROBERTO FRANZOSI, review of Jeremy Suri, *Power and Protest: Global Revolution and the Rise of Détente, American Journal of Sociology* 111, no. 5 (March 2006), 1589, https://www.journals.uchicago.edu/doi/full/10.1086/504653.

8. MEREDITH BOX AND GAVAN MCCORMACK, "Terror in

Japan," *Asia-Pacific Journal: Japan Focus* 2, issue 6 (June 25, 2004), 1570, https://apjjf.org/-Gavan-McCormack/1570/article.html.

9. AMY D. MCDOWELL, "Contemporary Christian Music," *Oxford Music Online*, 2013, https://doi.org/10.1093/gmo/9781561592630.article.A2234810.

10. WHITE HOUSE, *Ending America's Opioid Crisis,* accessed April 29, 2020, https://www.whitehouse.gov/opioids/.

11. US NATIONAL INSTITUTE ON DRUG ABUSE FOR TEENS, *Drug Facts: Marijuana,* last revised December 2019, accessed April 29, 2020, https://teens.drugabuse.gov/drug-facts/marijuana.

12. US DRUG ENFORCEMENT ADMINISTRATION, *2019 National Drug Threat Assessment,* December 2019, 9, https://www.dea.gov/sites/default/files/2020-02/DIR-007-20%202019%20National%20Drug%20Threat%20Assessment%20-%20low%20res210.pdf.

13. NATIONAL INSTITUTE ON DRUG ABUSE, *Overdose Death Rates,* revised March 2020, accessed April 29, 2020, https://www.drugabuse.gov/related-topics/trends-statistics/overdose-death-rates.

14. AMANDA HOOVER, "110 Pounds of Fentanyl Seized at Port in Shipment from

China," *New Jersey Advance Media*, July 2, 2018, https://www.nj.com/news/index.ssf/2018/07/110_pounds_of_fentanyl_found_in_philadelphia_port.html.

15. "Zhongguo dupin baogao: quanguo xidu renshu yu 1400 wan" 中国毒品报告：全国吸毒人数逾1400万 ["China Drug Report: More than 14 million drug users nationwide"], BBC Chinese, June 24, 2015, http://www.bbc.com/zhongwen/simp/china/2015/06/150624_china_drugs_report. [In Chinese]

16. ZHANG YANG 张洋, "Quanguo pohuo dupin xingshi anjian 14 wan qi" 全国破获毒品刑事案件14万起 ["140,000 Drug Criminal Cases Cracked Across China"] in "2017 nian Zhongguo dupin xingshi baogao 2017" 年中国毒品形势报告 ["China's Drug Situation Report 2017"], *People's Daily*, June 26, 2018, http://yuqing.people.com.cn/n1/2018/0626/c209043-30088689.html. [In Chinese]

17. "Things Are Looking Up in America's Porn Industry," NBC News, January 20, 2015, https://www.nbcnews.com/business/business-news/things-are-looking-americas-porn-industry-n289431.

18. "Boy, 12, Repeatedly Raped Sister After Becoming Fascinated With Internet Porn," *New Zealand Herald*, November 7, 2016, https://www.nzherald.co.nz/world/news/article.cfm?c_id=2&objectid=11743460.

19. INGA MARGRETE YDERSBOND, "The 'Promiscuous' and the 'Shy': Denmark and Norway: A Historic Comparative Analysis of Pornography Legislation," *NPPR Working Paper Series: The Politics of Commercial Sex* (March 2012), https://www.duo.uio.no/bitstream/handle/10852/34447/NPPRWP201201.df?sequence=1.

20. LARS GRAVESEN, "Taxpayers Foot Bill for Disabled Danes' Visits to Prostitutes," *The Daily Telegraph*, October 2, 2005, https://www.telegraph.co.uk/news/worldnews/europe/denmark/1499735/Taxpayers-foot-bill-for-disabled-Danes-visits-to-prostitutes.html.

21. CHEN JING 沉靜, "Fanrong changsheng de chaoji xingdaguo" 繁榮娼盛的超級性大國 ["Prosperous Prostitution in a Sex Industry Superpower"], *The Epoch Times*, September 25, 2009, https://www.epochtimes.com/b5/9/9/25/n2668274.htm. [In Chinese]

22. TAKUDZWA HILLARY CHIWANZA, "Thousands of Chinese Prostitutes Are Flocking to Africa for Lucrative Fortunes," *African Exponent*, May 7, 2018, https://www.africanexponent.com/post/8965-chinese-prostitutes-have-joined-the-scramble-for-africas-fortunes.

23. PAT FAGAN, "The Effects of Pornography on Individuals,

Marriage, Family and Community," Family Research Council (March 2011), accessed April 29, 2020, https://downloads.frc.org/EF/EF11C36.pdf.

24. US CONGRESS, SENATE, SUBCOMMITTEE ON THE CONSTITUTION, CIVIL RIGHTS, AND PROPERTY RIGHTS, *Hearing on Pornography's Impact on Marriage and the Family,* 109th Cong., November 9, 2005, https://www.judiciary.senate.gov/imo/media/doc/manning_testimony_11_10_05.pdf.

25. DAVID SHULTZ, "Divorce Rates Double When People Start Watching Porn," *Science,* August 26, 2016, http://www.sciencemag.org/news/2016/08/divorce-rates-double-when-people-start-watching-porn.

26. GEORGE AKERLOF, et al., "An Analysis of Out-of-Wedlock Childbearing in the United States," in *Explorations of Pragmatic Economics* (New York: Oxford University Press, 2005), 120.

27. JOSEPH CHAMIE, "Out-of-Wedlock Births Rise Worldwide," YaleGlobal Online, March 16, 2017, https://yaleglobal.yale.edu/content/out-wedlock-births-rise-worldwide.

28. ERIK HURST, "Video Killed the Radio Star," *Chicago Booth Review,* September 1, 2016, http://review.chicagobooth.edu/economics/2016/article/video-killed-radio-star.

29. MARK AGUIAR, Mark Bils, Kerwin Kofi Charles and Erik Hurst, "Leisure Luxuries and the Labor Supply of Young Men," The National Bureau of Economic Research, Working Paper no. 23552 (June 2017): 1, http://www.nber.org/papers/w23552.

30. TOM WIJMAN, "Mobile Revenues Account for More Than 50% of the Global Games Market as It Reaches $137.9 Billion in 2018," Newzoo, April 30, 2018, https://newzoo.com/insights/articles/global-games-market-reaches-137-9-billion-in-2018-mobile-games-take-half/.

31. "United States Crime Rates 1960–2018," FBI UCS Annual Crime Reports, DisasterCenter.com, http://www.disastercenter.com/crime/uscrime.htm

32. BONNIE BERKOWITZAND CHRIS ALCANTARA, "The Terrible Numbers That Grow With Each Mass Shooting," *The Washington Post,* updated March 4, 2019, accessed April 29, 2020, https://www.washingtonpost.com/graphics/2018/national/mass-shootings-in-america/?utm_term=.f63cc1b03c0b.

33. "Global Terrorism Database," University of Maryland: National Consortium for the Study of Terrorism and Responses to Terrorism, accessed on April 29, 2020, https://www.start.umd.edu/gtd/.

34. JACQUE WILSON AND WILLIAM HUDSON, "Gun Violence in PG-13 Movies Has Tripled," CNN, November 11, 2013, http://www.cnn.com/2013/11/11/health/gun-violence-movies/index.html.

35. ASSIL FRAYH, "Gun Violence Keeps Rising in PG-13 Movies, Study Says," CNN, January 20, 2017, https://www.cnn.com/2017/01/20/health/gun-violence-pg-13-movies-study/index.html.

36. "Violent Video Games and Young People," *Harvard Mental Health Letter* 27, no. 4 (October 2010), http://affectsofvideogames.weebly.com/uploads/6/4/3/3/6433146/medical_journal.pdf.

37. MARY GARDEN, "Why I Bobbed My Hair," *Pictorial Review,* April 1927, 8.

38. "Long Hair for Men," Encyclopedia of Fashion, accessed April 29, 2020, http://www.fashionencyclopedia.com/fashion_costume_culture/Modern-World-Part-II-1961-1979/Long-Hair-for-Men.html.

39. "Hip Huggers," Encyclopedia of Fashion, accessed April 29, 2020, http://www.fashionencyclopedia.com/fashion_costume_culture/Modern-World-Part-II-1961-1979/Hip-Huggers.html.

40. KATHRYN BROMWICH, "Groupies Revisited: The Women with Triple-A Access to the 60s," *The Guardian*, November 15, 2015, https://www.theguardian.com/music/2015/nov/15/groupies-revisited-baron-wolman-rolling-stone-pamela-des-barres.

41. NEIL ERIKSEN, "Popular Culture and Revolutionary Theory: Understanding Punk Rock," *Theoretical Review* 18 (September-October 1980), accessed via Marxists Internet Archive on April 29, 2020, https://www.marxists.org/history/erol/periodicals/theoretical-review/19801802.htm.